Meeting the Physical Education Needs of Children With Autism Spectrum Disorder

Melissa G. F. Alexander, Ph.D

Susan M. Schwager, Ed.D

National Association for
Sport and Physical Education
*an association of the American Alliance for Health,
Physical Education, Recreation and Dance*

NASPE Sets the Standard

To order more copies of this book (stock # 304-10515):
Web: www.naspeinfo.org
E-mail: customerservice@aahperd.org
Phone: (800)321-0789; (412)741-1288 outside the United States
Fax: (412) 741-0609
Mail: AAHPERD Publications Fulfillment Center, P.O. Box 1020, Sewickley, PA 15143-1020

ISBN: 978-0-88314-965-2

Printed in the United States

Suggested citation for this book:
Alexander, M.G.F., Schwager, S.M. (2012). *Meeting the physical education needs of children with autism spectrum disorder.* Reston, VA: National Association for Sport and Physical Education.

Table of Contents

Chapter 3. Instructional Strategies for Enhancing Student Learning

Chapter 4. Integrating Social-Skills Development

Chapter 5. Physical Education Curriculum Models: Implications for Students With ASD

Chapter 6. Behavior Management: Proactive Strategies

Chapter 7. Behavior Management: Reactive Strategies

Chapter 8. Working With Others

Preface

The purpose of this book is to provide physical education professionals with information and resources to help them accommodate the instructional and programmatic needs of students with autism spectrum disorder (ASD) both in self-contained and inclusive class settings.

ASD encompasses a range of developmental disabilities that affect a person's verbal and nonverbal communication, understanding of language and socialization with peers. Other characteristics of ASD can include engagement in repetitive activities, resistance to environmental change and unusual responses to sensory experiences. The range of severity can run from extremely mild to severe. ASD, however, is a neurodevelopmental disorder, not an illness, disease or behavioral disorder. ASD is a lifelong condition with which some children are born, even though it's typically not diagnosed until age 3 or older. It has no known cure, although one can find documented cases of symptoms being reduced and even of some children being re-diagnosed altogether.

As a physical educator, you are likely to encounter students with ASD in inclusive class settings and, possibly, in self-contained classes. Meeting the physical education needs of children with ASD can be very challenging, and the information in this book is intended to help you meet that challenge.

The book contains eight chapters. Chapter 1 introduces readers to ASD and describes the characteristics of those with the disorder. The chapter also describes — and dispels — myths commonly associated with ASD. Chapter 2 describes instructional strategies intended to enhance the abilities of students with ASD to cope with two issues that they typically face: communicating with others and managing sensory perception problems.

Chapter 3 outlines strategies to teach motor development and sport-related skills to children with ASD. It also discusses other instructional techniques to enhance the ability of students with ASD to reach the learning goals set for all students in physical education classes. Chapter 4 describes how to provide instruction, in the context of physical education class, to help students with ASD develop the social skills necessary to succeed in life.

Chapter 5 describes curricular approaches used commonly in physical education programs and how those approaches can best meet the developmental needs of students with ASD. The chapter also provides teaching considerations to address some of the challenges that may be associated with these models. Chapter 6 provides strategies to apply within self-contained or inclusive classes to promote an environment that is conducive to learning for all students.

Chapter 7 presents strategies to encourage appropriate behavior and to address those behaviors that interfere with learning. Chapter 8 describes ways in which physical education teachers can work effectively with others (e.g., classroom teachers, paraprofessionals, other students, parents) to help students with ASD learn and develop.

To make the best use of the information in the book, we recommend reading Chapter 1 first, even for those who are somewhat acquainted with the nature of ASD. The descriptions of the characteristics of children with ASD in the introductory chapter include commonly held myths about children with ASD that sometimes affect our ability to meet the needs of these children. Being well acquainted with the characteristics of people with ASD will help you to choose strategies from the remaining chapters that are best suited to your students.

Keep in mind that the strategies suggested in the remaining chapters depend on context. If you teach students with ASD in a self-contained class, some of the strategies might be more attractive to you than if you teach an inclusive class. In addition, your students' spectrum of abilities will influence the strategies that are appropriate in your setting. Although this book is focused on meeting the needs of students with ASD in physical education class settings, many of the activities and strategies described in the remaining chapters are effective with all students in inclusive class settings, in the classroom as well as in the gymnasium.

The strategies and sample activities in the book are intended to get you started. The best strategies and activities are the ones that *you* design to meet the needs of the students in *your* school.

Chapter 1
Characteristics of Students With ASD

Content

Introduction

Definitions

    Autism, Asperger's Syndrome & PDD-NOS

    Autism Spectrum Disorder After 2013

Prevalence

Characteristics

    Social Interaction

    Nonverbal Cues

    Communication

    Need for Schedule & Routine

    Sensory Perception

    Obsession With an Object or Topic

    Lack of Imaginative Play

    Repetitive Movements or Self-Stimming/Self-Soothing

    Cognitive Functioning

    Motor Development & Motor Performance

Myths About ASD

    Myth 1. ASD Can Be Cured

    Myth 2. People With ASD Have Savant Abilities

    Myth 3. ASD Is a Result of Emotional Neglect

    Myth 4. ASD Is Caused by Vaccines

    Myth 5. ASD Is Caused by "Spoiling" the Child

    Myth 6. Children With ASD Can't Build Social Relationships

Conclusion

Introduction

Since 1943, when Leo Kanner, M.D., first described "autism," (Ozonoff, Dawson & McPartland, 2002), our understanding of the disorder now known as autism spectrum disorder (ASD) has taken tremendous leaps. Yet, despite a growing body of research on the disorder and the increasing incidence of which it has been diagnosed over the past 20 years, we still don't know what causes ASD, nor have we discovered a cure. What we do know is that teachers — including physical education teachers — face a huge challenge in providing a high-quality education for children with ASD. And the first step in meeting a challenge is to develop an understanding of what one is up against.

The purpose of this chapter is simply to explain the characteristics of ASD. Specifically, this chapter will discuss what ASD is, its prevalence in the United States and the characteristics that are often associated with it. Lastly, the chapter will help clarify some misconceptions about the disorder.

Published by the American Psychiatric Association (APA), *The Diagnostic and Statistical Manual of Mental Disorders* (DSM) is used in psychological clinical settings and research settings to identify and describe specific neuropsychological disorders, including ASD. The current version of the DSM — DSM-IV-TR (APA, 2000) — uses the term "pervasive developmental disorders," which includes autistic disorder (also called "classic" autism), Asperger's disorder (commonly referred to as Asperger's syndrome), Rett's disorder, childhood disintegrative disorder, and pervasive developmental disorder – not otherwise specified (PDD-NOS) (otherwise known as "atypical" autism). This book focuses on disorders commonly termed as "autism spectrum disorders," which include autism, Asperger's syndrome and PDD-NOS. Rett's disorder and childhood disintegrative disorder are outside the scope of this book.

An updated version of DSM — DSM-V, due in 2013 — proposes a significant reorganization of those labels. Under DSM-V, all children who previously had been labeled as having autistic disorder, Asperger's syndrome, childhood disintegrative disorder or PDD-NOS would be placed in one large category, termed "autism spectrum disorder." Therefore, while children who are diagnosed before 2013 still will have the disability label "Asperger's syndrome" or "PDD-NOS," those who are diagnosed after 2013 most likely will have the disability label "autism spectrum disorder." For the purpose of this book, we will use the term "autism spectrum disorder" (ASD) to reference all children on the spectrum (including those labeled before 2013 as having autistic disorder, Asperger's syndrome or PDD-NOS). Regardless of the terminology, the strategies and suggestions provided in this book are designed to assist all students on the spectrum.

Definitions

Autistic Disorder (Autism), Asperger's Syndrome & PDD-NOS

Even though the DSM-V proposes not to recognize autism, Asperger's and PDD-NOS as separate disorders, it's likely that schools and community agencies will continue for some time to use the current definitions. So, it's important to understand the differences among the disorders.

While autism and Asperger's have some similarities, they also have unique differences. Figure 1.1 shows the similarities and differences between the two disabilities. Both disorders are characterized by a significant impairment in social interaction and a preoccupation with a specific pattern of behavior, area of interest or activity. To be labeled as having autism, a child also must show significant delays in communication skills, imaginative play and self-help skills. Children who are labeled as having Asperger's syndrome typically participate in imaginative play, show no delay in communication skills and demonstrate a normal cognitive level, leaving them with few challenges regarding self-help skills (APA, 2000).

The PDD-NOS label is given to children who demonstrate some characteristics associated with ASD, but who don't meet enough diagnostic criteria to warrant a diagnosis of autism or Asperger's (APA, 2000). Therefore, while children diagnosed with PDD-NOS might demonstrate some of the characteristics of autism and/or Asperger's — and they need appropriate services — they don't fit within the ASD or Asperger's syndrome categories. *Example:* Jose has significant social delays that interfere with his everyday activities but has no problem with verbal and nonverbal communication, has a normal cognitive level and doesn't show any stereotypical behaviors, interests or activities. After it's determined that no other medical issues are causing his social-skills deficiency, Jose could be diagnosed as having PDD-NOS. Still, the strategies used to work with children with PPD-NOS overlap with those implemented for children with ASD or Asperger's.

Autism Spectrum Disorder After 2013

As discussed earlier, DSM-V will combine current disorders under the label "autism spectrum disorder," but it will reorganize some of the diagnostic criteria. Figure 1.2 on p. 6 outlines the proposed criteria that medical professionals would use to diagnose a child with ASD.

Figure 1.1 Characteristics of Autism & Asperger's Syndrome

Both Autism & Asperger's Syndrome
Difficulties with social interaction (must display at least two):
• Does not use or has difficulty using and interpreting nonverbal communication (e.g., eye contact, facial expressions, body postures, hand gestures). • Lack of peer relationships that would be appropriate for age. • Lack of initiating or responding to others' interests, excitement or enjoyment. • Lack of social or emotional reciprocity.
Demonstrates restrictive repetition of behavior, interests and activities (must display at least one):
• An abnormal obsession with a particular topic, object or area of focus (e.g., cars, dinosaurs) that becomes restrictive to lifestyle. • Inflexible toward changing a specific, nonfunctional routine or ritual. • Persistent preoccupation with topics or objects (e.g., string, dinosaurs). • Stereotypical or repetitive motor behaviors, also called self-stimming/self-soothing (e.g., rocking back and forth, spinning, flapping fingers).

Autism	Asperger's
Impairment in communication (must display at least one):	• No delay in language or communication skills.
• Delay or no use of spoken language.	• No delay in cognitive abilities or age-appropriate self-help skills (e.g., ability to dress oneself or make a snack).
• Typical speech development, but an inability to initiate or maintain a conversation.	• No delay in curiosity about the environment.
• Abnormal use of language (e.g., simply repeating certain phrases or what someone else says).	
• Lack of self-initiated make-believe play or age-appropriate imitative play.	

Adapted from DSM-IV Diagnostic Criteria for Pervasive Developmental Disorders *(APA, 2000).*

Figure 1.2 Proposed DSM-V Diagnostic Criteria for Autism Spectrum Disorder

A. Persistent deficits in social communication and social interaction across contexts, not accounted for by general developmental delays, and manifest[ed] by all three of the following:

   1. Deficits in social-emotional reciprocity; ranging from abnormal social approach and failure of normal back-and-forth conversation through reduced sharing of interests, emotions and affect, and response to total lack of initiation of social interaction.

   2. Deficits in nonverbal communicative behaviors used for social interaction; ranging from poorly integrated verbal and nonverbal communication, through abnormalities in eye contact and body language, or deficits in understanding and use of nonverbal communication, to total lack of facial expression or gestures.

   3. Deficits in developing and maintaining relationships, appropriate to developmental level (beyond those with caregivers); ranging from difficulties adjusting behavior to suit different social contexts through difficulties in sharing imaginative play and in making friends, to an apparent absence of interest in people.

B. Restricted, repetitive patterns of behavior, interests or activities, as manifested by at least two of the following:

   1. Stereotyped or repetitive speech, motor movements or use of objects (such as simple motor stereotypes, echolalia, repetitive use of objects or idiosyncratic phrases).

   2. Excessive adherence to routines, ritualized patterns of verbal or nonverbal behavior, or excessive resistance to change (such as motoric rituals, insistence on same route or food, repetitive questioning or extreme distress at small changes).

   3. Highly restricted, fixated interests that are abnormal in intensity or focus, such as strong attachment to or preoccupation with unusual objects, and excessively circumscribed or perseverative interests.

   4. Hyper- or hyposensitivity to sensory input or unusual interest in sensory aspects of environment, such as apparent indifference to pain/heat/cold, adverse response to specific sounds or textures, excessive smelling or touching of objects, and fascination with lights or spinning objects.

C. Symptoms must be present in early childhood, but might not fully manifest until social demands exceed limited capacities.

D. Symptoms together limit and impair everyday functioning.

Adapted from "A 09 Autism Spectrum Disorder," DSM-5 Development, American Psychiatric Association, www.dsm5.org/ProposedRevisions/Pages/proposedrevision.aspx?rid=94. Retrieved February 24, 2012.

Prevalence

Each year, about one in every 88 children is diagnosed with an autism spectrum disorder. Because of that high rate of incidence, it's estimated that 1.5 million Americans have been diagnosed with ASD. In addition, ASD is four to five times more likely to affect boys than girls. But there's no evidence to suggest that it occurs more often among different social classes, different races or different cultures. While the number of children diagnosed with ASD increases each year, experts have not been able to give a definitive explanation for the cause of the increase (CDC, 2012).

Characteristics

The following characteristics are associated with ASD. Some of the characteristics are related directly to the disorder's definition, while other characteristics are not currently within the definition of ASD but are seen commonly in people who have been labeled as on the ASD spectrum.

It's absolutely essential to recognize that children with ASD — just as children who *don't* have disabilities — are individuals. Therefore, each child has a unique presentation of the following characteristics. And not every child with ASD displays all of these characteristics. It's also important to remember that each of the following characteristics falls along a spectrum. Just because a child has been labeled with the disorder doesn't mean that he or she will present a characteristic in the same manner or to the same extreme as another child with an ASD diagnosis. One child might display extreme sensitivity to sound and have only moderate difficulties with communication, while another child might display mild sensitivity to sound but have extreme difficulties with communication. Each child is a unique case and should be approached as an individual, not a disability label!

Social Interaction

Evan is in a 4th-grade PE class. The teacher has broken the class into groups to complete stations on manipulative skills such as throwing and catching. Evan instantly moves to the corner of the gym and starts analyzing the floor. The aide tries to direct Evan to the group by engaging him with another student. Evan turns his body away from his peers and looks at the floor. When a student asks whether Evan wants the ball, he doesn't respond. The other student hands Evan the ball and Evan walks away from the station. When the aide redirects Evan again, he starts to scream and throws the ball into the middle of the room. He then runs over to a different station, where he finds another ball.

Camille walks into the gym eager to start her 9th-grade PE class. She runs up to some girls who are chatting about their weekend plans while they wait for the rest of the class to finish changing. Camille stands close to one of the girls and starts talking to her about her favorite TV show. The girls ignore Camille and move away from her. Camille follows the group, talking louder over some of the girls engaged in the conversation. One of the girls humors Camille and asks a question about the TV show, but then tries to talk about her weekend. Camille instantly jumps on the TV show conversation but doesn't stop talking so that the other girls can talk, and doesn't pick up on the change of subject. She then notices that the teacher has brought out the balls, and she runs away in the middle of her sentence without saying "Goodbye." The girls start laughing and make fun of Camille.

By definition, one of the most significant areas of difficulty for children with ASD is with the ability to engage in commonplace social interaction (APA, 2000). Children without ASD tend to pick up socially acceptable behaviors by observing people around them; they learn from their parents, teachers and peers starting at a very young age. Children *with* ASD, however, tend not to learn these behaviors simply through observation and interaction with other people during daily activities. As a result, they can demonstrate social skills that are not considered age-appropriate, and/or they demonstrate social skills in an odd manner.

While each child will struggle in different areas, some social skills seem to present a consistent problem for people with ASD. *Example:* Many children with ASD struggle to make eye contact when they talk. They might look at the floor or to the side of the room, or they might turn their bodies away from the person they're addressing. Other children with ASD struggle with starting or ending a conversation. They might walk up to a person and start talking without any form of greeting or transition. A few minutes later, they simply walk away, without saying "Goodbye" or any other form of concluding statement.

Children with ASD also tend to struggle with taking turns in a conversation (i.e., either dominating the conversation or not contributing at all), with contributing relevant information to a conversation (e.g., talking about food when the group is talking about sports) and with standing an appropriate distance from the people to whom they are talking (e.g., stands too close or many feet away). There is no one master list of all the social skills that present problems for children with ASD, because each child is unique. Nevertheless, Figure 1.3 contains a list of social skills that often present challenges for children with ASD.

Figure 1.3 Sample Social Skills
That Present Challenges for Children With ASD

- Taking turns while talking together.
- Making eye contact.
- Standing an appropriate distance away from others while talking.
- Using appropriate voice tone.
- Recognizing different voice tones.
- Using appropriate voice volume.
- Listening to the other person.
- Taking turns in play.
- Sharing equipment, responsibilities, etc.
- Introducing oneself.
- Greeting someone.
- Starting a conversation.
- Entering a conversation.
- Maintaining a conversation.
- Staying on topic in a conversation.
- Shifting the conversation to a different topic, when appropriate.
- Ending a conversation.
- Giving and receiving compliments.
- Introducing topics of interest to others.
- Asking for help.
- Offering help.
- Compromising.
- Dealing with mistakes, winning and losing.
- Using appropriate touch.

Note: *This is not an inclusive list. Just because a skill isn't listed doesn't mean that it might not present a challenge for the child.*

Nonverbal Cues

Theo runs into the gym and, instead of going to his poly spot, he starts rummaging through the equipment cart. The teacher calls Theo's name and shoots him "the look." Theo smiles and waves back to her and continues to dig through the equipment. The teacher tells everyone to form into their groups. Theo then runs over to his poly spot and starts jumping up and down while he yells at the top of his lungs. The teacher again shoots Theo "the look" and shakes her head "No," but Theo doesn't respond to her actions. Instead, after about a minute, he starts biting his hand and rocking. Theo's aide explains to the teacher that Theo is excited to start class.

Kaitlin walks into the gym and is crying. She tells the teacher that her grandmother passed away yesterday. Joshua runs over and starts talking over Kaitlin, asking the teacher about the day's schedule. He obviously does not recognize that Kaitlin is upset. When the teacher suggests that Joshua say something nice to Kaitlin, he replies, "I have a cool hat."

Much of our social interaction and social etiquette is based on body language (Rink, 2010). A child with ASD, though, often doesn't notice a person's body language and facial expressions. If the child does notice such nonverbal communication, he or she typically has difficulty interpreting and applying it to the social situation (Koning & Magill-Evans, 2001). *Example:* When someone shifts her weight a few times, glances at her watch and stops adding to the conversation, it often means that she's bored with the conversation or needs to leave. A person with ASD often won't notice those gestures and simply will continue talking. Even when the person suggests politely that she needs to leave, a person with ASD still won't recognize the social cue.

Because of their difficulty in reading body language, it's common for people with ASD to put themselves into difficult situations in which they unknowingly are asking inappropriate questions or contributing inappropriate information (Wicks-Nelson & Israel, 2000). Because they don't pick up on the cues that the other person is uncomfortable with the topic, they simply continue talking.

Children often will taunt children with ASD or avoid social interaction with them because of past experiences in which social cues were missed (Nadel, 2005). *Example:* Allison really likes the color pink. So, whenever she sees a person with a pink shirt, she goes over to him or her and starts stroking the shirt while asking questions about it. Her peers have tried to have Allison focus on something else, have moved away from her, and have even turned their backs to her as if to shut her out of the conversation completely. Allison doesn't seem to notice, though, and continues to stroke the clothes. Eventually, one of her peers turns around and screams at her. From then on, Allison's peers intentionally stand far away from her. *Another example:* A student in a 10th-grade PE class has put on some weight recently. Kevin goes over to the student, points to her stomach and asks, "Are you pregnant?" The student looks horrified and her eyes well up with tears. Because she doesn't respond, Kevin repeats himself, this time a little louder: "When are you having a baby?" Even as the student runs to the locker room crying, Kevin still just repeats, "Baby?"

Sharing Emotions With Others

A student is excited because he has tickets to a big concert. He expresses his excitement to classmates while they're sitting in their floor spots for attendance in their PE class. When the student expresses his excitement to Joshua, a student with ASD, Joshua stares at him blankly then starts talking about his bike.

Children with ASD often come off as being aloof and uncaring. In large part, that comes from their difficulty in sharing enjoyment or interests with others (Kasari, Chamberlain & Bauminger, 2001). Children with ASD often don't recognize if someone is interested in a specific topic or whether he or she is experiencing a specific emotion, such as excitement. Therefore, they don't respond to the person's emotional state or try to connect with the person about his or her interest.

Appropriate Conversations

Jeffrey has been learning about healthy eating and the consequences of an unbalanced diet in his health class. At the beginning of his English class, he goes up to Miss Jefferson (who is obese) and informs her that she needs to start eating more fruits and vegetables and not eat junk food. Jeffrey continues to tell her that she is fat because she doesn't eat well.

Children with ASD also might not recognize when and where it's appropriate to talk about a specific topic (DSM-V, in-press). In the example above, Jefferey provides his teacher with accurate information, but it's obviously not appropriate. Children with ASD don't recognize when it's socially acceptable to communicate information, particularly when it's factual information that they perceive as "black and white." (e.g., when you eat unhealthy food, you become obese).

Children with ASD who are verbal also can be very blunt. They tell you exactly what they see and what they're thinking. While that can be humorous, sometimes, it also can hurt other children's feelings. *Example:* At the school pool, in the beginning of swim class, a boy is staring at another student's feet. He then walks up to the student and says, "You really need a pedicure." When the student smiles and agrees, the boy elaborates about the student's rough heels and then points out each toe that has chipped nail polish. While some people might be able to laugh at this foot analysis, it's easy to see how it could cause a problem. *Another example:* A new student has joined the PE class in the middle of the semester. In an attempt to make the new student feel welcome, the teacher states: "We all really enjoyed having Monica in our class today. We are thrilled that you have come to our school." As soon as the teacher finishes, Max — who has ASD — raises his hand and says, "I don't like Monica."

Blunt statements also can cause problems when a child with ASD is asked his or her opinion. The response is usually straightforward, even if it hurts the other person's feelings. The child with ASD is not trying to be mean, just honest. *Example:* During a dance unit, one of Yvonne's peers asks her: "Do I look silly when I'm doing that dance?" "Yep," Yvonne says without hesitation, and then walks away.

Expressing Emotions Appropriately

The teacher is taking students outside for field day. Tia, a student with ASD who enjoys physical activity and competition, is very excited but also a little nervous because of the change in routine and her general uncertainties. She starts jumping up and down while laughing and flapping her hands. When Tia reaches the field, she sees a ball lying on the grass. She runs over and kicks it into another field, then resumes jumping up and down while yelling.

Later on during the day, while Tia is participating in a relay race, she drops the ball, which causes her team to lose the race. She becomes very disappointed. Her whole body becomes rigid, with her fingers and elbows locked. The teacher can see the muscles in Tia's neck strain, and sees her jaw clench. Tia refuses to listen or respond to anyone and will not participate in the next activity.

A child with ASD also might struggle to express the emotion that he or she is feeling in an appropriate manner (DSM-IV-TR, 2000). Children with ASD can find excitement, frustration and disappointment overwhelming and difficult to express (Coyne & Fullerton, 2004). While some children with ASD might express their emotions only when they are extreme (e.g., incredibly excited or very sad), others might express their emotions but do so inappropriately (e.g., laughing when they're sad or scared). Children with ASD also might not use facial expressions to show emotions, but instead use vocal sounds or motor movements (Nadel, 2005). In the PE setting, this often is seen as poor sportsmanship. Much of the difficulty that children with ASD have in expressing emotions comes from their lack of ability to express their feelings vocally. They also might not know how to control the internal sensations that accompany these emotions. Young children learn what different emotions feel like internally (e.g., nervousness leads to butterflies in the stomach) and how to respond to these sensations by watching how others respond and portray the emotion. But, just as children with ASD don't always pick up on socially acceptable behaviors, they also don't always learn how to express their emotions. They also can feel overwhelmed by the physiological sensations associated with different emotions because of their increased sensory perception.

Children with ASD who have difficulty expressing their emotions might engage in activities such as rocking their bodies back and forth, yelling/screaming, kicking, or biting (usually, their own hands or arms). *Example:* Katie would grow very excited when it was her turn to lead warm-up. While waiting for the teacher to begin class, she often would bite her forearm while pacing around the gymnasium. As soon as the class started with warm-up, that behavior stopped. *Another example:* Jacob was very competitive in soccer. If he shot the ball toward the net but missed, he would yell incoherently while rocking back and forth. After two minutes of that behavior, Jacob would return to the game.

Communication

The teacher tells the class: "Go get a jump rope and then return to your poly spot. We will do 20 jumps in place with the rope swinging forward and 20 jumps swinging backward. Does everyone know what you're supposed to do?" The teacher hears Clark echo in a high-pitched voice: "Does everyone know what you're supposed to do?" Clark then runs over and grabs a rope, which he proceeds to swing around like a lasso. The teacher directs Clark to his spot and repeats the instructions. Clark stares at the teacher, then says "20 jumps." Assuming that Clark is all set, the teacher says to the class: "Hit me with your question." Clark hits the teacher in the arm, then starts swinging his jump rope like a lasso again.

Kramer does not speak. He has an iPad that he uses to communicate. On his first day of class, the teacher greets him at the door and tells him how excited she is to meet him. Kramer instantly puts his hands over his ears, starts yelling and runs away.

There are two different types of communication: expressive and receptive. Expressive communication is the ability to communicate one's thoughts to others. We often consider expressive communication the person's ability to verbalize, but vocalization is not the only form of expressive communication. It also includes body language, facial gestures and alternative means, such as using a computer.

Receptive communication is a person's ability to understand what others are trying to communicate to him or her. Many children with ASD have significant problems with both expressive and receptive communication.

Expressive Communication

Many children with Asperger's syndrome experience no problems with expressive communication. Other children on the ASD spectrum, however, will have significant difficulties with verbal communication. In fact, it's estimated that almost 50 percent of children with autism don't speak at all (Friend, 2007). Children who don't speak might be completely silent, or they might use a series of grunts and groans. They can live their entire lives without saying a word. But a child who doesn't speak *can* develop some spoken language much later in life. *Example:* Mark was completely silent until about age 15. At that time, he slowly started making one-word statements. Now, at age 22, he can produce three- and four-word sentences.

Other children with ASD have limited vocal skills; they talk, but only in two- to three-word utterances, and they can't speak in complete sentences. *Example:* A child with ASD might say "Hungry cookie." Or, the child might use one word (e.g., "Want"), accompanied by grunting, pointing or other gestures (e.g., pointing to the container of balls, pulling the teacher by the sleeve toward the container).

Some children with ASD demonstrate echolalia, or repeating what one has heard, as in an echo (Auxter, Pyfer, Zittel & Roth, 2010). *Example:* The teacher asks Jonathan: "How was your weekend?" Jonathan answers, "How was your weekend?" Children with ASD might echo what they just heard, or something they heard hours ago. In some cases, they might repeat phrases or statements that are irrelevant to the topic at hand but are familiar to them. When the teacher asks Mohamed what he did over the weekend, for example, Mohamed answers, "That's a nice boulder" in a voice that he wouldn't use typically. He's citing a line verbatim from the movie "Shrek" (his favorite), while trying to imitate the donkey character's voice.

It's important to recognize that, even though students with ASD might not be expressing themselves vocally, that doesn't mean that one can't communicate with them. Many children with ASD use sign language, gestures or augmentative and alternative communication devices as ways to communicate. Teachers also should never underestimate the value of facial expressions or physical gestures. While children with ASD might have difficulty recognizing what the teacher's gestures mean, they still are able to produce their own gestures. Just as with most children, a child with ASD who is smiling is in a very different emotional state from a child whose facial expression shows pain or discomfort.

Chapter 2 explores how to break down communication barriers.

Voice Tone

Another part of the expressive communication is the voice tone that a child uses. It's common for children with ASD to speak in a monotone, with the voice inflection not changing to indicate whether they're asking a question or emphasizing a point. Some children with ASD sing what they want to say; others might use a voice tone or pitch that one would not expect, given the child's age or body size (Auxter, Pyfer, Zittel & Roth, 2010). *Example:* Jack is 6'1" and has no problems with his vocal cords. When he speaks, though, he talks in a high-pitched voice like that of a 3-year-old girl who is excited. Jasmine, a 16-year-old girl, speaks primarily in a deep growl.

Receptive Communication

Receptive communication is just as important as expressive communication. While it's important for people to be able to express their own thoughts, it's also important that they understand what's going on around them. Children with ASD often encounter difficulties with receptive communication, including processing spoken conversations, interpreting pronouns, interpreting words or phrases literally, and understanding abstract concepts. Teachers should note that most aspects of receptive communication are not a problem for children with Asperger's, although they might struggle with abstract concepts and might interpret words literally.

Processing Spoken Conversations

Spoken language tends to overwhelm some children with ASD (Coyne & Fullerton, 2004). The more words directed at the child, the more overwhelmed he or she becomes. One of the common images associated with autism — a child rocking back and forth, hands over his or her ears — often stems from the child's being overwhelmed by spoken language or loud noises. Imagine that you're in a foreign country and someone starts talking to you in a language that you don't understand. For the first second or two, you try to understand. Then, you stop listening and most likely become frustrated as you realize that you have no idea what the person is saying. Eventually, you become overwhelmed. The same thing occurs for a child with ASD. It's unclear whether the child's distress stems from his or her becoming overwhelmed by the auditory stimulus of the person's voice or from the child's difficulties in processing spoken language. It might be a combination of both.

Whatever the reason, conducting a conversation with a child with ASD can cause great stress to the child.

Interpreting Pronouns

Children with ASD also tend to struggle with applying pronouns (e.g., he, she, you, me). They have difficulty understanding to whom one is referring (Coyne & Fullerton, 2004). *Example:* The teacher asks Ken to pass the ball to the boy next to him by saying "Pass it to him." Ken freezes and scans the class, while he continues to hold the ball. When the teacher repeats the instruction, Ken passes the ball to a girl three rows over. Most likely, Ken was unclear as to which student the teacher meant by using the word "him."

Interpreting Words or Phrases Literally

Children with ASD often tend to take things literally. So, when encountering slang or common expressions, children with ASD often interpret the statement very differently from how it was intended (Coyne & Fullerton, 2004). *Example:* Jessie's classmates urge him to "Run downfield." Jessie freezes in place for a few seconds with a confused look on his face. He then starts to run in place, while also attempting to crouch down. He was trying to "run" and "get down on the field" at the same time. *Another example:* The teacher stands by the bleachers and tells the class to sit down. Students start to climb up on the bleachers, but Jessie does exactly what is asked and sits down right where he is standing.

In cases in which a statement, when interpreted literally, seems unrealistic or out of place, a child with ASD can become distracted by the statement, causing him or her to ask repeatedly for clarification. *Example:* The teacher responds "Cool beans!" to one of her students who has completed a task correctly. A student with ASD overhears that and starts asking: "Where are the beans? I don't see any beans." The child with ASD stops performing the activity and continues to ask numerous questions about the "cool beans."

Because children with ASD tend to take phrases so literally, sarcasm can be very difficult for them to understand. They often miss the fact that the person is being sarcastic and take the statement at face value. *Example:* Jackie makes a mistake while playing tennis, and the ball goes flying over the fence. A teammate says, sarcastically, "Nice hit!" For the rest of the unit, Jackie continues to hit the ball over the fence, thinking she has made a "nice hit."

Understanding Abstract Concepts

Along with taking statements literally, children with ASD tend to struggle with abstract concepts (Auxter, Pyfer, Zittel & Roth, 2010). They do much better with concepts that are concrete. If they can see a representation of the concept, they find it easier to understand it. In general, children with ASD tend to be visual learners, so the more visual representations of the concept they encounter, the better. Therefore, concepts such as "teams," "running as fast as you can" and even the concept of time can be difficult for a child with ASD to grasp because they're difficult to visualize.

Example: If the teacher tells a class of 4th-graders to "Practice throwing and catching with your partner for a few minutes," most students will practice with their partners until the teacher tells them to stop or to begin a different activity. A 4th-grader with ASD, though, can have difficulty interpreting the phrase "for a few minutes" and won't know what he or she is supposed to do. So, instead of telling the students "… for a few minutes," the teacher might say "… for five minutes." The teacher then would start an egg timer or set the clock on the scoreboard so that the child with ASD could see the amount of time remaining for the activity. More suggestions of how to make abstract concepts more visual and concrete are provided in Chapters 2 and 3.

Need for Schedule & Routine

As a reward for good behavior, the teacher decides to give students a "choice day," for which she sets up several stations with different favorite activities that have been part of the unit. Students are allowed to pick whichever stations they like. The teacher explains the rules of the class and then yells "Go!" Students jump up and start running to their desired stations, while yelling to their peers. A student with ASD starts yelling and rocking. He refuses to move from his warm-up spot.

Because it was such an unusually nice spring day, the PE teacher decides to hold class outside. When she announces to students that they will go outside, most of the students cheer. However, Talihia (a student with ASD) starts asking numerous questions. "Why are we going outside?" "What are we going to play?" "When are we coming inside?" The aide redirects Talihia and they proceed outside with the class. For the whole period, Talihia appears anxious and distracted. She asks continually when the class will be going back inside.

Most children with ASD have an extreme need for consistency in their environment. They thrive on the use of schedules and the predictability of their environment (DSM-V, in-press). Because of their need for a predictable schedule, many children with ASD have specific routines that they follow throughout the day. Their routines break down every aspect of the day and, often, are very rigid. *Example:* When Ricardo wakes up, he goes to the bathroom, brushes his teeth, washes his face, brushes his hair, puts on his underwear, puts on his socks, puts on his pants, etc. Ricardo would never consider dressing before brushing his teeth. Depending on how rigidly Ricardo follows his schedule, he might not even consider changing the order in which he puts on his clothing.

Without a routine, or when the routine is changed, children with ASD can feel anxious and disoriented. In fact, one of the most common causes of outbursts in children with ASD is caused by a change in the schedule (Coyne & Fullerton, 2004). *Example:* The teacher tells students that they will be going outside, so they should wait in a line by the exit door. The class's normal routine, however, is to sit in teams in the middle of the gymnasium. When a student with ASD enters the gymnasium, he walks past the line of waiting students and sits in his team spot, where he sits every other time. When the teacher asks him to join the line by the door, the child starts screaming and rocking. This response stems from the disorientation he feels from the change in routine. When a child with ASD doesn't know what to expect or what is coming next, he or she often grows anxious. As a result, the child might disengage from the activity, ask off-topic questions or try to revert to a routine that is familiar.

Children with ASD see every aspect of their environment as part of their routine. Where they participate in the activity, what they are wearing, what the teacher is wearing and whom they are with are all important aspects to their routine. *Example:* Billy wore a blue pinnie on the first day of class, so he now expects to wear a blue pinnie in every class thereafter. Asking him to wear a yellow pinnie can disorient him.

Even small details that you don't see as relevant — the order in which the class performs stretches, which direction the students face while warming up, where the equipment is laid out, etc. — can make a big difference to a child with ASD. Adding to the challenge: Because each child is different, what might be a big deal for one child with ASD doesn't faze another child with ASD. *Example:* While Billy wants to wear his blue pinnie, he doesn't care about what position he plays. On the other hand, Caleb will wear any-color pinnie the teacher wants, but he refuses to play any position other than defender.

Changes with people and their appearance also can be distressing. *Example:* If the teacher always wears her hair in a ponytail and then one day comes to class with her hair down, that can be perceived as a dramatic change. Another potentially difficult situation can stem from a change in staffing. *Example:* If the PE teacher is out sick and a substitute takes his or her place, that can disorient a child with ASD.

Sensory Perception

Leonard is in 7ᵗʰ-grade PE class. One day, during PE class, the school's athletic director tested the sound on the scoreboard for the big game. When Leonard heard the buzzer, he ran into the locker room and refused to come out. Now, when Leonard enters the gym, he walks over to the wall with the scoreboard, puts his fingers in his ears and proceeds to hum and rock. As the teacher aide redirects Leonard to his poly spot, the teacher starts the music that accompanies the class warm-up. Leonard starts to rock more vigorously, while screaming in a high-pitched tone. After a few minutes, he runs back to the locker room. Meanwhile, Devin is having a great time with warm-up. As the warm-up progresses, though, the teacher notices that Devin is moving closer and closer to the speakers. By the end of warm-up, Devin has stopped participating and is standing near the speakers, mesmerized by the music.

An unusual response to sensory stimulus — a heightened response (hypersensitivity) or low response (hyposensitivity) — is to be added next year to the definition of ASD (DSM-V, in-press). For a child with heightened sensory responsiveness, for example, the noise of a balloon popping sounds more like a small explosion (or, in some cases, even a large explosion), whereas a child who is hyposensitive to sound might gravitate toward loud music and find it appealing. This unusual response to sensory input can include all five senses (hearing, sight, touch, taste and smell) or only one or two.

Sensory perception runs on a spectrum, from extreme sensitivity to an extreme *lack* of sensitivity to a stimulus or sensation. Think about a person's general sense of touch. People with a "typical" level of sensitivity don't really notice the texture of a cotton sweatshirt touching their skin. For people who are extremely hypersensitive, that cotton sweatshirt can feel more like they're wearing a shirt made out of a steel-wool pad. On the flip side, people who are hyposensitive won't feel the texture of the sweatshirt even if they were asked to think about it. Many children, though, fall somewhere in between those two extremes. So, the cotton shirt might feel more like an itchy wool sweater or it might just feel like a rough, old cotton sweatshirt that has lost its fuzz. The interpretation of the sensation varies from child to child. Sensory sensitivity also can vary, depending on which sense is being stimulated. A child with ASD might be hypersensitive to sound and touch but have typical sensitivity with his or her sense of sight.

One's vestibular system — responsible for balance and general spatial orientation — and proprioception — understanding where each component of one's body is in space — also can be affected by sensory perception. For children whose vestibular system is hypersensitive (also called vestibular defensiveness), motor movements such as running and jumping seem frightening and might even be nauseating. (Think of the feeling one experiences on a rollercoaster.) Children with sensitivity often experience vertigo (similar to what one experiences with a severe ear infection).

While children without a disability will develop an understanding of gravity through exploration, children with ASD who have a hypersensitive vestibular system often avoid activities in which their feet have to leave the ground, and stay away from playground equipment. They also struggle with activities such as fielding a ground ball because it requires them to bend over and then stand up quickly while also throwing a ball. In more severe situations, these children will feel uncomfortable even moving between a standing and sitting position. As a result, they sometimes might lie on the floor in a starfish position in an attempt to feel grounded.

Children with a hyposensitive vestibular system often seek out sensory experiences in which they are moving their position in space (e.g., jumping up and down, hanging upside down from monkey bars while swinging back and forth, rocking back and forth while standing or sitting).

While it's not so common for children to experience hypersensitivity in proprioception, it *is* possible. These children are constantly aware of the position of their bodies and cannot ignore it. Therefore, they tend to have difficulty sitting still for any length of time. They also find some positions incredibly uncomfortable because of the constant feedback that they're receiving from their muscles and ligaments. So, they tend to avoid and/or dislike many physical activities that require their bodies to remain in positions (e.g., batting stances, overhead soccer throw-in) that are not typical of daily activities. Stretching is another activity that they might not enjoy, because even a light stretch can feel uncomfortable.

A child with proprioception hyposensitivity often is not aware of where his or her body is in space. Therefore, the child tends to be clumsy and has difficulty developing motor skills (particularly fine motor skills or more complex motor skills). Because they can't feel where their limbs are in relation to the rest of their bodies, it's difficult for children with proprioception hyposensitivity to reflect on how a motor behavior feels. Typically, when we perform a motor behavior correctly, we think about how the body felt and then replicate the motor pattern. When one isn't able to reflect on the sensation, though, it's difficult to learn through experience and replicate a previously successful attempt.

Obsession With an Object or Topic

Graham is obsessed with train schedules. As he walks into the gym, he tells the teacher that the Metro North Train is currently arriving at Grand Central Station and will be departing again in five minutes. Throughout the class, Graham continually mentions trains, train schedules and train engineers. About every five minutes, he looks at the clock and announces a train's arrival at some station in the United States. When the teacher tries to cover the clock, Graham becomes frantic.

Children with ASD can display a preoccupation with a particular object or category (DSM-IV, in-press). It's not uncommon for them to be enthralled with a topic such as dinosaurs, cars or "Star Wars." Children who don't have an intellectual disability along with ASD can learn an extensive amount of information about a subject, to the point that they become experts. *Example:* Jeremy is obsessed with frogs. He can tell you both the common names and scientific names of most species, where they live, their life expectancy, what they eat and predators they have to avoid.

When children with ASD become interested in a topic, they tend to relate everything in their world to that topic. For children with ASD who have some verbal abilities, they often will strive to bring a conversation back to their topic of interest. *Example:* The class is talking about basketball. Jacob raises his hand and states: "Frogs have teeth in the roof of their mouths called vomerine teeth." Students with ASD also often try to arrange it so that everything they play with will relate somehow to their topics of interest. *Example:* When the class is practicing a running drill, Jacob starts hopping across the floor like a frog.

In other instances, it might be less of an obsession with a topic and more of an obsession with a specific object. *Example:* Jennifer was obsessed with a red string. When she accidentally left her red string at home, she spent the entire day looking for it while constantly repeating the word "string." Even when she was provided with a piece of string that looked identical (at least to the teacher), Jennifer would not accept it as a replacement. It's not simply the obsession with the concept of "red string" but that very specific piece of string.

Lack of Imaginative Play

The teacher has decided to change the warm-up activity for her 3rd-grade class by having students act out the different animals that she calls out (Animal Walks). Students spread out in the gym. The first animal called out is an elephant. Elliot, a student with ASD, stands in his spot staring at the other children. The teacher then calls out "snake." Elliot proceeds to sit down on the floor and play with his shoe. The teacher walks over to Elliot and says, "Can you act like a snake?" But he stares at her blankly and then returns his attention to his shoe.

Children are known for their amazing imaginations and creative play. Many children with ASD, however, don't participate in spontaneous, imaginative play (DSM-V, in-press). That can manifest itself in different ways. It might be that the child simply doesn't initiate play. *Example:* A child with ASD put into a room filled with toys and children might simply sit there. When a ball is rolled toward a child with ASD, he or she is likely just to sit there holding it. It's unlikely that the child will jump up and engage in an activity or roll the ball back to another student.

When children with ASD do engage in play, they often don't use toys as other children of similar age typically use them (Auxter, Pyfer, Zittel & Roth, 2010). Instead of stacking the blocks to build a tower, for example, children with ASD tend to sort them into piles by color and shape. Or, when given a bucket filled with small cars, a child with ASD might stack the cars like blocks.

A child with ASD also might perform the same movement over and over again, with no change in behavior (DSM-V, in-press). Instead of creating a game or progressing the movement into a more deliberate activity, children with ASD tend to repeat a simplistic version of the motor task. *Example:* Josh has learned how to throw the ball. Instead of engaging another student in a game of catch or throwing the ball at different targets (maybe even trying to put it into a basket), Josh throws the ball at the wall over and over again for more than an hour, without interacting with anyone.

Many of the games played in physical education require children to "pretend _____," which can be difficult for children with ASD. *Example:* The class is playing a cooperative game in which students try to cross a moat filled with alligators by staying on a flat board that represents a bridge. Baxter is quick to inform the teacher that the flat board is not a bridge, there is no moat in the classroom and there are no alligators. Because of their difficulties in processing imaginative activities, children with ASD often insist that people recognize "reality" and admit that a board is just a board.

Repetitive Movements or Self-Stimming/Self-Soothing

The class is starting a new unit. In an attempt to provide a multi-disciplinary approach to the unit on soccer, the teacher has brought in different pictures of soccer being played all around the world. After three minutes, Sergio starts rocking back and forth while making a constant monotonous sound. The teacher ignores his behavior and starts to talk about the rules of the game. Sergio stands up and continues with his previous behaviors but also starts to flap his hand in front of his face. At this point, the other students are staring at him and not listening to the teacher's instructions.

Many children with ASD repeat a movement over and over again (DSM-V, in-press). Many different terms are used to refer to this repetitive behavior, including repetitive movements, self-stimming/self-soothing behaviors and stereotyped and repetitive motor mannerisms (e.g., hand or finger flapping or twisting, complex whole-body movements). A child with ASD might demonstrate those behaviors without any sort of prompting and often favors one or two specific movements. Some of the most common self-stimming/self-soothing behaviors are rocking the body, flapping the fingers in front of the face, spinning around in circles, walking on the toes, wringing the hands and playing with an object such as a string or a zipper. Some of the repetitive movements — such as head banging, biting oneself, picking at the skin, pulling out the hair or hitting oneself — can cause harm.

A few different theories attempt to explain why children with ASD use self-stimming/self-soothing behaviors. The most common belief is that a child uses it as a coping strategy to address being under- or over-stimulated (autismspeaks.org). *Example:* If a child is visually hyposensitive, he might flap his fingers in front of his face to create more visual stimulus. It's a self-stimulating technique that seems to make him feel at ease. Therefore, children with ASD often self-stim/self-soothe when they're stressed or when they don't have the appropriate amount of external stimulus.

Actually, self-stimming/self-soothing is a behavior that is seen regularly in people *without* disabilities; it just isn't as extreme. Think of the person who taps his pencil or shakes his leg when he's bored, or the person who twirls her hair while she's thinking. These people are also providing themselves with a form of sensory stimulus. For children with ASD, though, self-stimming/self-soothing behaviors often are much more noticeable than simple pencil-tapping, and they occur more often.

The disruptive nature of the self-stimulating/self-soothing movements often leads people to stare at a person with ASD and think something is wrong. As a result, educators often try to teach self-stimming/self-soothing behaviors that are more acceptable in society. Another strategy to help contain such behaviors is through the use of physical activity. When a person with ASD participates in physical activity, we often see a decrease in the amount of self-stimming/self-soothing behaviors, even after physical activity ends (Levinson & Reid, 1993). So, educators would do well to encourage students with ASD to be physically active, especially before engaging in a learning situation.

Cognitive Functioning

Some children with ASD have an intellectual disability, but not all do. The empirical data supporting the correlation between the two disabilities are mixed and limited. Currently, it's unclear whether people with ASD have an intellectual disability or the problem lies with how the standardized tests used to identify intellectual disabilities are administered. It might be that a student has no intellectual disability; it's just that he or she has great difficulty performing within the structured school setting (Auxter, Pyfer, Zittel & Roth, 2010).

An intellectual disability (ID) is defined as having an IQ that is two standard deviations below what is considered normal, accompanied by difficulties in activities of daily living (DSM-IV-TR, 2000). A child with an intellectual disability might have difficulty performing life skills and activities of daily living, such as dressing or showering independently. It also can affect the child's ability to learn new skills. The level of the child's ID would determine how much it affects him or her. If the child has a mild intellectual disability, he or she would have far fewer delays than a child with a more moderate to severe intellectual disability.

Keep in mind that intellectual disability does not equal an inability to learn! Particularly for people with mild to moderate ID, it simply means that they take *longer* than average to learn, they might need extra guidance or they might not be able to learn the skill in its most complex form. With help and training, children with an ID are able to learn to perform many activities independently. *Example:* At age 14, Adriane could turn the shower on and rinse her body, but efforts to wash her hair often resulted in her jumping out of the shower screaming because she had gotten shampoo in her eyes. Within a few weeks and with a few key words (e.g., tip your head back) to help her remember what to do, she had no problem.

ASD also is associated with other learning disabilities, including dyslexia (difficulty with reading and deciphering symbols), dysgraphia (difficulty putting thoughts on paper, writing and spelling), dyscalculia (difficulty with numbers and mathematical concepts) and attention deficit hyperactivity disorder (National Center for Learning Disabilities Inc., 2011).

Motor Development & Motor Performance

Jaxson is in a grade 10 PE class that is completing a unit in soccer. During game play, Jaxson struggles to participate. When the ball is kicked to, him he kicks his leg too early, missing the ball entirely. When Jaxson attempts a throw-in, he raises the ball in front of his shoulders and then rigidly throws it to the ground right in front of his feet. When he runs down the field, he bumps in to three different players without acknowledging the contact. The teacher places Jaxson in the goal to see whether he will be more successful there, but Jaxson refuses to jump up to stop the balls above his head.

While some children with ASD are very athletic, many are delayed in reaching their motor skill development milestones and have general motor problems later in life (Manjiviona & Prior, 1995; Provost, Heimeri & Lopez, 2007; Reid & Collier, 2002; Staples & Reid, 2010). These delays are seen as early as the basic milestones such as sitting and crawling, and the delays then continue through childhood. It appears that gross motor skills are affected more significantly than object-control skills, although available research is limited (Staples & Reid, 2010).

In general, people with ASD tend to be robotic in their movements (Auxter, Pyfer, Zittel & Roth, 2010). These rigid movements can occur while performing any motor skill, from running to kicking and throwing. The rigidity is particularly noticeable in motor skills that require coordination of both sides of the body or both the arms and legs at one time. These movements tend to be broken down into pieces and be very choppy (Staple & Reid, 2010). *Example:* When jumping, a student with ASD bends his knees, then swings his arms back, then straightens his knees as he tries to jump. *Another example:* When Bobby runs, his arms become stiff, with his shoulders pulling up toward his ears, his fingers bent tensely into a claw and his arms swinging only a little. His legs are stiff, with little bend in the knees, and almost all of his weight on his heels. (Picture the Tin Man running.) When Bobby throws a ball, he refuses to bend his arm, instead throwing with more of a windmill movement.

Applying the arms to create momentum or balance is another area in which many children with ASD struggle: often, their arm movements are not beneficial or functional. In fact, they often hinder the child's performance (Staples & Reid, 2010). For example, the arms of a child with ASD often tend to flop around when the child hops, rather than being useful for balance and momentum.

Children with ASD also tend to struggle with motor planning. A significant delay has been observed in the ability of children with ASD to plan how to move their bodies in space, especially when planning a motor movement that requires them to reach and grasp an object (Mari, et al., 2003). If not instructed specifically on how to approach a motor task, children with ASD often choose energy-inefficient options or just don't approach the task at all. *Example:* A child with ASD is completing an obstacle course and comes across a bar that is at hip height. Instead of trying to climb under the bar (as most children without a disability would), the child attempts to climb *over* the bar or just stands there and stares at it.

Determining how much force to put behind an object they are propelling also can prove difficult for children with ASD (Auxter, Pyfer, Zittel & Roth, 2010; Morin & Reid, 1985). They might put far too much force behind the object, resulting in its overshooting the target, or put far too little force behind the object, resulting in its falling short of the target. *Example:* The teacher asks

Norman to toss him a ball. Norman throws the ball a good 20 feet past where the teacher is standing. Howard, on the other hand, tosses the ball so lightly that it lands about two feet in front of him and seven feet short of the teacher. Part of the problem also could stem from the fact that children with ASD often don't follow through after kicking or throwing a ball. They tend to stop the limb when it's perpendicular to the ground rather than when it's extended toward the target.

Some other motor performance difficulties that children with ASD encounter include:

- General delay in response time, resulting in difficulties with kicking, catching and striking. *Example:* The ball rolls past a student with ASD before he recognizes the need to move his leg, or he tries to respond but is ineffective.

- A lack of age-appropriate opposition between arms and legs when running and jumping, and the arm movements are not coordinated with the body.

- Immature throwing and catching patterns are demonstrated throughout adolescence and, sometimes, into adulthood.

- Great difficulty in running up to a ball and kicking it or dribbling the ball while running. When approaching a ball to be kicked, children with ASD often stop running, stand on two feet and then kick the ball.

- Struggling to rotate the body and transfer weight when striking a ball.

Jumping and running are two basic skills that are particularly difficult for some children with ASD. The skills are difficult because of the fluidity that's required for the motion to occur, but also because they can affect the child's proprioceptive sense, making the tasks unappealing. While many children with ASD struggle with these tasks, however, others use jumping up and down as a self-stimming/self-soothing behavior. It just depends on how the child perceives the environment.

One factor that teachers need to consider here is that a child's motor development delays could be related more to his or her ability to understand the task than to perform the skill. Some researchers have questioned whether part of the reason that students with ASD score so poorly on motor performance tests is that they lack the motivation to perform (Houston-Wilson, 2010). It's also been observed that many children with ASD focus on the general goal of completing a task and don't pay attention to the process that they've been asked to use on the task. For example, when asked to gallop from point A to point B, children with ASD tend to run or walk. It's unknown, though, whether the children run because they can't gallop or because they interpret the goal of the activity as moving from point A to point B, and pay little attention to the means for doing that (Staples & Reid, 2010).

Myths About ASD

A number of myths are associated with ASD that can influence one's interactions with children with ASD, as well as their families. The following section lists some of the most popular myths about ASD and some of the facts that can help dispel those myths.

Myth 1. ASD Can Be Cured

As of this writing, ASD has no known cure. A variety of interventions and treatments have been suggested to help lessen the effects of ASD, including behavioral intervention programs, special diets, homeopathic remedies and medications. Those approaches have yielded varying levels of success, but none of them has been found to "cure" a child of ASD. While one strategy might significantly decrease ASD characteristics in child A, it might have no effect on child B. Even when a treatment or strategy has helped a child decrease the characteristics of ASD, the child is not cured or free from the characteristics entirely.

Myth 2. People With ASD Have Savant Abilities

People with ASD often are portrayed in motion pictures and on television as having some amazing talent or savant characteristic, as did Dustin Hoffman's character in "Rain Man." They're often shown as having an unnatural ability to count objects, memorize extensive amounts of information on a particular topic or demonstrate an extreme talent in a skill such as music. While some people with ASD *do* have these talents, they're actually quite rare. In fact, only about 1 percent of people diagnosed with ASD demonstrate savant abilities. It's also important to note that these skills often are referred to as "splinter skills": skills that apply to one or two very specific areas in life, but not to other domains. Therefore, the savant skills often don't help the person in most everyday activities and might even interfere with the person's quality of life.

Example: Josh has an amazing ability to memorize. He has memorized the contents of all the phone books in the state of Michigan. If someone gives Josh a Michigan resident's name, he can recite that person's address and phone number purely from memory. But Josh isn't able to dial that person's phone number and have a conversation with him or her on the phone. In fact, Josh refuses to go near a phone. His ability to memorize information is impressive, but it doesn't help him with his everyday activities.

Myth 3. ASD Is a Result of Emotional Neglect

In the 1940s, some doctors believed that autism was caused by parents — particularly mothers — being cold toward their children. It was believed that, when a mother didn't interact enough with her child or provide a nurturing environment, the child would develop autism. Since then, we've come to realize that absolutely no evidence exists to suggest that parenting practices lead to autistic tendencies. Autism affects children who come from some of the most nurturing families.

Myth 4. ASD Is Caused by Vaccines

The original study linking autism to the measles/mumps/rubella (MMR) vaccine was based on falsified data. Many studies since have shown no correlation between vaccinations and ASD, and the medical community supports that conclusion (AMA, 2004).

Myth 5. ASD Is Caused by 'Spoiling' the Child

Sometimes, children with ASD appear to be throwing temper tantrums or meltdowns similar to what we see when a 3-year-old wants candy at the supermarket. The difference is, the child with ASD might be 15 years old. As a result, people sometimes conclude that a temper tantrum simply represents a child's desire for attention, or that it's the result of parents' spoiling their children. The reality is that how a parent disciplines a child has nothing to do with the development of ASD. Because they lack many of the communication and social skills needed to express themselves, children and adolescents with ASD often resort to other ways of expressing their needs, and that sometimes results in socially unacceptable behavior.

Myth 6. Children With ASD Can't Build Social Relationships

Because children with ASD often display aloofness and odd social behaviors, it's often assumed that they can't feel emotions or establish meaningful relationships with people. That's definitely not the case! Most, if not all, children with ASD are perfectly capable of feeling emotions. They're also capable of building social relationships with others. The catch is that children with ASD often express their love and appreciation for other people in a manner that's different from what we expect. Instead of giving someone a hug, for example, they might hand the person a piece of string or play with the person's hair. Unfortunately, when children with ASD use these types of behaviors to try making friends, they're often branded as "weird" and are dismissed or taunted.

Children with ASD have difficulty creating social relationships that many other children develop because their peers don't understand the relationship. However, when children with ASD interact with one another over time, they often develop meaningful friendships. The manner in which they interact might seem foreign to a person without ASD, but the children seem to understand one another and not notice the social oddities.

Social relationships also can take root when a child with ASD receives effective social skills training and is in an environment in which people understand that the child might express social skills in a manner that's different from other children. Many parents of children with ASD see that their children are very affectionate; some even say that their children with ASD are more empathetic toward them than their other children. Keep in mind that this is another area in which one will see a wide spectrum of abilities. Some children with ASD are able to express their emotions more so than others.

Conclusion

This chapter has provided a definition of ASD, a description of the common characteristics of people with ASD and how those characteristics can be misinterpreted by others. It also has tried to dispel some myths typically associated with autism. Having an understanding of the common characteristics of students with ASD will help teachers design appropriate learning activities. Providing all students — including students with ASD — meaningful and developmentally appropriate learning activities that contribute to their attaining physical education program goals is a major theme of this book. Subsequent chapters will offer suggestions on how to apply curriculum models and choose teaching strategies that will help students with ASD achieve the learning goals that teachers have for *all* students in physical education classes.

Chapter 2 ——————————————
Instructional Strategies for Enhancing Communication & Managing Sensory Perception Disorders

Content

Introduction

This chapter describes strategies that will be particularly useful when teaching students with ASD, both in inclusive and self-contained physical education classes. The chapter begins with some basic tips for helping PE teachers meet the learning needs of students with ASD in their classes, then offers strategies for handling situations that occur within a physical education setting involving communication and managing sensory issues. Applying these strategies successfully depends on adapting to the characteristics of each student with ASD.

General Considerations

The strategies that follow address the importance of being consistent, finding out what strategies other stakeholders are using, having a toolbox ready and providing the assistance that students need, but no more than necessary.

Be consistent. With everything you do, it's important that you're consistent. Use consistent terminology, keep your routine the same, use the same behavior-management strategies, etc. The more predictable you make the environment for a child with ASD, the better.

Find out what strategies other stakeholders are using. This is not the time to reinvent the wheel! Feel free to ask parents what strategies work for their children. Many parents are happy to share communication strategies, as well as helpful tips. Also, talk with classroom teachers, paraprofessionals, child-study team members and past teachers to see whether they have any ideas. It's much easier to incorporate a previously established system into your routines than to start from scratch. It takes less time to prepare, and students with ASD will respond much faster (and will appreciate the consistency).

Have a toolbox ready. Especially when first getting to know the student, you really have no idea what is going to work. So, go into class with Plans A through G. If one approach doesn't work, then it's time to move on to the next approach. Having the equipment and ideas in place before trying to manage a classroom of students will make it much easier. *Example:* Have an array of different types of balls that are different textures, weights and sizes. That way, if a student really dislikes the texture of a ball, or he or she isn't skilled enough to use the smaller ball, you don't have to dig through the closet looking for an alternative. The more options you make available, the easier it will be to accommodate and assist a student while still attending to the rest of the class.

Find a healthy balance. As educators, our primary goal is to help students learn and be successful. Don't assume that, just because a child has ASD, he or she needs every accommodation mentioned in this chapter. For students to develop skills, they need to have some sort of challenge. The accommodations are in place only to help children thrive in the environment and to help them cope with their situations. If you make too many accommodations, it actually does students a disservice. Start with the accommodation that you know the child needs — based on what is identified in the student's individualized education program (IEP) and what others have suggested — and then add or subtract, as needed. There's nothing wrong with adding more accommodations if a student is struggling. Just remember that the ultimate goal is creating and maintaining a productive learning environment.

Make it work for you and the student! Remember that the accommodations suggested in this chapter are simply recommendations. You can modify the approach to fit the child in whatever way is needed. You also need to consider your own teaching style and class structure. Every teacher has his or her own style and personality. Therefore, you might need to modify a strategy for it to blend in with the rest of your teaching toolbox. So long as the student's needs are being met, feel free to add your own personal touch!

Communication

Students with ASD might have limited verbal abilities or might be nonverbal. Because communication goes both ways, think about how you're going to communicate with all of your students — particularly with your students with ASD — and how they're going to communicate with you. Remember that, because each child is unique, there isn't one best strategy or tool. Different children prefer different strategies. Still, some commonly used communication techniques and devices can be helpful.

Augmentative Communication Systems

Sign Language

What It Is: Because of their difficulties with verbal communication, many students with ASD use sign language to communicate. Most children use American Sign Language (ASL), although some might use a modified version.

How to Apply It: It might be helpful for you to know some of the basics of ASL so that you can communicate with the students who use it. You don't need to become fluent, but basic signs such as "good," "bad" and "sit" can come in handy. *(For some common ASL signs, see the CD-ROM that accompanies this book.)* Most teachers will agree that knowing the sign for "bathroom" is also essential ... for all students! Some children with ASD might not actually sign to you, but they can recognize signs directed to them. Particularly for students who become overwhelmed with auditory stimuli (including the sound of your voice), sign language provides a means to communicate your thoughts and desires in a manner that doesn't overwhelm the students.

Use the ASL sign while you vocalize your thought. You don't need to sign every word, just the important concept that you're trying to communicate. *Example:* While you tell the class to "Sit down on the floor next to your partner," you can sign "Sit" to help clarify your instructions. *Remember:* Visual aides are very helpful!

Considerations/Helpful Tips

- You can find a few of the signs that you might commonly use in a classroom on the CD-ROM that accompanies this book. Also, some great Web sites — including www.alsopro.com — are available to help you out. You can find those sites at the end of the book on the CD-ROM, as well.

- Make sure that students can see the signs you use so that they can respond. Always stand in front of the student and ensure that no barriers (other students) obscure the child's line of sight.

Pick-a-Hand

What It Is: Pick-a-Hand is a commonly used strategy for students who are nonverbal or who have limited verbal abilities. Use it to allow students to choose between two different options. They point to one of your hands to signify their option, instead of verbalizing what they would like.

How to Apply It: Stand in front of the student when asking him or her a question with two options. When you describe option 1, extend your left hand in front of your body. Still holding your left hand out, describe option 2 and extend your right hand. Then, instruct the student to touch the hand corresponding to the option he or she wants to choose.

Pick-a-Hand is useful in a variety of situations. You can use it for everyday communication when you want to know what the child wants. *Example:* "Do you want the racket or the bat?" You also can use it when the student is flustered and you don't know why. *Examples:* "Do you need to use the bathroom?" "Are you thirsty?" In the last two examples, a student might not pick either hand, because you might not have identified the problem. In that case, provide other options until you identify the student's need or desire. Start with what you know normally causes the behavior (e.g., Jeff usually yells like that when he has to use the bathroom), and then go from there (e.g., maybe he is hurt or hungry).

You also can use Pick-a-Hand to gauge a child's understanding, by saying, "Touch my hand if you understand." Then, wait until the student touches your hand. If he or she doesn't touch your hand, you'll know there is still a communication barrier.

Considerations/Helpful Tips

- If you use Pick-a-Hand to gauge a child's understanding, it might be necessary to change the parts of your body that the student taps to demonstrate understanding. While we've emphasized the importance of consistency throughout this book, this is one instance in which some alteration is necessary. Otherwise, the technique might not gauge understanding, but rather elicit a rote response. If students have learned that when they touch your nose, you go away, they might do so even if the instructions are unclear. To prevent that, you can say, "Touch my arm if you understand" and then, in a later instance, say, "Touch *your* nose if you understand."

- It also might be that a student touches your hand because you said, "Touch my hand" and not because he or she understands the directions. This isn't a perfect science; you need to watch students to gauge whether they really understand the instructions.

Communication Board

What It Is: The general purpose of a communication board is to provide people with ASD with a way to express their thoughts or desires without having to speak. There are many different types of communication boards. The simplest communication boards consist of pictures that are attached to a plastic board or a flipbook from which the child chooses pictures to communicate.

The most complex communication boards are computers, through which the child either types in words or selects pictures on a touch screen. The computer then composes a statement and provides an automated message. The iPad has become a popular communication-board platform among students with ASD. Also, some cell phone applications serve the same function. Some students use a combination of computer technology and flipbook images, depending on the environmental circumstances.

Another type of communication system that is similar to communication boards is the Picture Exchange Communication System (PECS). Students have a notebook with a series of different images and words attached by Velcro®. Students also have a strip of cardboard that also contains Velcro® or there may be a blank strip of Velcro® on the front of the notebook. To communicate, the student selects the appropriate cards from the notebook (e.g., "I want" and "ball"), and attaches the cards to the blank strip of Velcro®. The student then gives the line of cards to the appropriate person (e.g., the teacher). One of the main differences separating PECS from other augmentative strategies is that a student using PECS is supposed to initiate the request as well as respond to questions and make social commentary (e.g., "I like _____."). Most other strategies are primarily reactive, in which the student responds after another person initiates the conversation.

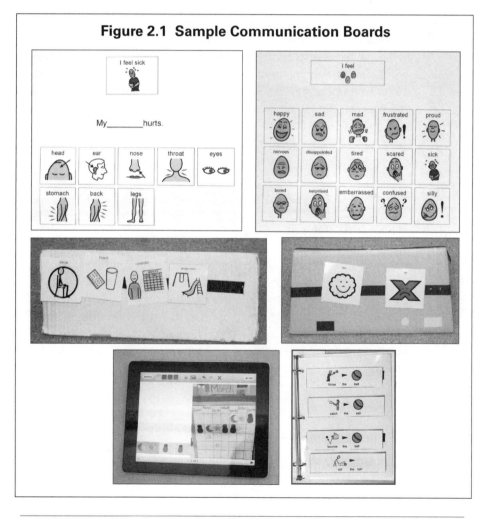

Figure 2.1 Sample Communication Boards

How to Apply It: Whenever you want to communicate with a student, make sure that he or she has access to the communication device. You need to be extra patient when a student is using a communication device. It often takes the student a little bit of extra time to select the icons/letters. Give the student plenty of time to respond. You can help the student by using yes/no questions or phrasing the question so that he or she can answer in only a few words. Avoid trying to guess what students are saying in the middle of their phrases or in the middle of typing/selecting an icon. If you guess wrong, the student has to stop what he or she was saying and choose "No" to answer you. He or she then has to go back to the original train of thought and start over. That often leads to frustration. Instead, wait until the child is finished with the entire statement.

Considerations/Helpful Tips

- One limiting factor with all communication devices that rely on icons is the icons that are presented. If students are trying to communicate a thought but don't have the appropriate icon, they are left with two choices: 1) choose an icon that is similar and hope that the person understands, or 2) don't communicate. Both options are far from ideal and can lead to frustration, wasted time and misunderstandings. Within physical education, students encounter many concepts and objects that they don't encounter in the typical classroom. Items such as bats, balls and pinnies probably aren't included on their communication boards. Some concepts, such as "team" and "warm-up," also might be missing. Usually, those symbols can be added to the communication board if they're requested in advance. Therefore, at the beginning of the school year, you might want to provide the child study team with a list of some basic symbols that will be essential for your class. If the student is able to handle changing the symbols on the communication board throughout the year, you might even provide the child study team with unit-specific lists and ask that the student's computer be updated appropriately. Keep in mind that the child study team needs to receive this list with enough time to add the icons. So, provide it to them well in advance of starting the unit and not the morning of.

- If you help pick out the symbols, make sure that they're as realistic to the action as possible. *Example:* If your class is playing soccer and you want to add an icon, use a picture of a soccer ball, not a tennis ball. If you choose an image of a person performing jumping jacks to represent warm-up, make sure that jumping jacks are in your warm-up activities.

- To help the child associate the symbol to the actual object, everything in the gymnasium should be labeled using the same images as are used in the communication device. *Example:* If the communication board has an image of a water fountain for when the student wants a drink, place that same image right on the actual water fountain where the student can see it. The more you label, the better. Place pictures on equipment carts, bathroom doors, where students line up, etc. Usually, you can request copies of the images used in the communication device from the child study team.

- When talking with a student who is using a communication board, remember to ask only one question at a time. If you ask a string of questions all at once, you won't know which question the student is answering. *Example:* Miguel walks into class and you say: "Hi! How was your weekend? Did you have fun? We're going to have a great class today! Do you need to go to the bathroom before we start?" When Miguel's computer says "Yes," you won't know whether he needs to use the bathroom or he had fun over the weekend.

- If you don't understand what the student is trying to communicate, that's okay! Ask him or her to try again. If the child is using a computer, it often comes with a "repeat" button. A paraprofessional who is familiar with the student's basic communication approach also might be able to help you until you become more familiar with the system. If you understood some of what the child said but not all of it, tell the student what you understood and then ask him or her to clarify what you missed.

- Never pretend that you understand what a student with ASD is saying if you're unsure! It's insulting and frustrating for the student. In some situations, pretending to understand can even lead to problems. *Example:* The swim teacher tells her students it's time to go to the locker room and change. A student with ASD asks a question, but the teacher doesn't fully hear her. In the teacher's haste to get things going, she smiles and says, "Yes." Imagine the teacher's shock when the student starts stripping down on the pool deck! Apparently, the student had asked, "Should I change here?" While this example is humorous, a situation like this can be embarrassing for the student and could have serious implications, depending on the child's age and the group's level of understanding.

- The only way the communication systems works is if you can see what students are pointing at or can hear what the computer is saying. In a classroom, this is a little bit easier to handle, because students are sitting at their desks and classroom noise generally is at a reasonable decibel level. In physical education class, though, you might be in a loud gymnasium or on a big, open field. And while you should always have your eyes on all students, you might not notice the student pointing to his or her communication device. Here are a couple of strategies to use:

- If the student has a paraprofessional, request that he or she helps the student draw your attention when trying to communicate with you.

- If you're standing in front of the group, it might be appropriate for the paraprofessional to repeat what the child's computer says so that the entire class can hear it. If the student is pointing at images, ask the paraprofessional to verbalize the student's message.

- If a paraprofessional is not available, you might want to consider using another peer to help out. While still participating in the class, the peer would verbalize the information from a child with ASD in the same way that a paraprofessional would. *Remember:* Teach the peer how to use the communication device. Also, use a variety of students as peers throughout the semester.

- Work out a system for students with ASD to attract your attention before trying to communicate. Students might need to raise their hands or walk up and stand in front of you.

- Remind the class of the importance of being quiet while a student with ASD is contributing to a class discussion. If students are talking or bouncing a ball, it will be difficult to hear the child's computer.

• In case the child's computer system freezes or crashes, have an alternative mode of communication (e.g., back-up cards) ready. The alternative mode doesn't have to cover all the typical vocabulary words, but it should cover the essentials so that the student is able to carry on some basic communication with you until the computer is fixed.

• Remember that the computer will need a power source. While many of the devices have a decent battery life, they might not be able to run an entire day without some sort of power charge. This becomes an important consideration when holding events such as field day, in which students are outside for an extended time.

- Remember that computers can do only what they have been programmed to do; they can't read a student's mind. Therefore, the computer message might not always represent exactly what the child wants to say. If the student makes a typo, the computer might not pick up on it and will repeat what the child has typed. *Example:* A student tries to type "I'd like" but types "Id like," instead. Looking at the screen, we would usually know what the student wants. But what the computer voices won't be correct. *Another Example:* If the student types "I want fall," instead of "I want ball." If you're balancing using a communication device with interacting with the rest of the class, you might not figure out the typo right away. This can be frustrating for students or can make it difficult for you to know what they want. If you have difficulty understanding, look at the screen to see whether the message is clearer when you read it. Also, consider the context of the message. "I want fall" doesn't really fit in the PE setting.

- While many new computers are small and portable, they're often too large to fit into a student's pocket. This is a challenge, particularly in physical education. When in the classroom, the computer sits on the student's desk and isn't a problem. When a student is running around a gymnasium, though, it's a different story. While it's important to always have a back-up system in case technology fails, most students don't like to use a system that's different from what they use on a day-to-day basis. We also want to encourage students to use their normal modes of communication to help strengthen their communication skills and to make them feel more comfortable. Therefore, you don't want to try to replace the student's computer with another form of communication. And a student should never be without a way to communicate! Therefore, you need to work out an alternative. Here are some suggestions:

  - Ask the paraprofessional to hold onto the computer throughout the physical activity.

  - Designate a spot (e.g., a folding chair) where the student can leave the computer. Try to keep this spot close to where the student is participating in the physical activity. A rolling stool and a technology cart with wheels are great options because you can roll them to wherever they're needed in the gymnasium. If you have several students using computers, the cart will have enough space to handle their computers.

- In some cases, students can carry their computers in a backpack, although that can impede their physical activity and it can be a hassle to take the laptop in and out.

- As with all pieces of technology, there is a risk that it will break during class. These computers are costly and, depending on how they're customized, they might take a considerable amount of time to repair. Because this is the student's primary means of communication, it's important that the computer is not put in a compromising situation. Within the physical education environment, that means you have a lot of things to consider! You can't completely avoid accidents, but here are some computer-protection tactics:

  - Make sure the computer isn't left on the ground where someone could step on it accidentally.

  - Keep it protected from flying balls.

  - Consider whether the child should keep the computer in his or her pocket, where it could be damaged if the child falls.

  - Try to keep the computer dry. A pool, rain shower, water fountain, damp field or a bathroom shower could spell disaster.

- When holding class outside, account for how the light reflects on the computer screen. Many screens become illegible when in direct sunlight, making it difficult for students to use them. You might consider staying close to a shaded area, or figure out a way to limit the amount of sun shining directly on the screen.

- What students wear also can affect the unit's efficiency. Many touch screens work from the heat of a person's hand. If the student is wearing gloves or has really cold fingers, the screen will not respond.

Resources

http://autism.healingthresholds.com/therapy/picture-exchange-communication-system-pecs

http://www.pecsusa.com/

Cohen, M.J. & Sloan, D.L. (2007). *Visual supports for people with autism: A guide for parents and professionals. Topics in autism.* Bethesda, MD: Woodbine House.

Figure 2.2 Tips for Interacting With Students Who Use Assistive Technology (Computers, Smart Phones, etc.)

1. Add icons that are specific to PE (e.g., bat, ball, pinnie).

2. Use symbols as realistic to activity as possible.

3. Ask one question at a time.

4. Don't be afraid to ask the student to press "Repeat."

5. Never pretend to understand!

6. Make sure that you can hear the computer or can see what the child is pointing to.

7. Have an alternative communication tool for when technology fails.

8. Have a power source available.

9. Remember that the computer reflects only what the student has input. Typos can interfere with communication.

10. Have a way to transport and store the communication device while students are engaged in activity.

11. Try to avoid sunlight reflecting directly on the screen, which can impede visibility.

12. Remember that protective clothing (e.g., gloves) or cold hands can interfere with students' ability to use touch screens.

Communication Strategies

Most often, you'll need to make only simple changes to your communication style to communicate with children with ASD. Each child will need his or her own combination of strategies to be successful. As with all accommodations, remember that you want to make as few of them as possible. When a student with ASD is out in the community, chances are that people will not modify how they speak to the child, so try to keep your speech pattern as natural as possible. That way, you help prepare the student for other experiences in life. But you also don't want to compromise the student's ability to understand and learn! If you need to make dramatic changes for a particular student to understand, then by all means, do so! What follows are some simple communication changes to consider.

Watching the Number of Words You Use

What It Is: For students who can become overwhelmed with spoken language, using a complete sentence might not be appropriate. Long sentences or phrases can lead children with ASD to shut down, which results in their not getting the information and experiencing frustration and/or fear. In most cases, some words within your sentences aren't necessary to communicating your meaning and can be removed to help enhance communication.

How to Apply It: When speaking to a student with ASD, think about how many words you are using. As a general rule, use only three or four words to describe what you want the child to do. *Example:* Instead of saying "Chimene, I want you to run around the gym five times," you might say simply "Run five laps." While you speak the words, you can show the movement of running, then point where you want the child to run, and hold up five fingers. When using such a limited number of words, choose them wisely. Using a verb (e.g., run, jump, swim) and a number or length that you want accomplished is usually easiest. If you want the student to run to a spot, clarify the destination. *Example:* "Dribble to red cone; back." Adjectives often are not necessary, and will be ignored by the child, anyway.

Considerations/Helpful Tips

- It's essential that you know how much the child can handle. While it's important to make accommodations for the student, you also want to use conversation styles that are as typical as possible to what he or she would see in society. By modeling typical conversation styles, you help students transition into other settings in the community and help them develop communication skills. Therefore, if the child can handle five- to six-word phrases, then use five- to six-word phrases. If the child can handle normal sentences, use them.

Avoiding Pronouns

What It Is: Many students with ASD have a difficult time understanding pronouns. Words such as "he," "she," "we," "you" and "it" often are too vague and abstract to a child with ASD. As a result, the student is unclear as to whom you are referring in a conversation. If the child doesn't know to whom you are referring, he or she can't complete the instructions you're giving them.

How to Apply It: Because pronouns are so difficult for children with ASD to grasp, it's often better to avoid using them entirely. To do that, simply replace pronouns with names. *Example:* Instead of saying "Your turn" to Caleb, you would say "Caleb's turn." Also, while you say "Caleb's turn," point at him. For children who struggle with pronouns, use everyone's name, including your own. *Example:* With a drill in which you and Caleb pass a ball back and forth, say, "Caleb's turn, Lissa's turn, Caleb's turn, Lissa's turn," again pointing at Caleb and then at yourself.

Considerations/Helpful Tips

- If you believe that a student with ASD can learn the pronouns (or the classroom teacher has asked you to work on it), use them interchangeably with names. Use the person's name first, then mix in the pronoun that's appropriate for that person, followed again by the person's name. You then can wean the student slowly from having to hear names.

- Point at the person to whom you're referring, as well as saying his or her name. A student with ASD might not know another student's name, or even *your* name. Providing the visual helps to clarify.

Using Your Words Literally

What It Is: Because students with ASD have such a hard time with sarcasm and slang, it can be very helpful to say exactly what you mean.

How to Apply It: Avoid commonly used sayings, slangs and sarcasm. Also, try to state explicitly what you want students with ASD to do. *Example:* If you want students to sit on the bleachers, tell them to "Sit on the bleachers" and not "Have a seat." When students misinterpret what you say, it can lead to hurt feelings, frustration and even dangerous situations. It might be that the student interprets what you are saying in an entirely wrong — and dangerous manner — or it might result in their doing something for which they will be teased. Either way, if you keep it straightforward, the students are better off.

Considerations/Helpful Tips

- Make a list of sayings that you use often in your class. Everyone tends to use at least a handful of phrases consistently. Figure out a more specific or direct way to deliver that information.

- Particularly for students who are verbal and who don't have an intellectual disability, you can teach them what some of society's common sayings mean so that they can understand and apply them. You will have to tell students with ASD explicitly what the saying means and give them an example of when they can use it. That not only helps to break down a communication barrier but also helps provide the student with another socially acceptable behavior. If you teach students with ASD a new phrase, though, be prepared to reinforce appropriate and inappropriate use of the term.

Figure 2.3 Common Physical Education Terms With Literal Alternatives

Category	Term	Alternative
PE General	"Hustle." "Chop-chop." "Pick up the pace." "Let's go."	Be specific; describe desired behavior (e.g., "Get dressed faster," "Stay with the class").
	"Show some effort."	Be skill-specific (e.g., "Run faster").
	"Chill out."	Describe desired behavior (e.g., "Take a deep breath and sit down").
	"Focus."	Specify what student should do (e.g., "Look at ___," "Watch the ball").
	"Back off."	"Move away from (student's name)."
	"Time out."	"Stop playing."
	"Warm up."	Define what this means at the beginning of the semester.
	"Cool down."	Same as above.
	"Bring it in."	"Everyone stand on the center circle."
	"Partner up."	"Stand next to the person who will be your partner."
	"Cut it out."	"Stop doing ___." Remind students of the appropriate behavior.
	"My bad."	"I made a mistake."
	"Line up."	"Stand in line by the door."
	"Q & A time."	"Time to ask questions."
	"Have a seat."	"Sit down." Specify a location (e.g., on the bleachers).
Sport, General	"Support your teammate."	"Say 'Nice job' or give a high-five to your teammate."
	"Pass the ball."	"Kick the ball to (name of teammate)."

Figure 2.3 *(Cont.)*

Category	Term	Alternative
Sport, General	"Run downfield."	"Run toward the goal," or "Dribble toward the net."
	"Beat the other team/crush the other team/kill 'em."	"Score more points."
	"Play through the whistle."	"Keep playing until you hear the whistle."
Sport-Specific	**Baseball:** "Steal second." "Run home." "You're out." "Take your base." "Choke up on the bat."	Be specific: "Run to second base." "Run to home plate." "Your turn is over; time to sit." "Walk to first base." "Hold the bat here" (demonstrate).
	Basketball: "Cut to the basket." "Plant inside foot." "Make a basket."	"Run toward the basket." "Put weight on L/R foot." "Throw ball into the basket."
	Football: "Soft hands."	"Catch the ball with your hands."
	Track: "Run through the line." "Run like the wind." "Run like gazelle."	"Keep running until you've crossed the line." "Run fast."

Making Instructions Specific & Positive

What It Is: Because students with ASD take instructions so literally, you need to tell them exactly what you want from them. Also, tell them the behavior that you want to see, so that they're not left guessing. Many times, teachers tell students only what they *don't* want them to do, not what they *do* want them to do. Students with ASD often don't know what behavior they should be demonstrating in place of the inappropriate behavior.

How to Apply It: Avoid telling students what you don't want to see (e.g., "Don't touch that"). Instead, tell them exactly what they should be doing (e.g., "Keep your hands on your hips while waiting your turn").

Considerations/Helpful Tips

- Provide students with a visual demonstration at the same time that you give the instructions verbally.

- Ask the child study team or classroom teacher what key phrases they use to communicate basic rules. Chances are, if a student is having difficulty keeping his hands to himself in PE, he also is having difficulty keeping his hands to himself in his academic classes. Find out what phrases are effective with the student to keep the terminology consistent.

Keeping Instructions Simple

What It Is: While some students with ASD have a terrific memory for long lists of instructions, others do not. For many students with ASD, giving them a list of four or five instructions is too much. They often will complete only the first item or the last item on the list, leaving out the items in the middle.

How to Apply It: Give students with ASD one or two tasks at a time. After they have completed those tasks, give them one or two more. Also, provide visual reminders of the tasks so that they're less likely to be forgotten.

Considerations/Helpful Tips

- If you have created stations and have five different activities planned, students with ASD probably will have a difficult time remembering all of the stations, and they most likely will become overwhelmed. That doesn't mean you shouldn't use stations! In fact, stations are a great way to keep children with ASD included in an inclusive classroom. Just keep these strategies in mind:

  - Go over one station at a time with students with ASD.

  - Keep the instructions short and simple, emphasizing one goal.

  - Post simple instructions and/or a picture of the task to be completed at each station.

  - Review the activity with the student, one station at a time.

Using Consistent Phrases

What It Is: As students with ASD get to know you and your routine, they will become much more comfortable in your class. This comfort level often will increase their productivity and cooperation levels. To help them become more comfortable, try to keep your terminology consistent.

How to Apply It: Decide on what key words and phrases you want to use at the beginning of the school year. From then on, make sure that you use the same words each time in class. *Example:* Always call drills by the same names, use the same adjectives to describe a motion (e.g., always use "fast" instead of interchanging "quickly," "speedy" and "fast"), and use the same key words to teach a skill. Particularly when you refer to a specific part of your routine, be sure to use the same name. Once students with ASD have learned what the words or symbol means, they will stick to it.

Considerations/Helpful Tips

- Abbreviating a term or using a shortened version of it is just like using an entirely different word to students with ASD. For example, interchanging the terms "abdominal muscle" and "abs" might not work. Be careful to not abbreviate terms as you progress through the school year or unit.

- When choosing terminology, consider the terms that students use. You might call the hamstring flexibility test the "V sit," for example, while students have always called it the "sit and reach." If you know that's the term they usually use, it only makes sense to use their words. Consistent terminology also helps with communication between students with ASD and their peers. If you teach the student with ASD "V sit" but peers without disabilities refer to it as "sit and reach," students with ASD are going to have some difficulties. This is of particular importance if you have students who spend some days in self-contained PE classes and other days in inclusive classes. You want to help make the transition back and forth as smooth as possible. One way to ensure the ease of transition is to use terms that students use.

- There are many words in our field that refer to similar motor skills. While the motor skills themselves might vary slightly, they generally revolve around the same concept. *Examples:* "jog" and "run," "throw" and "toss," "sit-ups" and "crunches." Using these different terms — even if you use them as intended — can be confusing to a student with ASD. Instead, use one word for both motor tasks (e.g., use "throw" to refer to both "throw" and "toss"), and then show the student exactly how you want the skill performed.

- Sometimes, you might use a phrase or provide students with instructions that a student with ASD doesn't seem to understand. If you hear the student use a different term to describe the action, and his or her wording doesn't alter the message you're trying to deliver, rephrase your directions to include the student's terminology. If you're trying to instruct students to walk backwards, for example, and you hear a student with ASD use the term "march," you can rephrase your directions to "March backward." Sometimes, students with ASD don't recognize when words are synonymous. By using their words, you break down that conceptual barrier. Once you figure out which words work, try to remember them for future use.

Using Visuals

What It Is: Students with ASD tend to be strong visual learners, particularly because of their difficulties with verbal communication. Therefore, it's essential that you integrate as many visual cues as possible into your lessons.

How to Apply It: No matter what you're trying to communicate, rely on your visual aids. Whenever you provide instructions, make sure that you are modeling the action, as well as saying it. Here are some ways to include visuals:

- Use cones and poly spots to mark locations. Also, use floor tape to designate general boundaries. Propping mats so that they are perpendicular to the ground, work to create makeshift walls when trying to divide large spaces.

- Hold up cue cards (see p. 52).

- Post instructions on the wall. Remember to consider students' ability to read. You might need to provide the instructions using images instead of words.

- Show short video clips of the motor skill or game.

- Hang pictures on the wall.

- Create a poster of acceptable behaviors.

- Draw hand prints on the ball to show students where their fingers should go on the ball. That's particularly useful in basketball and football.

- Attach stickers to a stationary ball to show students where the foot should make contact with the ball.

- Place stickers on students' shoes to show them which part of the foot to use when kicking the ball.

- Place an image or somehow highlight which part of the target the student should aim at. In archery, for example, don't assume that all students know the bull's eye is the ideal target. Put numbers in each ring of the target to show the point value system. (You will need to provide some verbal explanation, as well.) If a student is not able to understand the point system, attach a picture of a character or object (e.g., a dinosaur) on the bull's eye and tell him or her to try to hit the picture.

Considerations/Helpful Tips

- Particularly with cones and poly spots, consider designating specific colors for specific purposes. *Example:* Always use green cones as the starting place and red cones for the spot at which you want students to stop.

- You also can rely on the "red light/green light" system. Every time you want students to start an activity, hold up a green poly spot. When you want them to stop moving, hold up a red poly spot.

- Keep in mind that, if you use a color to designate a purpose (e.g., red = "Stop" and green = "Go"), you shouldn't use the color anywhere else. Therefore, don't use red cones in an obstacle course unless you want students to stop there.

- When trying to communicate where you want students to step (e.g., teaching to step with the opposite leg when throwing), place an image of a foot on the ground where you want the student's foot to go. This technique is particularly helpful when teaching basic motor skills such as jumping (feet where they start and then feet where they finish), sliding, hopping and galloping.

- You also can assign students a consistent color. The color should stay consistent throughout all activities and should show students where they should be going. *Example:* The starting place for a squad would have a yellow poly spot, and students on the squad would use a yellow ball, throw at a yellow target, run through yellow cones, etc. A different squad would have all red items. That will help students with ASD remember to stay with their squads.

- Be creative! Wherever and whenever you can, incorporate a visual. When planning your unit, try to think of ways that you could communicate your intentions to students without saying a word. Incorporate these strategies on the first day of the unit and keep them in place throughout.

Resources

Coyne, P., & Fullerton, A. (2004). *Supporting individuals with autism spectrum disorder in recreation*. Urbana, IL: Sagamore Publishing.

Cue Card

What It Is: A cue card is a piece of paper/poster board that has a single image on it to represent the current activity. Just as you can hold red and green poly spots in the air to communicate "Stop" and "Go," you can hold up a cue card to remind students of the activity that the class is currently completing. You can use the cue card to show general activity transitions (e.g., attendance, warm-up, practice kicking), or you can use it to show more specific activities within a piece of the lesson (e.g., jumping jacks, running in place, sit-ups, arm stretch). You also can use it to show behavior expectations (e.g., listening).

How to Apply It: Hold up the card so that the entire class can see it, and announce the activity. You can continue to reinforce the activity by hanging the cue card where students can see it.

Considerations/Helpful Tips

- Cue cards work particularly well when you use them to show general activity transitions. *Example:* You might make a poster board to hang on the wall that students typically face. On the poster, you draw a picture frame and then attach a piece of Velcro® inside the picture frame. On the back of each cue card, place the opposing piece of Velcro®. Once you have announced the activity (e.g., "Time for warm-up"), put the cue card inside your picture frame. Students can look to it when they need redirection.

- The suggestions on how to make an effective cue card are the same for how to make an effective task card (*see p. 94*).

- The accompanying CD-ROM contains images of some cue cards that often are used in a PE setting.

- Make sure that the images used on the cue card are the same as images used elsewhere in the class.

Modeling What You Want to See

What It Is: Because students with ASD are such strong visual learners, you need to model exactly what you want them to do.

How to Apply It: Modeling a behavior has four steps:

1. Before demonstrating the motion, tell students what you are going to demonstrate.

2. Tell students that they will perform the same movement when you're finished.

3. Tell students what they should focus on. Be specific. *Example:* "Watch my hand that is holding the ball." Otherwise, students might watch something entirely irrelevant, such as the way your ponytail swings when you shift your weight or the way you pinch your lips together. When demonstrating the task, provide students with a few cue words as you perform the motion. *Example:* When you teach throwing, say, while performing the motions: "Step (step with opposite leg), back (move arm back), throw (throw ball)." Make sure that your motions show exactly how you want the task performed.

4. Have students perform the task themselves. Verbalize the cues as students perform the task.

Considerations/Helpful Tips

- If you're having difficulty working with the class and giving the cues, have students partner up and give the cues to each other. This is an ideal time to incorporate a paraprofessional.

- Make sure that everyone uses the same cue words. Using different words can be confusing to students with ASD. The only exception to this rule is when you discover that a student does better with a different set of terms.

- It might be helpful to provide the paraprofessional with a handout that states the cue words associated with each component of the skill.

- You can help draw a student's attention to the spot on which you want him or her to focus by adding something that is visually appealing. For example, you could wear a bright-colored bracelet if you want a student with ASD to watch your hand, or you could put a sticker on your shoe when you want a student to focus on how you kick a ball with the inside of your foot. You still will need to tell the student what to look at, but the extra visual reinforces the behavior.

- Don't exaggerate the movement or modify the skill's appearance when trying to model it in slow motion. Teachers often make the mistake of exaggerating their movements when they're trying to teach or encourage a skill such as running. They try to demonstrate the motion while standing next to the student but, because the student is moving slowly, the teacher either moves in slow motion or does more of a high-knee run. That modified demonstration teaches the student an odd gait pattern. Instead, run in place or move at a normal pace and then return to the student. Keep everything as close to "normal" as possible.

- Students with ASD might do well watching a video because the visual is contained, and they can view the same example numerous times, without any variation. Try to use videos of people similar to the student in age and appearance. Check YouTube or PELinks4U. org for examples. Or try this:

  - If you have some athletically skilled students who are looking for a fun community-service project, have them make their own series of videos showing different motor skills. With a little guidance about what to include on the video, these volunteers can make an excellent teaching tool that will benefit all students, not just those with ASD.

- When modeling, choose words to describe actions that are specific and not too abstract. Typical cues such as "open and closed" that we use when teaching locomotor movements such as sliding, for example, are too abstract. Instead, try using terms such as "apart and together," which suggest the actual motion the students should be completing with their bodies.

Limiting Your Use of Abstract Concepts

What It Is: Many aspects of physical education involve rather abstract concepts. Some of the concepts are difficult for many people *without* a disability to understand fully (e.g., off-sides in soccer or hockey). But there also are many other concepts that we generally take for granted (e.g., teams). For students with ASD, these concepts can be a real struggle. Therefore, it's important to make the concepts as concrete as possible.

How to Apply It: The best way to help with abstract concepts is to provide a visual representation of the concept. To help clarify the concept of "team," for example, have all students wear pinnies. It also can help to assign the teams names. You can keep it simple and use "red team" and "blue team," or you can have students come up with their own team names. Out of bounds can be another abstract concept. Line markers are more helpful than cones when it comes to marking out a specific space, such as a field, because it's much easier to see when you have crossed a line than to recognize that four cones placed in corners make up a rectangle. If need be, use floor tape or paint. If you can't mark the lines for the long term, make a line of cones down the sidelines to emphasize the boundary.

Sometimes, the rules of a game can seem abstract and confusing. In soccer, for example, teachers harp on not using one's hands, but then instruct the goalie to pick up the ball. To help clarify this rule, tell students that only the student wearing gloves or only the student wearing the special shirt can touch the ball with his or her hands. Then, provide the goalie with some sort of gloves (any cheap, stretchy gloves will work) or a different-color pinnie. Students with ASD also might struggle with knowing which net to shoot at. It isn't uncommon for them to shoot on their own net because they see a teammate (the goalie) there. To help clarify, tie pinnies on the corners of each goal to show which team should shoot at it. *Example:* The team wearing red pinnies should shoot at the goal sporting red pinnies.

Time is another abstract concept used in PE. While children with ASD generally are schedule-oriented, the concept of "a few minutes" can be difficult for them to grasp. Use the student's need for schedule and his or her desire for visuals to your advantage. *Example:* If you tell the class to work on a drill for 10 minutes, use an egg timer so they can see how much time they have remaining. A scoreboard or a large digital clock with a timer also work great. *Note:* Remember that the noise a scoreboard makes might be too loud for some children with ASD.

Considerations/Helpful Tips

- Don't be afraid to try teaching an abstract concept while providing a more concrete visual. Just because students with ASD struggle with the abstract doesn't mean that they shouldn't try to learn it. This is particularly true for students who do not have an intellectual disability.

Sensory Perception Disorders

Students with ASD might be either hyper- or hyposensitive to various forms of sensory stimuli. Children who are hypersensitive will need a way to decrease the sensory overload to their systems. Students who are hyposensitive might resort to self-stimming behaviors to provide the stimuli they perceive as missing from their environment. These sensory perception difficulties are common in people with ASD, although each student with ASD will have different responses to different stimuli. Therefore, it's best to find the strategies that accommodate the needs of each individual student. The following section provides some examples of how you can help students deal with their sensory perception.

Hypersensitivity

For students with ASD who are hypersensitive to stimuli, physical education is often a nightmare. If you think about it, a lot goes on in your gymnasium, with all of your students' senses being challenged. Whistles blowing, balls bouncing, students yelling and running, the smell of perspiration and the smell of rubber balls all combine to create a sensory overload. *(See Figure 2.4 for examples of some common causes of sensory overload in PE.)*

Figure 2.4 Sensory Overload in PE

Sound: Whistles, balls bouncing, kids yelling, music playing, starter's gun firing for a race, lockers slamming, using "gym voices," scoreboard horn, balloons popping.

Sight: Bright sunlight, lighting in gymnasium, overabundance of bright posters, general motion of everyone running around.

Touch: Contact with other kids, pinnies, grass (might be moist from dew or long and touching ankles if unmowed), ball textures, sensation of sweat, water (if in pool), cold or heat (if outside), pressure from fitness equipment.

Smell: Rubber balls, disinfectant, finish on floor (if recently redone), body odor, food (if gymnasium also serves as cafeteria), perfumes and deodorants used in locker room.

Proprioception/Vestibular: Tumbling, jumping, climbing (ropes, cargo nets, adventure education elements), dancing that requires spinning, movements that require moving up and down (touching toes, sit-ups, fielding a ground ball).

Assessing and Adjusting the Environment

What It Is: First, identify what could be causing sensory overload. Remember that some students might have hypersensitivity with one sense (e.g., sound) while others might have it with two, three or all five senses. You need to address only the sense(s) that are being over-stimulated.

How to Apply It: To start, identify which senses are problematic for each student. Then, in your mind, go through a typical class. Write down everything you can think of that is related to that sense. Then, imagine each related stimulus heightened by 500 percent. For example, for a child with ASD who is sensitive to sound, the sound of your whistle blowing to signify the start of an exercise is like an ear-piercing siren.

Once you have identified what stimuli could be overwhelming for a child with ASD, figure out how to decrease its effect on the student. In some cases, you can remove or change the stimulus so that it isn't quite so strong. Instead of using your whistle to draw the class's attention, for example, you could use a visual cue such as holding up a card or poster, or dimming the lights. You also might be able to use a less-abrasive stimulus, such as playing music at a reasonable decibel level. If the music is still a little too much, place the student with ASD in the farthest corner of the gymnasium, away from the speaker. For the times that you can't change the stimulus, you can help students with ASD cope with an overwhelming sensation.

For students who are sensitive to sound, for example, suggest that they wear earplugs. Or, give them the option of always standing in the back of the group so that your voice is not so loud and oppressive.

For some other ideas of how to address over-stimulus, see Figures 2.5 – 2.9.

Considerations/Helpful Tips

- Ideally, you want to get rid of the overwhelming stimulus before the student arrives. But realize that everyone is different, so you probably will have to solve some problems on the spot or recognize that it's a problem in one class and address it for future classes.

- Think about the small things as well as the obvious. For example, many high school PE teachers will tell you that they have smelled their share of body odor and would agree that it's offensive to anyone's nose. But how many people complain about the offensive smell of playground balls? While the smell of rubber doesn't bother most people, it can be incredibly overwhelming to someone with ASD. (Think about when you're in the tire section of an auto shop.) The stimulus also might be something small that you don't notice, but it drives a student with ASD to distraction. *Example:* A flickering or humming light bulb might be all a student with ASD can focus on.

Hyposensitivity

Children who are hyposensitive are looking for additional stimulus to feel comfortable or tend not to respond to typical levels of stimulus (e.g., pain). Therefore, you need to help provide them with extra sensations and ways to better interpret the sensations.

Using Texture

What It Is: Because students with hyposensitivity want additional stimulus, they gravitate toward different textures. Use different-textured equipment or environments to help keep them focused or interested.

How to Apply It: Balls that have different textures — including balls with nubs, rubber balls, yarn balls and squishy balls — are all very appealing. Some students might prefer only specific textures, while other students will want to try all textures. Allowing students to use balls with different textures helps them remain focused.

One example of using the environment to provide texture comes from grass. While some students with ASD hate the feeling of grass touching them, others

Continued on p. 65

Figure 2.5 Helping Children Cope With Sensitivity to Sound

Stimuli: Whistle, scoreboard horn, starter's gun for a race

Strategies:

- Visual cue, such as a red card for "Stop" and a green card for "Go."
- Hand signals.
- Use voice; warn students with ASD so that they can cover their ears.
- Lower-toned noise such as a drum, which often is less offensive.

Stimulus: Music playing

Strategies:

- Place student far away from speakers.
- Encourage student to wear earplugs.
- Turn music down a little.
- Avoid music with high-pitched notes.

Stimuli: Kids yelling, lockers slamming, balls bouncing

Strategies:

- Remind students to be respectful.
- Space students so that they aren't right on top of one another.
- Hold class outside, when possible, where noise doesn't echo.
- Encourage use of earplugs.
- Allow student with sound sensitivity to use MP3 players while dressing so that they can play music that is soothing, covering loud slams.

Stimulus: Your "gym voice"

Strategies:

- Warn students before you yell so that they can cover their ears.
- Don't stand directly in front of a student with sound sensitivity when talking to the group.
- Enforce the "Class is quiet" rule, so that you don't have to yell so loudly.

Stimuli: Noise in hallways or other places, noise of traffic/commotion outside

Strategies:

- Close the gym door.
- Encourage students with sound sensitivity to wear earplugs.
- Use part of the field that is farthest away from the road.

Figure 2.6 Helping Children Cope With Sensitivity to Visual Stimuli

Stimuli: Sunlight, lighting in the gymnasium

Strategies:

- Allow students to wear sunglasses or a hat to help reduce the light on their eyes.
- Dim the gym lights, if possible.
- Place students in shade.
- Make sure that, when you give instructions, students aren't looking into the sun.

Stimuli: Visual distractions/chaos from posters

Strategies:

- Give class directions from in front of a blank wall.
- Try to limit number of colors used for posters, balls, etc.

Stimulus: Motion of students

Strategies:

- Space students and stations so that they aren't too close.
- Have students face a wall (and not open, chaotic gym) or a single partner, during their activities.
- Create barriers to help break up the gym and create some order.

Figure 2.7 Helping Children Cope With Sensitivity to Smells

Stimulus: Rubber balls

Strategies:

- Air out new balls for a few days before using.
- Soak balls before inflating to decrease intensity of smell.
- Try balls made of different materials.

Stimulus: Disinfectant, finish on floor (if recently redone), food (if gym also serves as cafeteria).

Strategies:

- Open a window.
- Use fans to push smells out of gym.
- Request that sensitive students not have PE the period after lunch.

Stimulus: Body odor

Strategies:

- Remind all students about personal hygiene.
- Place sensitive students by an open window or door where there is ventilation.
- Allow children to leave and get a break from the smell.

Stimulus: Perfumes & deodorants used in locker room

Strategies:

- Assign sensitive students to lockers by a window or some sort of ventilation.
- Tell students to use sprays only in a specific section of the locker room.
- Provide an alternative changing location.

Figure 2.8 Helping Children Cope With Sensitivity to Touch

Stimulus: Kid contact

Strategies:

- Modify activity so that contact is not needed. *Example:* Instead of requiring students to make physical contact in a game of tag, have them pull a pinnie from the person's pocket, or use flag football belts.
- Remind students about personal space for drill activities.
- In contact sports, acknowledge to the class that the student needs personal space.

Stimulus: Pinnies

Strategies:

- Have one team wear pinnies and the other team not wear them. Place children with sensitivity on the "no pinnies" team.
- Use wrist bands instead of pinnies.
- Allow touch-sensitive children to tuck their pinnies into the waistband of their shorts, or into a pocket, instead of wearing them.

Stimulus: Grass (might be moisture on grass or grass touching ankles)

Strategies:

- Encourage the child to wear pants or socks that he or she can pull up to limit skin contact with the grass.
- Allow the student to stand (instead of sitting) while you give instructions.
- Use a baseball diamond, where there is less grass.

Stimulus: Ball textures

Strategies:

- Have a variety of textures available so that a student with ASD can find one that is least offensive.
- Ask if the student uses a texture at home that he or she prefers.

Stimulus: Sensation of sweat

Strategies:

- Discuss how it is a good thing to sweat. (Sometimes, students with ASD fear sweat because they are unfamiliar with the sensation.)
- Provide a means for cooling (e.g., a fan), when possible.

Figure 2.8 *(Cont.)*

- Encourage the use of sweatbands.
- Allow the student to have a towel to wipe sweat from his or her face.

Stimulus: Cold or heat (if outside)

Strategies:

- For cold, make sure that the student has extra layers of clothing.
- Consider staying indoors.
- For heat, stay in the shade, when possible.

Stimulus: Pressure from fitness equipment

Strategies:

- Use free weights instead of machines.
- Place a textured item (e.g., a towel) that the student is comfortable with over the pad of the machine.
- Use a Thera-Band® instead of machines.

Figure 2.9 Helping Children Cope With Sensitivity to Vestibular System & Proprioception

Activity: Locomotor skills

Strategies:

- Allow students to do a large step instead of jump.
- Provide students with something to hold onto or lean against (e.g., a folding chair, a person's shoulder) to help feel grounded.

Activity: Low & high elements in adventure education

Strategy:

- Activities probably not appropriate.

Activity: Tumbling/gymnastics

Strategy:

- Focus on rhythmic gymnastics instead of apparatus gymnastics.

Activity: Stretching

Strategies:

- Teach what is "okay" pain and what is "dangerous" pain as a result of stretching (recognizing that even a slight stretch will may cause discomfort).
- Avoid dynamic stretching.
- Provide a visual of how far to stretch (e.g., tape on the floor or wall), so that students have a target.

Activity: Yoga/Pilates/aerobics

Strategies:

- Allow for modified positions that accomplish same goals but are physically comfortable for students with ASD.
- Provide an extra-soft mat with padding (to make for less contact with floor).
- Provide padding (e.g., pillow, folded blanket, sweatshirt) for sitting on gymnasium floor.

Note: PE teachers can do only so much to help with proprioception. It's more important to recognize that the sensitivity exists and makes particular activities problematic.

love it. Allow students to sit in the grass and run their fingers through it while you're providing instruction. Most likely, you'll need to remind them to leave the grass in the ground and not pull it up, but grass is a great texture for them.

Considerations/Helpful Tips

- Don't be afraid to make your own textures! You don't have to spend money on fancy equipment just to get texture. You can create it using inexpensive supplies or items in the closet. For example:

  - Make a pompon ball out of yarn. Vary the length of the yarn to change the ball's texture as well its size.

  - Take an old Nerf® ball and cut chunks out of it.

  - Duct tape over beads or bells that you have placed on a ball to create a bumpy surface.

  - Glue felt or shag material onto a basic rubber ball.

  - Attach strips of Velcro® directly to the ball.

    The possibilities are endless. Dig out some old equipment from your closet and get creative. Just make sure that whatever texture you create is secure and will not become a hazard when the ball flies through the air.

- If you do want to buy some items, dollar stores are great for textured balls. Look for balls that have nubs, plastic strings hanging from them, Koosh® balls, stress balls, etc.

- It's difficult to predict what texture a student will prefer. Your best bet is to have a few different textures available, and let students pick what they like. Once they've found a texture they like, make that particular piece of equipment available to them always. But you still can offer different textures to help increase their perception of textures.

- If a student is fond of a particular texture but it's not something that can be integrated into the physical activity, use the texture as a reward. If the student completes so many minutes of an activity, he or she can play with the textured item. *Example:* Jason really likes the feel of the goop he has in a little plastic container. You tell him: "If you throw the ball at the target 15 times, you can play with the goop for one minute."

- If you use textures as a reward, don't base the reward on successful trials, but on effort. In the previous example, then, you would never say: "If you hit the target in the middle five times, you can play with the goop." It's not fair to demand expertise in a skill as qualification for a reward. Instead, place emphasis on effort and on trying to complete the task.

Increasing Stimuli Around Them

What It Is: For students who are hyposensitive, take the opposite approach from one you would take with children who are hypersensitive: Try to increase stimuli around them to help stimulate the sense that is hyposensitive.

How to Apply It: Identify the sensation that needs further stimulation. Then, increase the stimulus levels in your classroom to help provide the additional stimuli that the student needs. If you know that a child is particularly focused on one sense, work on increasing the stimuli involving that sense. If you're not sure what sense is hyposensitive, or if the student has the need in multiple senses, increase stimuli in all areas. *Example:* Increase auditory stimulus by playing music; schedule activities that incorporate a lot of physical contact with the equipment; use visual stimuli such as bright posters, bright-color pinnies, cones and balls, etc. When the class is outdoors, allow the child to sit in the grass while you provide instructions, so that the child has additional sensory stimulus.

Considerations/Helpful Tips

- Be sure that any stimulus you add doesn't take away from the lesson or create a distraction. If you use music, for example, ensure that students still can hear your instructions and feedback. If students focus on the music too much and don't pay attention to the lesson objective, the stimulus is defeating its purpose.

- Once you have established the stimulus that a student with ASD responds to, try to incorporate it as part of your class routine.

Allowing a 'Waiting Tool'

What It Is: Waiting your turn or being patient while a teacher gives instructions can be exceptionally difficult for children with ASD, especially when they're not being provided with enough stimuli. In an attempt to compensate for the lack of stimuli, a student with ASD might start demonstrating self-stimming behaviors (e.g., rocking), wander to find something to play with or poke at other students around him or her. One way to prevent that is to provide the student with a small object to play with while not actively engaged. The object provides the student with stimulation while not distracting other students or taking away from the student's ability to learn.

How to Apply It: Introduce a waiting tool at the beginning of the semester or as soon as you notice that the student will need it to be successful. Examples of using a waiting tool might include allowing a student to play with some Silly Putty®, a yarn pompon or a squishy ball. The waiting tool should be an object that provides just enough extra stimulus to keep the student focused on the class. Introduce the waiting tool to the student at the beginning of class and then explain exactly how to use it. Explain to the student that he or she may play with the object while you are providing instructions and while awaiting his or her turn. When it's time to be physically active, the waiting tool must be placed in its designated spot. It's essential that students understand that the object must be put down when it's time to participate in the activity. Therefore, it's helpful to have a place that the waiting tool is kept in between uses. *Example:* Jillian plays with a yarn pompon while she is waiting. The teacher places five plastic bins around the edge of the gymnasium. When it's time for Jillian to be active, she puts her pompon in one of the plastic bins.

You also can incorporate the waiting tool into the activity. *Example:* If the class is playing basketball, allow students to retrieve basketballs before you give instructions. You then instruct a student with ASD to sit on his or her ball while you speak. Allow the student to rock back and forth on the ball, providing him or her with the necessary additional stimulus. This technique often helps many students, not just those with ASD.

Integrating or Redirecting Self-Stimming Behaviors

What It Is: Children who are hyposensitive often demonstrate self-stimulating behaviors. They might rock, spin around in circles, flap their hands in front of their faces, scratch their arms, wring their hands, hum, jump up and down, or even hit their heads and undertake other self-injurious actions. These behaviors can make it difficult to perform physical activity. For example, it's difficult for a child who is flapping his fingers in front of his face to throw or catch a ball. As a result, you might try to integrate the self-stimming behavior into the motor activities that the class is engaged in. If integrating the behavior is not possible, try to redirect the behavior by providing a similar replacement stimulus.

How you approach self-stimming behaviors depends on what the child's teachers, parents and study team feel is best for the child. In some cases, it's recognized that the behaviors help the child cope with the environment, and the child is allowed to continue with the behaviors. In other instances, the team might try to decrease the incidence of these behaviors because they make it difficult for the child to be integrated into society without being perceived as "odd." The team also might be working to teach the child a less intrusive or harmful self-stimming action. Before doing anything, find out what approach the child study team is taking toward his or her behaviors.

The only exception to that rule is if the child is hurting himself or herself (e.g., banging his or her head against the wall) or is hurting another student. In that case, try to stop the action as quickly as possible. Usually, you can do that by removing the child from the current environment and putting him or her in a spot with fewer stimuli (e.g., a quiet hallway or room).

How to Apply It: If everyone has agreed that the self-stimming may continue, you need to find out how to ensure that it doesn't interfere with the student's learning. First, identify what purpose the stimming is serving. For example, by flapping fingers in front of his face, the child is providing himself with a visual stimulus. When a child jumps up and down, he or she is providing himself or herself with a proprioceptive or physical stimulus. Next, identify how you can replace that stimulus with a similar stimulus that complements your lesson. For a child who flaps his or her fingers, try using a bright-color ball or having a bright, interesting target to throw at. For a child who jumps up and down, try to incorporate the behavior into the motion. Include jumping jacks in the warm-up or have the student undertake activities that provide a similar sensation.

Researchers have found that self-stimming behaviors tend to decrease when the child participates in physical activity (Levinson & Reid, 1993). So, keeping the student engaged in the activity might help decrease the behavior. If you plan to give instructions for a short period of time and find that the student's self-stimming distracts the class, consider having the class perform some physical activity before you deliver instructions. You might need to have the class run two laps around the gym and perform warm-up activities before having students sit for instructions.

Considerations/Helpful Tips

- Just because a student's self-stimulating behavior is large and distracting, that doesn't mean you have to replace it with another large behavior. You just need to match up the sense that needs extra stimulus. For example, letting a child hold a squishy ball might be enough stimulus to keep him or her from slapping his or her arm.

- Before trying to provide a replacement stimulus, remember to find out what the child's parents and other teachers have discussed as an acceptable approach. You don't want to counteract what the team is trying to instill at home and in other classes.

- Sometimes, self-stimming can be inappropriate (e.g., fondling genitalia). Before you jump to conclusions, first confirm that the child actually is doing something inappropriate. It might be that the child actually is playing with a piece of string inside his or her shorts that tightens the waistband. If it *is* something like a string inside the shorts, just make sure that the string is not tucked inside the shorts. If the child is doing something inappropriate, try to redirect the behavior. Do that by giving a short prompt to take the child's hands away from the location and then providing the child with another option for stimulus. *Example:* "Jason, no touch," then hand him a squishy ball. Again, refer to the child study team.

- Watch to see when self-stimming behaviors occur. Many children with ASD demonstrate one particular self-stimming behavior when they become overwhelmed or over-stimulated. If you notice the behavior starting, you can help take away some of the stimulus or even direct the child to a quiet location before the problem escalates. *Example:* Katie often rocks and wrings her hands. When she starts to rub her upper lip repeatedly, though, it's a sign that she is over-stimulated and close to having a meltdown. If Katie is directed into the hallway as soon as she starts to rub her lip, she usually is able to calm down and then return to the class without incident.

Identifying Cues Other Than Pain to Indicate Limitations

What It Is: Students who are hyposensitive might not perceive mild pain or discomfort, so some students might not recognize how far to stretch safely, when they need to slow the pace and/or rest, or when they have a minor injury. Therefore, you need to teach children with ASD other cues to help them determine when they might need to back off an activity.

How to Apply It: First, determine to what extent the child is hyposensitive. Some students might not be aware of superficial pain (e.g., a scrape to the skin) but are aware of internal discomfort. Other students might be slow to recognize any kind of discomfort.

For students who are not aware of superficial pain, you must be more vigilant about monitoring them for injuries. For students who have trouble recognizing overexertion, identify some cues that they can use to identify discomfort. Instead of saying "Stretch as far as you can," for example, have a student stretch first under your supervision and take note of how far he or she can reach. Then, give the child a visual marker (e.g., "Stretch until your fingers touch your shoelaces") to use in the future. Given that the student's flexibility might change, you should reassess periodically.

For a running activity, bring attention to some of the physiological changes (e.g., perspiration, heavy breathing) that occur when a person exerts himself or herself. Have the student wear a heart rate monitor, if one is available and the student will tolerate it, and provide the student with a target heart rate zone. You also must be vigilant about monitoring students with ASD for injuries.

Considerations/Helpful Tips

- Creating a visual poster of some cues might be helpful. For physical exertion, for example, having pictures of a person sweating and a person breathing hard might help clarify physiological changes. Keep in mind, though, that on a hot day, students might exhibit some of those symptoms without having to exert themselves.

- When doing stretching activities, it often helps to put a marker (e.g., a sticker, a line from a pen) on the spot you want the student to reach for.

Teaching Classes With Both Hyper- and Hyposensitive Students

When you have a gym filled with some children who are hyposensitive and others who are hypersensitive, you face a double challenge. It's important to recognize that both groups need their optimal levels of stimuli to perform. To do that, you might need to be creative. For example, for auditory stimulus, you might allow some students to listen to music on headphones during warm-up. Or, you might play the music at a reasonable level, and then place the students who are hyposensitive close to the speakers and the students who are sensitive to the noise as far away from the speakers as possible. To accommodate touch, you might have a large assortment of textures, with some balls having dramatic textures and others having very little.

Conclusion

This chapter offered general tips for teaching students with ASD in either inclusive or self-contained settings. In addition, it described strategies and tools to enhance the teacher's ability to communicate with students with ASD, as well as students' abilities to communicate with the teacher and others. Students with ASD also struggle with sensory perception, and this chapter described strategies for helping students manage their sensory interpretation. You are encouraged to choose from the strategies and tools suggested in this chapter to best meet the needs of the students with ASD in your classes.

Chapter 3 —————————
Instructional Strategies for Enhancing Student Learning

Content

Introduction

Chapter 2 presented strategies and tools to help you communicate effectively with and manage the sensory perceptions of students with ASD in your physical education classes. This chapter presents specific considerations and suggestions for teaching motor skills and describes a variety of other techniques that will help facilitate instruction within the gym.

Providing effective instruction lies at the heart of what you do as a physical educator. The overarching goal is to provide all students with the skills, strategies and dispositions they need to engage in a healthy and physically active lifestyle as adults. Students will benefit from developing a repertoire of skills that provide them with the opportunity to participate in different activities.

All students benefit from well-planned, sequential and developmentally appropriate instruction, and students with ASD are no different. In fact, students with ASD will thrive in a class environment that takes into account some of their unique needs. The information presented in this chapter is meant to help you design effective learning experiences for your students with ASD. After a description of how to teach basic movement skills, games and fitness, you will find strategies for accommodating the abilities of students with ASD to receive and process instruction.

General Considerations Revisited

The general considerations suggested in Chapter 2 hold true when considering all instructional strategies, and they bear repeating here:

- Be consistent.

- Find out what strategies other stakeholders are using.

- Have a toolbox ready.

- Provide the assistance that students need, but no more than necessary.

Teaching Basic Movement Skills

Typically, physical educators teach basic movement skills in the elementary grades, Pre-K–3. It's likely, though, that students with ASD will need additional time to master these basic skills. In fact, some students might not be able to master all of the basic skills commonly taught at the elementary level.

Therefore, the suggestions regarding teaching basic movement skills to students with ASD can prove useful beyond the elementary grades.

As discussed in Chapter 1, children with ASD might have difficulty performing many of the common motor skills efficiently or successfully. It's important to acknowledge that children with ASD might never fully develop an efficient form of motor skill performance. While some students with ASD are very athletic, other students with ASD will always appear rigid and robotic in their movements. For children who struggle to develop motor skills, consider incorporating the suggestions that follow into your instruction.

Balance & Transfer of Weight

Balance and transfer of weight are necessary for the performance of all motor skills. Given that children with ASD might have difficulties with these skills, it's incumbent upon you to provide students with opportunities to develop and practice the skills in a variety of contexts. Activities that develop balance and the ability to transfer weight should be included throughout the K-12 curriculum (or the duration of time that the student is at the school). *(See Figure 3.1 for some ideas on how to practice these activities in your class.)*

Locomotor & Manipulative Skills

Many of the common cue words that are used to teach motor skills might need to be modified for students with ASD. Ensure that the cue words are not only simple but also that they give a clear explanation of what the student should be doing with his or her body. *Example:* The cue for galloping, typically, is "open and closed." But those words don't clearly define what the student should be doing with his or her legs. Instead, use the cue "apart and together."

Having an opportunity to learn and practice basic motor skills in a variety of contexts will be important for students with ASD throughout the physical education program. It's important for teachers to acknowledge that not all students will master every basic motor skill, but all students will be able to perform these skills at some level of competence, and many students will be able to go on to learn subsequent sport-specific and game-related skills. *Example:* Having learned throwing and catching, a student might be able to participate in a recreational game of baseball. *(See Figures 3.2 and 3.3 on pp. 76-83 for sample performance cues and tips.)*

Figure 3.1 Practicing Balance & Weight Transfer

Static Balance

- Provide a count for how long each student needs to balance.

- Stand on a poly spot. Students may stand on two feet and then progress to standing on one foot.

- Cue is "knee to hand." (Have a paraprofessional hold his or her hand in front of the student with ASD, and have the student touch his or her knee to the hand.)

- Have students balance on one foot, using the wall or some other support (e.g., chair) to help maintain their balance.

- Play "I'm a statue," in which the student freezes like a statue.

- Play "Freeze Dance." When then music stops, students must freeze and maintain their positions.

Dynamic Balance

- Have students walk a line on the floor using "heel to toe."

- Have students walk on their tip-toes across the gymnasium.

- Balance beam. Put a poly spot or marker on each end on the beam and put markers where students need to step. Have them move heel to toe.

- Play "Follow the Leader." Manipulate skills as they go (e.g., walking on toes, walking in different pathways, walking "heel to toe").

Transferring Weight

- Have students sway to music (placing emphasis on shifting weight).

- Play "Monster Walk." Have students take wide, giant steps across floor. Encourage them with a visual, such as placing poly spots where they're supposed to step.

- Play "Twister." This activity combines a visual with a specific instruction, with no ambiguity. *Example:* "Place your left hand on the blue dot."

- Play "Animal Imitation." Call out the name of an animal, and students imitate that animal's movements. *Examples:* penguin, elephant, frog, rabbit, snake, lion. Have students imitate other things, depending on interests or themes. *Some possibilities:* pirate-related activities, aliens/ robots, Halloween characters, different sports.

Figure 3.2 Teaching Locomotor Skills

Skills	Performance Cues	Tips for Students With ASD
Walking & Running	**Step:** Put foot in front of body. **Swing:** Swing opposite arm while stepping. If walking on toes (very common), try: **Heel:** Step onto heel. **Toe:** Roll up onto toe.	• Consult a physical therapist and/or occupational therapist regarding specific suggestions for improving fluidity of walking/running movements. • Students might respond to stickers placed on the part of the foot that typically is not used. Emphasize stepping on the sticker. *Example:* Put a bug sticker on the heel of the student's shoe and say, "Squish the bug!"). • Toe-walkers can practice walking backward, with emphasis on contact with the heels. • Heel-walkers/runners can practice "tip-toeing" on poly spots.
Sliding & Galloping	**Apart:** Step with lead foot. **Together:** Touch trailing foot to lead foot.	• After showing students the skill, physically move their feet. • Provide objects for students to step on to help with the motion. *Example:* Place pictures of bugs on the floor and have students squish the bugs; place outlines of feet and have students line up their feet with the pictures.

Figure 3.2 (Cont.)

Skills	Performance Cues	Tips for Students With ASD
Sliding & Galloping *(Cont.)*		• If students have difficulty bringing feet together, put a sticker on the inside sole of each shoe and encourage each child to make the stickers touch. Or, attach a slightly deflated balloon on one foot and encourage students to squeeze the balloon. *Note:* This is not a good option if the student is hypersensitive to noise, because the balloon might pop. Deflating the balloon a little will help prevent it from popping, but it isn't worth risking if you know that noise is a problem.
Hopping** (in place or moving forward)	**In Place** **Bend:** Bend the knee of the standing leg. **Up:** Straighten the knee of the standing leg.	• Hopping forward: Provide a visual (e.g., masking tape on the floor, jump rope on the floor, crack in the pavement) over which to jump. • Provide a visual take-off and landing (e.g., draw an x with chalk on pavement, make an x with masking tape on ground, put fun stickers on ground).

Continued on next page

Figure 3.2 *(Cont.)*

Skills	Performance Cues	Tips for Students With ASD
Hopping** *(Cont.)*	**Moving Forward** **Bend**: Bend the knee of the standing leg. **Swing**: Swing arms back. **Jump**: Swing arms forward and up while jumping. *Note:* If "Jump" is unclear, try "Up."	• Model the skill while providing verbal cues. • If the child understands imaginative play, compare the skill to the way a frog or rabbit jumps.
Skipping**	**Step**: Step with the right foot. **Hop**: Hop on the same foot. **Step**: Step with the left foot. **Hop**: Hop on the same foot.	• Skipping can be difficult for students with ASD to master. If a student becomes frustrated after successive unsuccessful attempts, consider moving on to other locomotor movements that are more transferrable to popular sports and games (e.g., running, sliding).
Jumping	**Bend**: Bend the knees and ankles before jumping. **Swing**: Swing the arms back, then forward at take-off.	• Provide a visual (e.g., masking tape on the floor, jump rope on the floor, crack in the pavement) over which to jump.

Figure 3.2 *(Cont.)*

Skills	Performance Cues	Tips for Students With ASD
Jumping *(Cont.)*	**Jump or Up:** Take off on both feet and land on both feet. If students are landing on straight knees, try "bend, swing, jump, bend."	• Provide a visual take-off and landing (e.g., draw an x with chalk on pavement, make an x with masking tape on ground, put fun stickers on ground). • Jumping for height: provide a target for the student to touch with his or her hand or head (e.g., hold your hand up above the student's head and ask him or her to touch his or her head to your hand).

Note: Students with ASD might not be able to master all of the locomotor skills. Decide what's reasonable for each student to achieve and what is a functional prerequisite to the student's participation in lifelong physical activity and/or sport.

**These skills can be particularly challenging for students with ASD, and teachers might decide that a skill is not appropriate for all students, especially if the skills are not used commonly in lifelong activities.

Figure 3.3 Teaching Manipulative Skills

Skills	Performance Cues	Tips for Students With ASD
Throwing: Overhand throw to a stationary partner __ feet away.	**Back:** Reach back with your hand **Forward:** Bring arm forward in front of body. **Let go (or release):** Let go of object.	• Have a variety of balls of different size, texture and color available from which to choose. • Put markers or poly spots on the floor where the student should put his or her feet. • Student touches hand to a paraprofessional behind him or her before reaching forward. (This is especially helpful if student is not extending his or her throwing arm.) Also can be done with the paraprofessional standing in front of the student to urge the student to extend all the way forward. • Throw at a target. • Vary the distance to perfect the amount of force to apply. • Put numbered poly spots on the floor to motivate students to continue to throw from various distances. • Provide student with verbal cue (e.g., "Now") when ball is to be released during performance.

Figure 3.3 *(Cont.)*

Skills	Performance Cues	Tips for Students With ASD
Overhand throw to a moving partner: The receiver initially runs slowly from left to right, then from right to left in front of the thrower, who must throw the ball in front of the receiver. Anticipate where the receiver will be when the ball arrives. The receiver then runs away from the thrower, and the thrower must throw beyond the receiver.	Same cues, but when giving instructions, emphasize throwing the ball in front of the partner's/receiver's hands.	• Have the partner hold out a hand for the student to aim at. • Put a poly spot in the path of the receiver. Have the student with ASD aim for the poly spot, releasing the ball when he or she thinks the receiver will be in place.
Throwing: Underhand throw	**Back:** Swing arm straight backward. **Swing:** Swing arm straight forward. **Let go:** Release the ball. If the student can handle abstract concepts, use cue words (e.g., "Tick, tock, toss," like a clock).	Have a paraprofessional or peer extend an arm in front of the student tossing to show where the movement stops and the ball is released. • If the student is able, have him or her count to three, with three being the number that cues the student to release the ball. • Use a squishier ball to provide a solid grip. • Have a target at which to aim, such as a basket or bucket.

Continued on next page

Figure 3.3 *(Cont.)*

Skills	Performance Cues	Tips for Students With ASD
Throwing: Underhand throw *(Cont.)*		• Use beanbags rather than balls. • Start with the target close by and facing a blank, solid-color wall.
Catching	**Watch the ball:** See the ball come into your hands. **Reach** to meet the ball.	• Use a squishy ball or a ball with extended texture (e.g., yarn ball, Koosh® ball). • Deflate the ball partially to make it easier to grasp. • Use a ball whose color is in contrast to the environment (e.g., dark-color ball if the gymnasium has white walls). • When using a larger ball, start with arms already extended and waiting to prepare for a "scoop catch."
Kicking	**Step:** Plant your non-kicking foot next to the ball. **Swing Back:** Swing the kicking leg back. **Kick:** Swing the kicking leg forward, with the foot striking the ball.	• If kicking a stationary ball, use stickers to mark the ball where the student should kick. • Provide someone or something on which to lean for balance. • Visual target: Give students a line that they want the ball to reach. • Start behind a line and step on the line to kick. • Face sideways when kicking with inside of the foot. Help direct student's shoulders.

Figure 3.3 *(Cont.)*

Skills	Performance Cues	Tips for Students With ASD
Sport-Specific Skills	Provide cues that are concrete and brief, and that describe the desired movement. *Example:* Dribbling in soccer: kick left foot, kick right foot or kick one foot, kick other foot.	• Place a sticker on the part of the body that you want to make contact with the ball (e.g., the instep). • With striking skills, provide a target at which to aim. • For slaloming around cones, use gym tape to show the path to follow. • Provide visual cue of where to place hands on equipment.

Techniques for Facilitating Instruction

Helping Students Interpret Cues & Body Language

What It Is: When a student doesn't recognize the teacher's cues, problems arise. Think of how many times you give your students "the evil eye" during class. One of teachers' most subtle, yet efficient behavior-management strategies is to make eye contact with a child and show him or her — through a shake of the head or a facial expression — that the behavior is unacceptable. At the same time, teachers continually use body language to support and encourage students. Basic gestures such as smiling, nodding the head or giving a thumbs-up can go a long way. Students with ASD, however, often don't recognize the message behind these nonverbal signals.

How to Apply It: For many children with ASD, you will need to avoid using visual cues and, instead, state your intended message directly. Don't leave a feedback statement open to interpretation; tell the student exactly what you are pleased or displeased with, followed by what the student should do next. *Example:* Instead of saying "Stop" or shaking you head "No" to a student with ASD who is bouncing a ball while you're talking, say: "Stop bouncing the ball. Sit down and put the ball in your lap."

Use a similar approach when you are pleased with a child's performance or want to provide encouragement. You need to express your thoughts verbally in a short, direct statement. *Example:* "David, good catching with your hands." General positive feedback statements such as "Great job" leave your message open to various interpretations. A student with ASD could interpret "Great job" in a manner that encourages appropriate behavior, such as catching a ball with his or her hands, or inappropriate behavior, such as talking over his or her peers.

Considerations/Helpful Tips

- Some children have a signal that they use every day to communicate when they have done something correctly or incorrectly. Commonly, parents and teachers will use a thumbs-up/thumbs-down system. If the child knows that cue, then you should use it. Ask parents, paraprofessionals or classroom teachers whether they use a cue that the child knows. If the child knows sign language, he or she might use the sign for "good" as a form of a positive reward. *(Find some basic signs on the CD-ROM that accompanies this book.)*

- Be sure that the student sees the cue. Remember that many children with ASD don't make eye contact, or they focus their attention on obscure objects. If children with ASD don't see you providing them with a cue, they can't respond. So, ensure that the cue is within their line of sight. That doesn't mean they have to look right at you. Many children with ASD rely heavily on their peripheral vision and will see things even when they are not making eye contact. Conversely, it sometimes looks as though they are staring right at you, but you then realize they didn't see a thing. As you get to know the student, you will know where his or her line of focus is.

- Use one or two signals consistently, avoiding a combination of different cues. *Example:* If you use a thumbs-up/thumbs-down cue, you can't shake your head "No" and expect the student to stop the behavior. You need to be consistent.

- Depending on the student's abilities, you might want to introduce a cue to the student specifically for your class. If you do that, recognize that it might take some time for the student to grow accustomed to the cue. To start, explain to the student that you will have a shared cue. Tell the student exactly what the cue will be (e.g., "Bobby, I will shake my head like this") and when you will use the cue (e.g., "I will use this cue when you are not waiting your turn"). Then, inform the student what behavior you want in response to the cue (e.g., "When I shake my head, I want you to stand behind Jamie and wait until it's your turn"). For the student to grasp your use of the cue, you have to use it consistently and often, especially when you first introduce it. You must use it to discourage or encourage the behavior every time it occurs. This means that, in the beginning, someone must monitor the student to be able to provide the cue every time the student performs the behavior. (This is a perfect time to incorporate a paraprofessional.) Also, be sure to provide the cue immediately after the action, so that the student can associate the cue with the behavior. As the student becomes comfortable with the cue, an immediate and constant response will not be necessary.

- If you use a cue to extinguish a behavior, be sure to provide positive feedback when you don't have to give the cue. That encourages the correct behavior. *Example:* If Bobby stands behind Jamie in line without being cued to do so, you would say, "Bobby, I really like how you are waiting your turn in line!"

Coping With Emotions

Teaching students with ASD how to express their emotions appropriately can seem like an overwhelming task. Remember that they aren't going to pick up on subtle modeling very well, so simply hoping that they will notice what other students are doing isn't going to work. Even saying "Look at what Cody does" won't work. But teaching children with ASD to cope with their emotions is far from impossible, and it's very important.

Before trying to implement your own strategies, find out what, if anything, the student is being taught to do at home, in the community or in other classrooms. Because of the nature of its activities, PE class is an ideal place for students to learn about disappointment, excitement and frustration. But it's far from the only environment in which they need to express their emotions appropriately. It's common for children with ASD to have something in their IEPs about expressing emotions appropriately. The child study team or the classroom teacher can inform you of how they are working with the student.

If a particular strategy has been identified on the IEP or by the child study team, you must use the same approach. The following suggestions are meant to complement existing behavioral plans and provide you with some options if a child with ASD does not have a plan in place.

Emotions Chart/Self-Regulation

What It Is: Using an emotions chart is a common strategy for helping students with ASD learn how to control their anger and emotions. Typically, an emotions chart is a rubric with visuals that illustrate different levels of emotions one experiences, from calm to rage. It might include colors (e.g., green representing calm to red representing out of control), numbers (usually 1 to 5, with 1 representing calm and 5 representing rage), or a general theme of interest (e.g., a parked car representing calm, a car crash representing rage). Encourage students who have pre-established emotions charts to use them throughout the class, particularly when they are struggling with their emotions. If a child doesn't have an emotions chart, consult with the speech therapist or the child's study team to design a system that works throughout the school day. *(See Figure 3.5 on p. 87 for an example of an emotions chart.)*

Figure 3.4 Using an Emotions Chart

1. The student identifies his or her current emotional level, either verbally while looking at the chart or by pointing to the appropriate level on the chart.

2. The student identifies an appropriate emotional level for the situation. If the child needs help, you can guide him or her to the appropriate level, providing the student with an example of how the behavior would look.

3. Identify how the student can reach the desired emotional level and can resume activity with the class. Usually, that entails calming down.

Figure 3.5 Sample Emotions Chart

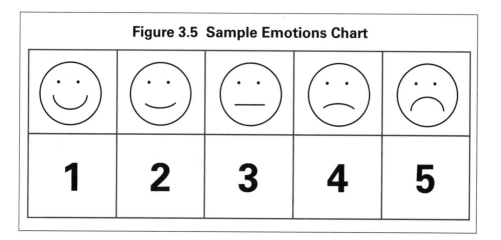

How to Apply It: Students use emotions charts when they are having difficulty expressing their emotions or are demonstrating inappropriate behavior because of their emotions.

Example: Your students are taking turns throwing for accuracy. Joe is having difficulty waiting his turn, and pushes peers out of the way. You ask the paraprofessional to show Joe his emotions chart and walk through the stages with him so that he can participate effectively. The paraprofessional has Joe point to the level of emotion he is feeling and verbalizes that emotion: "Yes, you are frustrated, like a car speeding out of control." The paraprofessional then asks Joe to identify where he should be. After a few seconds, the paraprofessional points to the car that is parked and says, "When waiting in line, we stand quietly, with our hands at our side, like a parked car." The paraprofessional then provides Joe with an idea to calm down: "Let's count to five, and then backward down to one."

Example: Gregory has been increasingly aggressive during game play, to the point that you are concerned for other students' safety. You establish an emotions chart with Gregory, his paraprofessional and the special education teacher. When Gregory starts to show frustration, you direct him to the Cool-Down Zone *(see p. 89)*, where he is told to follow the steps when using the emotions chart. The paraprofessional walks Gregory through the emotions chart until he is ready to resume game play.

Considerations/Helpful Tips

- Providing the student with a visual representation of each emotion level is very helpful. The visual can be pictures of the student or it can be generic pictures of people experiencing different emotions. If the student understands analogies, you can incorporate an object of interest. *Example:* If the student loves dinosaurs, you can say that "resting," or Level, 1 is when the hadrosaur is sleeping. Level 2, or "calm," is when a stegosaurus is eating leaves. You then move up the scale, ending in 5, or "out of control," which would be when the tyrannosaurus rex is roaring loudly. If you are using pictures of the student, discuss with the student what he or she feels like at each level. Have the student act out each level for you, and then take a picture of the student's face. Only students with some understanding of imaginative play can do this. Several Web sites offer help in creating an emotions card. For links to some of these sites, see the CD-ROM that accompanies this book.

- It might be helpful to accompany colors with the visual images and the description. Start with green as representing the calmest; use yellow in the middle and red for the last level.

- This system works best if it's incorporated throughout the student's day and not just in one class. Talk with the other teachers to determine whether you all can implement the same system.

- For some students, you might want to use only three levels of emotion. Too many levels can be difficult to comprehend, and the student might struggle with delineating one level from the next. When the student tries to identify where his or her level of emotion falls on the spectrum, the number of options might overwhelm him or her, rendering the tool counterproductive.

- Try to use an odd number of levels on the chart. By using an uneven number, you identify the middle of the spectrum with a specific level.

Cool-Down Zone

What It Is: It's a small section that you designate as the place where students can take themselves to regain their composure. It isn't a place to go relax with friends when one doesn't want to participate, nor is it intended to be where students are sent for a "time-out." Rather, a Cool-Down Zone is a spot where students can go for a minute or two to put emotions back in check.

Obviously, for everyone's safety, it's essential that the Cool-Down Zone is someplace you can monitor while you're still working with the class. Therefore, it's often a corner of the gymnasium or field. While the spot should be in your line of sight, it also should be removed enough from the class environment to ensure a decrease in stimuli and no interaction with peers. Some students with ASD might need a location that is completely removed from the group. That's often needed when the setting is still too chaotic (e.g., too loud), even when the student has moved to a corner of the gymnasium. In that case, consider having a paraprofessional sit with the student in the hallway or another designated spot that is quiet (e.g., the nurse's office).

How to Apply It: Using the Cool-Down Zone is a process that you develop over time. Introduce the concept by telling students that they can go to the Cool-Down Zone when they feel frustrated or overwhelmed, and they think they need a few minutes away from the class. (Allow the entire class to use the Cool-Down Zone, so that all students can work on managing their emotions and so that unnecessary emphasis is not placed on the student with ASD.) It's important to emphasize that this is not a "time-out" or a punishment, but simply a place to allow students to recompose themselves. Also, emphasize that it's not a social hang-out or somewhere students go when they don't want to participate. If a child is young or has moderate levels of an intellectual disability, he or she might not be able to handle a full explanation of the Cool-Down Zone's purpose. In that case, provide the student with the essential information. Show him or her the Cool-Down Zone and use a word that you've established for calming the student (e.g., "Calm," "Quiet," "Okay").

At first, students with ASD probably won't recognize when they are experiencing an overwhelming emotion. They just recognize discomfort and often start to demonstrate behaviors that interfere with learning (e.g., yelling and rocking). While they might not recognize the emotion, you as the teacher will be able to see the distress through their facial expressions and body language. Students with ASD often give subtle physical cues to show when they're losing control. They might fidget with a piece of clothes or a body part, cover their ears, wring their hands or start to hum. You also will learn specific triggers that often lead to specific emotions. When you start to notice that a student is becoming frustrated or agitated, start to direct him or her toward the Cool-Down Zone. To prevent the problem from escalating, it's best to intervene as soon as you see a signal of distress. You can take the student by the hand, gently direct him or her by the shoulders or tell them to follow you to the designated area. Use a method that won't add to the child's stress or discomfort.

While you're directing a student to the Cool-Down Zone, help identify the emotion that he or she is experiencing and then provide the student with a way to calm himself or herself. *Example:* When Jason grows frustrated, he starts rocking, flapping his arms and yelling at the top of his lungs. The teacher goes over to Jason and starts to direct him toward the Cool-Down Zone. The teacher says to Jason: "You are frustrated. Breathe in and breathe out." The teacher says this in a firm, yet calm voice while also demonstrating the deep breathing. At the Cool-Down Zone, a paraprofessional stands with Jason for a minute, reminding him to breathe. Meanwhile, the class continues the activity. Once Jason shows that he is breathing and calm, he returns to the activity. The teacher repeats this procedure as many times as needed. The paraprofessional also can walk a student through these steps and help him or her regain composure.

Figure 3.6 Components of a Successful Cool-Down Zone

- A place for the child to sit. Often, an object on which the child can rock (e.g., rocking chair, exercise ball) is best.

- A few items that the child can play with in his or her hands to relieve stress and provide sensory stimuli (e.g., squishy ball, stress ball, yarn pompon, Silly Putty®).

- A timer — an egg timer is perfect — to help remind the student to return to activity.

- A visual reminder (e.g., poster) of good ways to calm down and/or relax. *(See the CD-ROM that accompanies this book for some samples.)*

Considerations/Helpful Tips

- The Cool-Down Zone is not supposed to be a spot that the child is in for a long time. Most students will need to be there for only about two or three minutes, but it varies for each child. If a student appears to have regained composure but hasn't chosen to return to the activity, invite him or her to return while providing a specific task. *Example:* "Jason, it looks like you are ready to come back and play. You can partner up with Jackie and finish the passing drill with the class." Vague statements such as "Come, join us" might cause confusion and lead to feelings of anxiety.

- With time, you will need to provide fewer instructions and less guidance. Depending on the child's ability level, he or she will start to regain composure independently. *Example:* After three weeks, Jason still needs to be directed to the Cool-Down Zone, but he starts the relaxation breathing by himself as he and the paraprofessional walk to the designated area. After six weeks, Jason starts walking to the Cool-Down Zone by himself and performs his relaxation breathing independently. He still needs some reminders from the teacher, but is able to initiate the process himself and regains composure much faster.

- Students who are higher-functioning might start to lose their composure but not demonstrate obvious behaviors that would catch your eye. When still learning how to identify their emotions, as well as how to use the Cool-Down Zone, students might not remove themselves from the class and go to the designated area. While they recognize that they are not comfortable, they're not sure how to react. In that situation, you might consider giving students some sort of cue that they can use to let you know they need help or need to go to the Cool-Down Zone. It can be a hand signal or an index card that they keep in a pocket and hold up when they are struggling. This provides them with a way to tell you that they need help, without having to verbalize their feelings and before they lose composure. The cue is nice, because the child can alert you quietly. A student can walk up and hand you the card without having to have a long conversation with you or without having to discuss things in front of other students. It saves time and also provides a sense of privacy.

Incorporating Objects of Obsession Into Instruction

What It Is: Students with ASD often have an object of obsession. It can be a specific object, such as a shoe lace, or it can be a theme, such as cars.

How to Apply It: There is only so much you can do about a child's obsession with a topic, but you can set some boundaries. For example, you can allow students two minutes at the beginning of class to talk about their topics of obsession. Then, you can require that they talk only about whatever topic you designate for the next 25 minutes. The topic you designate could be the sport the class is playing or a random topic. If a student reverts to his or her topic of obsession, remind the student that the class won't discuss that topic until the designated discussion time.

You also can try to use the obsession as a motivator or an instructional tool. For example, if the child is obsessed with "Star Wars," try to relate the concept of sportsmanship with being a Jedi. Or, you might relate a motor pattern to a motor pattern that relates to the obsession (e.g., jumping like a frog). Try incorporating the object of obsession into the activity in a visual manner. *Example:* If the obsession is with the color green, use a green ball or, if a student is really into "Finding Nemo," you can put pictures of Nemo and friends on the target that the child is aiming at. You also can incorporate the obsession as a reward. *Example:* If the child does well that day, provide him or her with a sticker that matches the obsession.

Considerations/Helpful Tips

- Relating the object of obsession to the activity works if the student is able to engage in imaginative play. Otherwise, it will be more of a distraction to the student.

- If a student is having difficulty not discussing his or her object of obsession during the time that you designated as "discuss anything but the obsession," you can provide a visual cue, such as a clock, that shows how much time remains before the student may discuss the object of obsession.

- If you're going to ban the object of obsession in the class, provide the student some time during the class — at the beginning, middle or end of class — to interact with the object. Allow the student to hold or play with the object, or discuss it if the obsession is with a topic. Banning the object of obsession completely is unrealistic and often leads a child with ASD to become distressed.

- If the object of obsession is a physical object, it might be helpful to designate a safe place to leave the object when you don't want the student interacting with it. *Example:* If the student has a toy car as his or her object of obsession, keep a little box in the equipment closet with a picture of the car on it. When the student walks into the gymnasium, have him or her leave the car in the box. That keeps the item out of sight and also creates some routine to help distance the student from the object.

- Recognize that some students (particularly those who are not as high-functioning as others) might not be comfortable in parting with their objects of obsession, which serve almost as a security blanket. Decide whether a student will be more distracted if he or she has the object or if you ask him or her to function without it. It might be best just to have the student put the object in his or her pocket.

- You can use locations/landmarks as visual prompts to where a student may and may not discuss his or her object of obsession. *Example:* Once you step into the gymnasium, discussing the topic of obsession is off limits; it can be discussed only when the student is standing outside the gymnasium or in a designated spot in the gym. Using that approach is much more effective for children who don't have an intellectual disability. Those who have an intellectual disability or who have difficulty with receptive language probably won't be able to follow through with that approach (although it's worth a try).

- If you have a number of students with ASD who all have different obsessions, it can be a challenge to incorporate all of the obsessions into one lesson. But you often can find some overlap in the students' interests. It might be possible to incorporate numerous children's interests if you use more vague images or objects. *Example:* If one student is obsessed with reptiles, another with the color purple, and another with Nemo, place a picture of the turtle from "Finding Nemo" on a purple ball.

- Giving students stickers that are related to their objects of obsession works only if the students like stickers, and it's appropriate for them developmentally. A 15-year-old student with ASD who doesn't have an intellectual disability probably won't want a sticker, but it might be appropriate for a child of a similar age who has ASD and is cognitively lower-functioning, leading the student to act more like a 6-year-old. You also must consider that some students with ASD don't like stickers on their clothes, because it changes their appearance. Instead, offer to put the sticker on the student's task card or on an index card that the child can carry around.

Maintaining a Predictable Schedule & Routine

As mentioned in Chapter 1, a lack of schedule and routine can lead many children with ASD to have full-fledged meltdowns. They need predictability. Therefore, it's important to keep your class as schedule-oriented and predictable as possible. Having a general outline of how your class will go each day can make a big difference. *Example:* Students know they come into class, you take attendance, they warm up for five minutes, do drills for 25 minutes and play games for 15 minutes. Once the routine is established, students with ASD will follow it closely and will tend to remain on task more than when they don't have a routine.

Task Cards

What It Is: While the general outline of class is helpful, many children with ASD need a little more elaboration to the schedule. This is where a task card is incredibly helpful. A task card, in this situation, is a little different from what we typically refer to when doing station teaching. In this case, it's a simplified lesson plan for the student. *(See pp. 95-96 for sample task cards.)* It consists of three columns. The first column is a check-off column for the student, the second column describes the activity and the third column is for recording the amount of time that the class will spend on the activity or the number of repetitions the student should complete. The purpose of the card is to let the students see what they have accomplished, as well as what they should expect next. It provides them with start and finish times, while also helping to make the class seem more concrete.

How to Apply It: Each student receives a task card at the beginning of class and then may refer to it throughout the class period. Many students with ASD will have task cards for the entire day. They also might have cards at home that help them complete their daily routines (e.g., getting ready in the morning), or they might have cards at school that outline their day (e.g., 8:15 homeroom, 8:30 math).

You can design your task card in many ways. It's usually best to keep it consistent with what the student is used to. Ask the child study team or classroom teacher whether they already have a general template. If they don't have a template or if you have many students with ASD who have different-style task cards, you can create your own format (or use the one provided on the CD-ROM). Once you have created a general template, be sure to use it consistently throughout the year.

Remember that the purpose is to help students understand what they should be doing and to let them know what is coming. So, your card should outline your class activities, starting from the second that students walk in and ending at the second before they leave the gymnasium. It should include items such as going to the locker room, forming into groups, lining up at the door and cleaning up. It should be relatively easy to understand and should show the progression of activities clearly. As students complete each task on the cards,

Figure 3.7 Sample Task Card

Completed	Activity	Time (in minutes)
	Attendance in squads	2
	Dance Party: Dance to music	5
	Warm-Up: Red Warm-Up Day	8
	Mrs. Smith gives instructions	5
	Two-foot jumps	5
	Jumping rope	15
	Mrs. Smith gives instructions	3
	Line up at door	1

they check it off in the column on the far left. Students can check off the boxes with a writing utensil (e.g., marker) or they can use stickers.

Considerations/Helpful Tips

- Task cards don't have to be used only for children with ASD. All children can benefit from task cards. Students can use them as an assessment tool to track how many successful reps they were able to complete, or they can use them to increase their own autonomy within the class.

- Task cards can be especially useful with station teaching. Students are able to see which stations they have completed and what they have left to do. At the end of class, students are able to see all that they accomplished.

- Task cards are excellent tools to incorporate into lesson closure because you can encourage students to reflect on what they've accomplished, as well as what they would like to improve on in future classes.

- You don't have to make hundreds of task cards. Make enough for one class and then have them laminated. If you can't afford to laminate them, slip each card inside a plastic sheet protector or cover it in clear shelving paper. Have students use washable markers instead of pencils to record their progress. After class, simply wash the task cards and use them again for the next class.

Continued on p. 97

Figure 3.8 Sample Task Card for Jump Rope Lesson

ANDREW

✓		🕐
	🧍‍♀️	2
	🕺💃	5
	🤸	8
	🧍	5
	🧒	5
	🪢	15
	🧍	3
	👨‍👩‍👧‍👦	1

- Create a class task card, using a large dry-erase board, a magnetic board, a bulletin board or a piece of poster board. Use whatever is available to you, so long as it's large enough for the class to see. As you complete each activity, remove the listed item or mark it off as completed. Be sure to remove or cross off each task as soon as it's completed and before moving on to the next task. That helps students recognize that they're about to transition.

- If using a class task card, use both words and pictures to represent the activities. For the dry-erase board, write the words out and draw a picture or attach pictures with masking tape. For a magnetic board or bulletin board, you can attach a picture of the activity and a typed word version of the activity (e.g., "warm-up," "throwing") using push pins or magnets. For a poster-board task card, attach images and typed words with Velcro®, which allows you to reuse the board for many other class periods.

- Use class task cards in conjunction with individual task cards. This approach is beneficial to all students because it encourages autonomy, yet provides a visual aid if a student falls behind or becomes confused.

- For children with ASD, you can change task cards in a number of ways to make them appropriate for each student. If a student isn't able to read, replace the words with pictures that represent what you want the student to do *(see Figure 3.8 on p. 96).*

- Modify the task card to avoid abstract concepts. If some students have difficulty with the concept of time, put a picture of what the clock — digital or analog — will look like when the allotted time has passed. Also, stipulate a number of minutes and give students an egg timer.

- Numerous computer programs, such as Boardmaker®, are designed specifically to help make task cards. Check with your special education department to see whether your school has a license for Boardmaker® software or a similar-type program. If not, clip-art images will work very well.

- Be sure to keep images consistent throughout the year. Always use the same pictures to represent activities such as warm-up and attendance. Also, if you use cue cards, keep the images consistent between the cue cards and the task cards.

- If a student is obsessed with a specific theme (e.g., fish), ask the child's family to provide stickers to mark off completed tasks, rather than using a pen. Or, print the task card on theme paper (e.g., ocean background).

- If students have difficulty making an "X" on the sheet to signify that they have completed the task, give them a Bingo pen so that they can just poke the paper.

- For students who are more advanced, include more details. *Example:* Instead of simply listing the drill, list the objective on which you want them to focus (e.g., keeping their heads up while dribbling), provide the performance cues or set a goal for them (e.g., jump rope 10 times without stopping). Also, encourage them to set their own goals.

- A flip book is another option to a task card, based on the same concept but a little less advanced. Instead of having a check-off sheet, the student sees only one picture of the task that he or she is performing at the time. Using Boardmaker® or similar software, print pictures that represent the activity the class is doing. Laminate the pictures and then hole-punch the upper left-hand corner. Put the pictures in the order of your lesson plan (e.g., warm-up, throwing, running, cool-down). Hold the cards together with a small metal loop, such as a key ring. Each student gets his or her own flip book. When the class has completed a task, students flip the picture of that task to the end of the book and then start the activity represented by the next picture.

Resources

www.usevisualstrategies.com/Welcome.aspx

www.angelfire.com/pa5/as/asteachersites.html

Boardmaker® and other resources: www.mighter-johnson.com

Coyne, P. & Fullerton, A. (2004). *Supporting individuals with autism spectrum disorder in recreation.* Urbana, IL: Sagamore Publishing.

Helping Students Adjust to Changes Within the Class

What It Is: While task cards are great for helping with the daily schedule, inevitably, you will make changes to your routine. You can't cover the same unit all year, and you should take students outside when the weather is nice. Such changes in routine can be very traumatic for a child with ASD. But you can use some strategies to significantly decrease the amount of stress that change causes children with ASD. It's also important to help teach children with ASD that change is inevitable and is not always a bad thing.

How to Apply It: Provide students with ASD time to process changes. As you approach the end of a unit, for example, forewarn students with ASD that the class will be starting something different. Tell them exactly when the class will be changing units, what new unit it will be doing and what to expect in this new unit. Take the same approach if you plan to change the environment; give students with ASD time to prepare for when the class moves to the weight room or goes outside. When explaining what will happen in the change, it also might help to show students where the class is moving so they can picture the new location.

The more rigid students are with their need for routine, the longer they'll need to adjust. If the class has to make an unanticipated change — the band needs the gym today to practice for a concert, for example — let students with ASD know about it as soon as you can. Ask the classroom teacher and/or paraprofessional to start preparing the student. Even with forewarning, the transition might be a little rocky, but that extra time to process the change often makes a world of difference.

Considerations/Helpful Tips

- Some students benefit from receiving a task card a few days before the class. So, if you know the class will be held outside on Friday, provide the student with a task card for the first outdoor lesson on Monday. That way, the student can look at the task card and prepare for the upcoming change. For this strategy to work, students with ASD need a few days' notice. Don't wait until the day before the change is to take place to alert students with ASD; often, that's not enough time for them to process the change.

- Send a note home so that the child's family can start to talk about an upcoming change in routine. Also, tell the child's paraprofessional, so that he or she can discuss it with the child throughout the day.

- If you have a picture of the new activity, show it to the child. Make sure that the image is as close to reality as possible. Try to use a picture that shows an environment that is similar to where the class will be held and that depicts students who are close in age.

- When change occurs, it's best to keep class basics the same. *Example:* Try to keep the warm-up the same throughout the entire year. To help students with ASD feel more at ease, point out the similarities in the schedule while trying to downplay the differences.

- Never assume that you can "trick" a student and that he or she won't notice the difference! Instead, try to help the student cope with the change. Talk briefly about how change is a good thing. Point out positives of the new activity or environment.

- Discuss with students that change is not a bad thing. Particularly for students who don't have an intellectual disability, it's important to introduce ways to calm themselves when change does occur. They also must recognize that, sometimes, we don't have control over when change occurs. Therefore, discussing positive aspects that come from the change might help students cope. *Example:* If the gymnasium is being used for a guest speaker, which will change the student's schedule, point out that the guest speaker might talk about a topic of interest to the student.

Incorporating Repetitive Activities

What It Is: People with ASD tend to prefer activities that are repetitive, most likely because the activities are predictable. *Example:* Closed skills such as swimming laps, running around a track and jumping on a trampoline are all activities that require little interpretation of the environment. Participants don't have to worry about interacting with peers, interpreting social cues or changing situations. On the flip side, team sports and open skills such as soccer and floor hockey often are very difficult for children with ASD because things are constantly changing and it is a more chaotic environment. So, it's important to offer some activities that are predictable in nature.

How to Apply It: Just because students with ASD struggle with team sports and group activities doesn't mean that they shouldn't participate in them! Team sports and group activities are very important for social-skill development, and many children with ASD enjoy them once they learn to cope with the unpredictable, chaotic nature of the activity. Instead of avoiding these activities, try to strike a balance of individual sports and team sports, as well as repetitive activities (closed skills) with those that are unpredictable (open skills). Also, recognize that on days when a student is particularly stressed (e.g., due to a change in their schedule earlier in the day), it might be more productive for him or her to take on a repetitive, individual activity instead of a varied, team activity.

Considerations/Helpful Tips

- Many team sports and group activities lend themselves to drills that require repetitive activities (e.g., passing the ball back and forth to a partner). When teaching an activity that is unpredictable in nature, always try to include at least one activity that is more repetitive.

- Remember that unpredictable activities can be more mentally draining than a predictable activity, so students with ASD might have a shorter attention span or need more frequent breaks. They are also more likely to become overwhelmed in these activities, so it's important to have resources such as a Cool-Down Zone available.

Increasing Transition Time

What It Is: Transitioning from one activity to another can be very challenging for children with ASD. They might resist the actual transition or take an extensive amount of time to transition. *Example:* At the end of class, you give the students seven minutes to change clothes. When the bell rings to go to the next class, Marcus, your student with ASD, is still in his underwear and is moving slower than a snail. Students with ASD often have their own sense of time, and it tends to be slower than one would like. Trying to rush them, though, will only lead to frustration, poor performance and meltdowns.

How to Apply It: Often, there's little you can do to change the sense of time for children with ASD. Instead, provide them with a little more time to transition. Allow students with ASD to end class five minutes early, so that they have more time to change clothes. Keep in mind that this is possible only when a paraprofessional or teacher is available to help supervise in the locker room. It also might take students with ASD a few extra minutes to transition into the "PE mindset." When they enter the gym, they might still be thinking about the class they've just come from. Give them a few minutes to switch gears. For the first five minutes of class, a student with ASD might need to observe the class from the sidelines or participate on the outskirts of the group.

It's also helpful to provide students with ASD with a warning that a transition is coming. *Example:* If students are playing a game, and the class will end in five minutes, tell the students with ASD that five minutes of class remain. Provide them with another reminder when only one minute remains. At the end of the period, inform them that it's time to transition to the locker rooms or to their next classes. By providing these verbal cues, you give students with ASD some time to prepare themselves mentally for the change.

Considerations/Helpful Tips

- Clarify when an activity is completed, and remind students of what they will be doing next. *Examples:* "We're done with physical education for today. You are going to reading next." "We've finished our warm-up and are going to practice catching next." Be sure to state exactly what students are now expected to do.

- Rely on visual aids to help enforce the transition. Refer to the student's task card, have diagrams on the wall that show the basic routine in class, use a visual countdown aid (e.g., egg timer, scoreboard clock, digital timer) to show the amount of time remaining in an activity, and show cue cards.

- Always have the next activity ready to go, to ensure little to no down time between activities. Having students stop an activity and then stand around and wait is disorienting to students with ASD; they often will revert to the previous activity while they are supposed to be waiting. If you can't transition right into the next activity, consider having all students (not just those with ASD) help set up the next activity so that they're not waiting around.

Using Video Feedback

What It Is: For students who have difficulty determining where their limbs are in relation to space and the rest of their body, it's often difficult for them to develop more complex motor tasks because they can't reflect easily on their bodies' movements. While they are able to see whether they performed the target behavior (the ball went in the net), they can't easily reflect on how their bodies felt so as to replicate the behavior. Therefore, video feedback can be helpful because students can watch themselves perform the task.

This strategy won't work for all students with ASD, however. The students need to understand that the video they are watching is of them. Some students won't be able to recognize themselves, as that is an abstract concept. Students also need to be able to understand and apply the information they obtain through observation.

How to Apply It: First, inform students that you're going to videotape them and that they are going to watch themselves. It's important that students are motivated to complete the task. Have students perform a few practice trials before videotaping them. When each student is ready, videotape him or her completing a few trials. Then, have students watch the videos of themselves performing the skills. You can provide students with feedback in a few ways. You can:

- Provide feedback directly to each student while he or she watches the video. This is very productive, but it's difficult to do when you have a large class.

- Have a paraprofessional review the video with the student. That, however, creates some segregation between the student and the rest of the class.

- Have students work in groups of two or three and provide feedback to each other, using a performance rubric. This is ideal for inclusive classrooms, because everyone benefits.

- Have students critique themselves. This might not be possible for all students with disabilities.

Considerations/Helpful Tips

- Using video feedback can benefit all students in the class. Many students tend to enjoy the activity and find it very helpful, but avoid embarrassment by making sure that each student is comfortable being videotaped and having people watch the video.

- You don't need to set up fancy video equipment or have expensive programs to implement this strategy. Webcams that record onto basic software work great. Students need only to be able to view the video in normal speed.

- It can be helpful to provide students with a rubric or some specific focal points if they critique their own videos or provide feedback to a peer. Be sure to explain exactly what each element will look like.

- Particularly for students with ASD who struggle with social skills but not with communication and don't have an intellectual disability, it's important to emphasize at the beginning of the activity that if a peer offers a suggestion, he or she is not attacking or picking on the student. The peer is only trying to make the student better. Sometimes, students can see critiques as personal attacks.

- You also might need to show students with ASD how to provide constructive feedback to others in a nice way. Students with ASD might not know how to suggest an improvement and should be provided with some scripted options, or they can be very blunt in

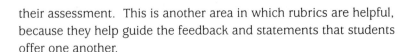

their assessment. This is another area in which rubrics are helpful, because they help guide the feedback and statements that students offer one another.

Conclusion

The various management and instructional strategies suggested in this chapter and Chapter 2 might seem overwhelming to implement. That's why it's important to choose the strategies that you feel will be most helpful to you and the students in your classes. If you would like to implement several of the strategies presented, we suggest that you start slowly. Pick one or two strategies that you feel will have a noticeable impact in your classroom. Implement one strategy and practice it until you're comfortable before adding another, unfamiliar strategy. *Most important:* Choose those basic and specific strategies that you feel will benefit you and your students most.

Chapter 4
Integrating Social Skills Development

Content

Introduction

A young man with autism once described his difficulties with social skills as "getting off of a plane in a foreign country without knowing the language, cultural gestures or cultural norms" (Coyne & Fullerton, 2004, p.19). With social skills presenting a universal struggle for people with ASD, it's important that we as physical educators work on developing social skills in all settings, including the PE classroom. This chapter discusses why it's helpful to practice social skills in physical education, which skills to teach and how to practice the skills, as well as offering helpful tips to make the experience more successful. It also offers some sample social skills activities to get you started. You can use the suggestions provided in this chapter in an inclusive or segregated classroom. Many students need help with social skills development, not just those students with ASD. Therefore, the strategies we suggest have been created to apply to all students, as needed.

Why Are Social Skills So Important?

Social skills are an essential component in our society. They are needed in almost every realm of life. In fact, according to Amy Wetherby and Juliann Woods of the Early Social Interaction Project at Florida State University's Autism Institute, "Communication competence may be the primary factor determining the extent to which individuals with ASD develop relationships with others and participate in daily activities and routines at school, at home and in the community" (Woods & Wetherby, 2003, p.180).

When compared to people with developed social skills, people with poor social skills are at much higher risk for having problems in school, being underemployed or unemployed, developing depression or other mental health issues, and having problems in the community (Elksnin & Elksnin, 1995, 1998, 2001). A lack of social skills also has been cited as one of the primary reasons that students are unsuccessful in their transition from school to employment and independent living (Chadsey-Rusch, Rusch & O'Reilly, 1991; Edgar, 1987; 1988). Therefore, it's essential that we work on developing social skills so that students have a greater chance of being happy and successful in all environments.

Why Work on Social Skills in Physical Education?

While physical education is designed to help improve students' fitness levels and motor skills, it's also an excellent setting for teaching social skills. Unlike most of the other classes your students attend, your class provides an environment that is filled with natural social interactions. Throughout the class period, students have spontaneous interactions with one person, small groups of people and even the entire class. These interactions provide a terrific opportunity for students to develop and practice numerous social skills. When it comes to social skills development, students tend to retain and apply the social skills they learn when they are given the opportunity to practice them in a natural environment, such as a sport program (Kohler, Anthony, Steighner & Hoyson, 2001). Your class can be that place!

Students with ASD need lots of opportunities to practice their social skills. Unfortunately, because they tend to be so delayed in their social skills, they don't tend to have many close relationships with peers their age. If they try to initiate a social interaction with someone, their novice attempts often lead to ridicule or teasing from people who don't understand the situation. This then creates a snowball effect: Students with ASD don't have age-appropriate social interactions with peers, which results in decreased time to practice their social skills. That lack of practice leads to a larger gap between their social skills and those of their peers, making future social interactions increasingly difficult.

Example: John sees some students talking on the playground. He approaches the students to try to start a conversation. Standing very close to one of his peers, John immediately starts talking about "Wheel of Fortune" (his favorite subject). The students are talking about a videogame and become angry that John is talking over them. At first, they try to ignore him, but John keeps talking. One of the boys makes a nasty comment to John, and the group walks away. John goes to the edge of the playground and plays by himself. Now, John not only was unsuccessful in practicing and developing his social skills, but he's also discouraged.

In your class, you can provide an environment where students can practice and develop their skills while receiving some feedback. Unlike the playground, where students with ASD are often dismissed, your class can help them recognize how to fix the social interaction while keeping the atmosphere positive. In your PE class, students with ASD can make mistakes without the fear of their peers' making fun of them. Therefore, they're more likely to risk more social interaction.

Another reason to teach social skills in physical education is that PE is fun! As human beings, we often associate fun activities with positive memories and feelings. If social skills development is made to feel like a chore that is tedious, as sometimes happens in a structured classroom setting, students with ASD won't want to continue applying the skills because they associate that with feelings of boredom and frustration. But if the setting is fun, and they associate positive, happy feelings with social skills, they might be more likely to try using those skills in other settings, such as home and in the community.

More important, you can incorporate social skills development into your class without interfering with motor skills development. It might even give you a new, fun game for practicing some of the routine motor skills. *Example:* If your class is focusing on dribbling in basketball, you could create a game in which students dribble a basketball in an open space. Students move from one peer to the next, asking each peer questions to learn new facts about one another. So now, you're working on dribbling and numerous different social skills (e.g., making eye contact, standing at an appropriate distance, staying on topic, asking questions, appropriate voice volume). You're also helping students learn ball control. Instead of having students dribble through a series of cones to practice ball control, which often becomes tedious, they're now using one another as barriers and learning to control the ball in a fun and realistic manner.

Do Students With ASD Even *Want* to Be Social?

Yes!!! People often assume that people with ASD don't want to be social because many of them come off as aloof. But, it isn't so much that students with ASD don't want to be social, as they don't know *how* to be social or how to express themselves in an appropriate manner. Once students with ASD start to develop their social skills, we often see them starting to initiate conversations and create friendships.

Which Social Skills Should I Teach?

The individualized education programs (IEPs) of children with ASD almost always have a list of targeted social skills. It's essential that you review a child's IEP to determine which skills should be of focus. While there is no master list of social skills that must be taught to student with ASD, there are some social skills that many people with ASD struggle with (e.g., making eye contact). Therefore, if you have several students with ASD in one class, it's highly likely that you will be able to identify two or three social skills that are listed as targeted skills in the children's IEPs. But if you find that each child has a unique list of targeted skills, that's okay! The type of activities that you will schedule to work on social skills development will address numerous skills at one time.

Figure 4.1 Common Social Skills on Which to Focus

- Taking turns while talking.
- Making eye contact.
- Standing at an appropriate distance while talking.
- Using appropriate voice tone.
- Recognizing different voice tones.
- Using appropriate voice volume.
- Listening to another person.
- Taking turns in play.
- Sharing equipment, responsibilities, etc.
- Introducing oneself.
- Greeting someone.
- Starting a conversation.
- Entering a conversation.
- Maintaining a conversation.
- Staying on the same topic in a conversation.
- Shifting the conversation to a different topic.
- Ending a conversation.
- Giving and receiving compliments.
- Introducing topics of interest to others.
- Asking for help.
- Offering help.
- Compromising.
- Dealing with mistakes, winning and losing.
- Using appropriate touch.

Note: This is not an inclusive list.

You also might find that skills that are fundamental components of etiquette in physical education/sports are not identified on a child's IEP. These skills can be important for children to develop because they're expected when participating in recreational activities throughout one's lifetime. *Example:* It's appropriate to clap and cheer when someone scores a goal, and it can be considered poor sportsmanship not to respond to a successful performance. That's probably not a skill that any IEP identifies as being important.

If you think that you can help develop this skill in a child with ASD, and it's a skill that you think will benefit the child long-term, talk to the child study team about making it a focus in your class. The team might be able to identify ways that the skill you've identified will complement target skills already identified, or team members might think that the skill is a good addition.

As a result, everyone would work to teach the student that cheering and clapping is perfect for the playground and for PE, but it's not appropriate when a classmate answers a question correctly or an employer compliments an employee on a job well done.

Check with the child study team before implementing the new skill so as not to confuse the student or counteract something else the team might be doing with the child. *Example:* If the rest of the school is teaching the student to shake a person's hand when greeting him or her, and you focus on giving a "high five," you're being counterproductive.

Figure 4.2 Prioritizing Social Skills

1. **Check students' IEPs.** Many times, a child's IEP identifies the primary social skill to be developed, followed by some secondary goals. You must focus on the skills identified in the IEP.

2. **Watch & listen.** On the first few days of class, watch how students with ASD interact with you, their peers and other teachers. Based on the list you have developed from the students' IEPs, determine which skills are most appropriate to incorporate into your environment. Consider which of the social skills occur naturally in physical education. While activities can be modified to include just about any skill, it's important for the skill to be happening naturally. *Example:* Taking turns in a conversation happens all the time during class discussions or when students are talking while they are practicing a drill or waiting their turn in line. Sitting quietly at a table, on the other hand, is not a skill that could be incorporated easily in a gymnasium.

3. **Talk with teachers and the child study team.** Feel free to pick other people's brains! Ask classroom teachers or special education teachers exactly what they are focusing on during that particular month. This is not the time to reinvent the wheel! See whether you can complement what they are doing in the classroom by focusing on the same skill sets and using the same information to present the skill (e.g., same cue words).

How Can I Teach Students Social Skills *and* PE?

Many different interventions are being used to teach social skills to children with ASD. One general technique that can work well within the physical education setting, both self-contained and inclusive, applies numerous strategies in two different contexts: 1) *casual skill development* and 2) *planned skill development*. Casual skill development provides students an opportunity to practice the social skills and learn through general experiences. Planned skill development is more of a structured activity, in which students receive feedback about their social skills development. Both types of experiences are needed for children with ASD to not only develop their social skills but also to retain and generalize the skills (Alexander, Dummer, Smeltzer & Denton, 2011).

Casual Skill Development

As mentioned earlier, PE presents lots of opportunities for students to engage in social interaction. Using casual skill development, you can tap into those times to help students develop social skills without really changing anything in your class. In other words, you encourage social interaction in your already-established routine. *Example:* During warm-up and cool-down, teachers often have students remain quiet or listen to music. Instead, consider having a class discussion about a current event in sports. If you find that a large-group discussion is a little too overwhelming, have students talk in small groups or with partners. The purpose is to take a time when students typically are quiet (or are talking quietly amongst themselves) and provide a little structure. With this technique, students continue with the normal warm-up routine, yet they get to enjoy talking with their peers while practicing and developing their social skills. It's a win/win!

Figure 4.3 Times for Casual Skill Development

- While walking out to the field at the beginning of class.
- During a warm-up and/or stretching activity.
- While waiting one's turn in line.
- When students are divided into teams and must come up with a team name or slogan.
- During cool-down.
- While waiting for the classroom teacher to pick up the class, or waiting for the bell to ring to change classes.

To create the structure, simply help students pair up and then, if needed, provide them with a discussion point. Students in the class who are social already will make their own little groups naturally. Students with ASD, though, might not initiate a social interaction, so provide the students with a little instruction (e.g., "Talk with the person next to you about … ") to help them start the social interaction.

If students need more help, provide a specific topic for discussion. A more detailed outline of how to provide instruction during these situations begins on the next page.

Figure 4.4 Encouraging Casual Skill Development During Physical Education

- Encourage students to talk about their favorite Olympics sport while walking out to the field at the beginning of class.

- Tell students during warm-up to think about one classmate they want to compliment at the end of class. During cool-down, have students volunteer compliments about one another. Help students word the compliment appropriately. Also, help the students being complimented to receive the compliment nicely. You can help them by demonstrating how to receive the compliment or by giving them some ideas of what you would say when someone compliments you.

- Have students brainstorm a team name during a tournament, as well as a team slogan or cheer. You can do this at the beginning of the tournament, and it takes only a few minutes.

- Hold a class discussion during cool-down about what teams did well in the scrimmage and what they need to improve in the future. If a whole-class discussion is too much, have them work in small groups.

- Have students partner up during stretching and discuss what they plan to be doing for Thanksgiving or another holiday. Then, ask whether any students want to share their partners' plans.

- Have students discuss their favorite TV shows while waiting for the bell to ring or for the teacher to pick up the class.

Planned Skill Development

With planned skill development, you plan an activity that can develop a specific motor skill and a social skill at the same time. The purpose is to provide a more structured activity in which you tell students to work on one or two specific social skills. *Example:* If you are in your basketball unit and want students to work on staying on topic in a conversation, pair up students to practice chest passes. Then, give them a general category (e.g., fruits). Before chest-passing the ball to a partner, each student must call out something in the category. Make it a little more challenging (and incorporate listening) by telling students that they may not repeat a word. So, if the theme is jungle animals, the first child might say "Tiger!" and the child's partner might say "Elephant!" and so on.

There are endless possibilities of activities you can create. When designing the activities, first identify what motor skill/sport skill you are covering. Next, identify general ways to practice that skill and how you normally would arrange the students (e.g., pairs, small groups, whole class). Once you have identified those variables, think of activities to incorporate that make the activity fun but also work on social skills development. The biggest challenge is being as creative as possible. At the end of this chapter, you will find some sample activities to help start your creative juices flowing.

Don't feel limited by students' abilities! If they can't read, use pictures. If they have limited verbal skills, allow them to use incomplete sentences or use their communication devices. If loud noises and chaos overwhelm them, make the activities more structured, use smaller groups of students, and expand the boundaries for the activity to provide more personal space for each student. Work with your students' strengths while still trying to improve their weaknesses.

Once you have come up with an activity, make it so that you can use it over and over again. If you're using cards with pictures on them, for example, have the cards laminated or stick them into plastic sheet protectors. Start a binder with all of your ideas, so that when you get stuck, you can just flip through your binder. This is a great way to add some new exciting activities to your lesson plan!

Providing Instruction

Because students with ASD tend not to engage naturally in these social interactions, they often need a little more instruction. Here are some key steps to follow:

- Remind students of one or two social skills to work on while they participate in the activity. Remember to be specific (e.g., "You need to stand an arm's distance away from the person next to you"). Take the time to demonstrate what the appropriate social skill should look like.

- Particularly for the casual skill development activities, you might need to give students a topic to discuss. You can suggest any topic you want (e.g., last night's football game, weekend plans, favorite holiday traditions, pets). You also can let a student pick a topic for each day/activity. If the student struggles to come up with his or her own topics, let the child pick one from a list of suggestions or a bunch of pictures. As students progress, they probably won't need you to suggest a topic for discussion.

- If you see students performing the skill well, provide them with positive feedback. If they are performing the skill incorrectly, provide them with some quick instruction. Remember to give short, specific feedback. *Example:* "You need to stand one arm's distance away from your partner. Right now, you are too far away. Take three steps in."

- Make sure that, while you provide some feedback, you also allow students to have as much of a natural interaction as possible. If you constantly intervene, they might feel discouraged or overwhelmed. Also, students will become distracted from the activity if you stop them continually to give them instructions.

Other Helpful Hints

Choosing When to Start Teaching Social Skills

The earlier you start to help students develop appropriate social skills, the better! Some students with ASD, however, might have a lot going on during their earlier years. One parent once described her son as "needing to learn how to live in his own skin before he could be social." If a child with ASD has a lot of sensory difficulties accompanied by extreme struggles with communication, it might not be appropriate to address social skills development right away. Helping the student become comfortable with simply being in the gym, being in a group of people or running might be a more appropriate priority.

Example: A 1st-grader with ASD runs into the gymnasium, starts rummaging through the balls and then starts screaming while she covers her ears and rocks in place. Her motor skills are what you would expect to see in a 3-year-old, she doesn't follow your verbal directions, and she tends to do inappropriate things with the equipment, such as put the balls in her mouth. You need to help this student learn how to be comfortable in the gymnasium and how to act safely in the gymnasium before you can focus on making eye contact. It's important that you recognize each child as unique and that, while some students are ready for social skills training as early as pre-school, others need a little more time.

How Many Skills at a Time?

For most students, it's usually best to focus on no more than two or three skills at one time. But if a student has an intellectual disability or a combination of other difficulties (e.g., difficulty managing sensory perception, significant communication difficulties and a large number of self-stimulating behaviors), it might be best to focus on only one social skill at a time. Whether it's one skill or a handful of skills, be careful not to address too many skills at once. If you take on too much, students are not likely to develop any of the skills. Instead, focus on a small number of skills so that students can improve in those areas. As students improve on one skill, you might be able to incorporate a new skill.

Working With Classroom Teachers & Paraprofessionals

Often, classroom teachers and aides are working on social skills development within their classrooms, as well. In some cases, a student might be seeing a specialist to work specifically on social skills development. Talk with your co-workers and other professionals so that you can complement one another's lessons. If you all focus on developing the same social skills at the same time, students will have a much greater chance of developing those skills. Your co-workers also might have ideas on how to incorporate a social skill into your class or might be able to share with you a reward system that they have established.

Using Consistent Cues

Another reason to speak with other people who are teaching the same skills is to ensure that you are using the same performance cues. Many different cues can describe the same basic social skill. To help a student with ASD be more successful, you must use the same performance cues that other teachers and professionals are using. That makes the student much more likely to learn the skill and generalize it to numerous settings.

Recruiting Students' Families

Don't be afraid to involve students' families. Many families are invested in helping their children develop new skills. Try setting up a system in which you can communicate exactly what social skills you are working on that week. *(See Chapter 8 for more suggestions on working with students' families.)*

Remember That It Takes Time

Keep in mind that students with ASD probably will not learn the skill in just one class; it's going to take a lot of repetition and practice. You might be able to help students develop only two or three skills within the entire school year.

Simplify

When it comes to students with ASD, some of the simplest activities are the most successful, so don't let your activities get too elaborate. Think about how much your students can handle cognitively, what your objective is and how familiar your students are with a skill (both the motor skill and the social skill). *Example:* If your class has never worked on making eye contact before, create an activity through which you can provide feedback easily to everyone and that doesn't require a lot of different steps for the students. So, you might choose a warm-up activity that students are familiar with and for which everyone is in groups. That way, students don't have to think about how to engage in the activity and make eye contact at the same time. They can focus more of their attention on making eye contact while performing a motor task that is familiar to them. As they become more proficient in the social skill, you can start incorporating it into new activities or more complex activities, such as an obstacle course.

Make Sure That Students Understand the Purpose

For students to develop a social skill, they must understand how it is relevant to their lives. So, take time to discuss briefly how the social skill can help with students' relationships and when they will be able to use it. As you continue to develop the social skill through practice, remind students how it can help them. When you see them have a positive interaction as a result of applying the social skill correctly, be sure to point out the positive experience so that students can recognize the benefit of performing the social skill.

Consider the Context

Think about where students are going to be demonstrating the social skill and with whom they will be interacting. *Example:* Teachers often emphasize to students that it's important to make eye contact with a person while conversing and that they always should face the person to whom they are talking. In the locker room, though, the unwritten rule is that you *don't* make eye contact with people when you talk to them. In fact, many people find it offensive when you look at them in a locker room setting. Imagine the implications to a high school boy if he tries to apply the eye contact social skill you taught him while he's changing in the locker room! You might need to clarify that, in certain situations, some social skills don't apply. If this is the case, provide the student with the culturally acceptable social skill, instead. *Example:* "When you are in the locker room, it's not polite to look at people changing. Instead, look at the floor or into your own locker." *(See Figure 4.5 on p. 119 for more guidance.)*

Conclusion

This chapter emphasized the importance of helping students with ASD develop social skills, and described how physical education classes offer ample opportunities for social interactions and, therefore, for developing social skills. Further, the chapter offered two different strategies — casual skill development and planned skill development — for incorporating social skills development in both self-contained and inclusive physical education classes. The most effective use of these strategies depends on the needs of each student with ASD in your classes. To help you, the following 12 pages offer sample social skills-building activities that you can incorporate easily in your class.

As you will see in Chapter 5, the use of certain curriculum models also can provide opportunities for students to develop their social skills. In particular, the Sport Education, Adventure Education and Teaching Personal and Social Responsibility models create contexts in which interaction among students plays an inherent part.

Adding yet another responsibility to your already-full plate of responsibilities might seem overwhelming, which is why you should seek collaboration among teachers, paraprofessionals, parents and classmates to help students with ASD develop their social skills.

Figure 4.5 Common Skills That Are Different in PE Compared to Society

General Etiquette	Locker Room Etiquette
Make eye contact with people when you speak to them.	Don't make eye contact or stare at a person while dressing.
Don't let other people see your private parts or undergarments.	It's okay for people in a locker room to see your body. *Note:* You still need to teach appropriate modesty.
Compliment someone if you think he or she looks nice.	Don't compliment someone who is naked or has little clothing on.
Stand next to people when you talk to them.	Put some space between you and the person you are talking to. Don't pick the urinal that is closest to another person unless it's the only one available.
General Etiquette	**PE Etiquette**
Don't yell when inside.	It's okay to yell in a gymnasium during game play.
Share toys with your friends.	When playing a team sport, share the ball only with your teammates.
Wait your turn to talk in a conversation.	When playing a game, it's okay to yell to a peer even if someone else is talking.
Stand next to people when you talk to them.	In a game, it's okay to yell to a peer from far away (e.g., "I'm open!").
Keep your hands to yourself.	In some games (e.g., tag), you will want to touch other people gently.

Sample Activities

Dribbling Bingo

Social Skills: Eye contact, starting a conversation, asking questions, listening, taking turns while talking, staying on topic.

Motor Skills: Soccer dribbling, ball control, stopping.

Equipment: Soccer ball for each student, modified Bingo card for each student, washable marker for each student.

Directions

1. Create a Bingo card *(see sample card on next page)* for each student, replacing numbers on the cards with different pictures. You can use any basic clip art images or use some of the software that is available (e.g., Boardmaker®) to make communication boards. The pictures should be of common objects that students can discuss.

2. Give each student a Bingo card, a marker and a ball.

3. Tell students that they each will dribble the ball to a peer, using their feet.

4. Upon reaching the peer, the dribbler asks a question based on one of the pictures on the Bingo card. *Example:* If the student has a picture of a dog, he or she could ask, "Do you have a dog?" The dribbler then crosses off that block on the card and moves on to another peer.

5. The first student to cross off an entire row or column of pictures wins.

Modifications

- Instead of having students complete a row on the Bingo card, have them dribble until one student marks off all the squares, or see who has the most checked off when you end the game.

- If competition is a problem or not understood, make it a little more structured. Have students dribble the ball until you yell "Talk." At that point, each student dribbles to the closest peer and asks a question based on a picture on the Bingo card.

- Instead of having students discuss their images, challenge them to find peers who have the same pictures on their cards. That helps students work on recognizing similarities.

Helpful Tips

- Make the Bingo cards reusable by laminating them or putting them inside plastic sheet protectors. At the end of class, just wash off the marks.

- Feel free to repeat the pictures on numerous cards. Also, think creatively when coming up with pictures. The cards can include almost anything!

Figure 4.6 Sample Dribbling Bingo Board

Get-to-Know-Me Freeze Tag

Social Skills: Eye contact, asking questions, listening, standing at an appropriate distance, taking turns while talking, tone, volume, introducing oneself, starting a conversation, staying on topic.

Motor Skills: Running, warm-up, balance.

Equipment: Two or three pinnies.

Directions

1. Set up a typical game of Freeze Tag, with two or three students as "it."

2. Explain to students that, when a peer becomes "frozen," they need to help the peer by unfreezing him or her.

3. The only way that a student can be "unfrozen" is by a peer asking the student a question. Encourage students to use the questions to get to know one another.

4. Make it clear that when two students are talking, they are in a safe-zone bubble and may not be frozen.

5. At the end of the game, ask students to share what they learned about their peers.

Modifications

- If you have students who are not comfortable being touched, have each student put a pinnie in his or her pocket (or use flag football flags) and have the students who are "it" pull pinnies/flags instead of tagging someone.

- Divide the class in half and have one team against the other. All rules stay the same, but no one person is "it."

Create a Silly Story

Social Skills: Taking turns in a conversation, listening, staying on topic, imaginative play.

Motor Skills: Passing (any sport), stopping the ball if controlling it with foot, catching if controlling ball with hands.

Equipment: Balls that are appropriate for motor activity (e.g., soccer ball, basketball).

Directions

1. Depending on the number of students, keep them in one large group or break the class into groups of five or six students.

2. Put students in a circle that leaves them enough space to pass the ball.

3. Tell students that they are going to create a silly story.

4. When a student has the ball, he or she adds one sentence to the story, then passes the ball to a classmate.

5. Emphasize that everyone must have a turn.

Modifications

-   Students often enjoy listening to their silly stories, so record the story and play it back, or jot down some notes and retell the story to the class yourself.

-   Encourage students with limited vocabularies to say one word or use the computer to add to the story. They can leave their communication boards/computers on a chair or table next to them.

Helpful Tips

-   The first few times, students might find it difficult making the story silly. They might have a hard time coming up with a sentence at all. Feel free to jump in and add a sentence every once in a while. Use crazy, silly sentences to emphasize how to make it silly.

-   Another way to make the story silly is to have some general unrelated topics in a hat. Have two or three students from each circle pull out the topic and challenge them to incorporate the topics into the story. It might be too challenging for some students with ASD to add to the story and include the topic they pulled from the hat, so use your discretion.

Clear the Ball

Social Skills: Taking turns while talking, staying on topic, listening.

Motor Skills: Passing the ball with arms, serving a ball (volleyball).

Equipment: Balls that are appropriate for motor activity (e.g., volleyball, basketball), small cards (about 2" x 3") with conversation topics on them.

Directions

1. Attach a bunch of different conversation topics to the ball with pieces of tape. The topics should be common things that students can talk about.

2. Put students into groups of two or three.

3. Tell students that they're going to pass the ball to one another. Each time a student receives the ball, he or she takes off one topic.

4. The student then makes a statement about the topic. *Example:* If the topic is favorite thing to do over the summer, the student could say, "I love to go swimming in my grandmother's pool."

5. Once a student has made a statement, he or she passes the ball to a peer in the circle, and it starts all over again.

6. The goal is to clear the entire ball of topics.

Modifications

- Use pictures for topics instead of words for students who cannot read or who struggle to read.

- Make it a race by giving students a time limit and then having them count how many cards they were able to take off.

- Let students work on listening by letting them ask questions instead of making statements. When a student receives the ball, he or she has to answer the passer's question before removing a tag.

- Have students work on recognizing similarities and categories. Put numerous cards on the ball that all fall into one category (e.g., animals). Then, put other cards on the ball that have nothing to do with the topic (e.g., fruit, family, colors). Instead of making a statement, students look to pull off a card that fits in the category.

Helpful Tips

- Laminate the topic/pictures so that you can reuse them or use them for a different activity.

- Have a large assortment of pictures so that you can mix it up and use a diverse set of topics.

Theme Flip Cone

Social Skills: Listening.

Motor Skills: Running, warm-up activity, balance.

Equipment: A large number of flat cones. See *Modifications* for other options.

Directions

1. This is simply a modified version of the basic warm-up drill Flip Cone (sometimes called Pancakes).

2. Put out a bunch of flat plastic cones, in at least four different colors. If you don't have that many colors, tape pieces of colored paper on each cone.

3. Break students into two teams.

4. Tell members of Team A the color cone they should flip over. Tell members of Team B to flip over a different-color cone.

5. Tell students that the goal of the game is to flip over as many cones as possible. But they may flip over only the colors they have been told.

Modifications

- If you don't have enough cones, you can use any sort of equipment. For finer motor skills, you can use playing cards. You can also use poly spots, plastic/paper cups or shuttle cocks. Use bean bags or tennis balls if you want students to gather colored objects instead of flipping them.

- Feel free to mix and match equipment, as well. Instead of focusing on colors, tell students to flip an item that you specify.

- Instead of using colors, put pictures on the cones and have students find specific themes (e.g., cartoon characters, jungle animals).

- You can have the entire class flip over one color. For every cone flipped that isn't the right color, the class loses points.

- If the concept of flipping a cone is too difficult, have students just pick up as many cones as they can.

- Add more challenge by allowing teams to flip over their own color and un-flip the other team's color.

Helpful Tips

- Spread the cones out far enough so that students won't run into one another.

- Use at least three times more cones/pieces of equipment than students.

Safari Run

Social Skills: Listening, imaginative play, standing at an appropriate distance.

Motor Skills: Running, warm-up, balance, spatial perception.

Equipment: Four cones to designate space within which to run.

Directions

1. Make a designated space for students to run.

2. Tell them to all run around until you yell out the name of an animal. When they hear the animal's name, each student moves to the person closest to him or her and acts out the sound/action that the animal would make.

3. Remind each student to face his or her peer when acting out the animal and to stand at an appropriate distance from the peer.

4. Have students start running. Randomly yell out the names of animals (e.g., elephant, lion, bear, alligator) that might be fun to act out.

Modifications

- You don't have to use just animals; you also can use letters, cartoon characters and mythical objects (e.g., monsters, dragons, "Star Wars" characters). Also, try to incorporate themes that students are working on in their classes.

Helpful Tips

- *Remember:* Some children with ASD have difficulty with imaginative play, so you might need to demonstrate the animal when you call out its name.

- You might need to remind them to keep running in between animal names.

Going Fishing

Social Skills: Staying on topic, eye contact, standing at an appropriate distance, voice volume, voice tone, listening, starting a conversation.

Motor Skills: Ball control, basic locomotor skills (e.g., running, skipping, hopping), warm-up activity.

Equipment: Four or five small buckets or containers; conversation topic cards.

Directions

1. Arrange students in teams of four to six. Divide each team in half. Have one half of each team (Group A) stand on one side of the gym or playing area, and have the other half of each team (Group B) stand on the other side. Next, have each Group A stand directly across from each Group B.

2. In front of each Group B, place a container that holds a bunch of conversation topics.

3. Have students from each Group A move to their Group B teammates while performing a motor skill (e.g., dribbling a ball, running, hopping, skipping, doing lunges).

4. When Group A students reach their Group B teammates, they pick a topic from the bucket, then tell a fact to Group B that is related to the topic.

5. The first person in Group B then runs to Group A and shares what he or she just learned.

6. Continue the game until each student has shared a fact that he or she has learned.

Modifications

- If some students can't read, use pictures in the buckets. You also can place random items in the bucket that the student needs to talk about.

- If you want to work on fine motor skills, as well, make the topic cards in the shape of fish. Then, place a large paper clip on each card. Using a stick, string and a magnet, create a fishing pole. Instead of having students reach in and grab a topic card, have them pick it up from the floor using the fishing rod.

- Have all students start out on the same side of the gym. Students run to the bucket, pick up a card, then run back to the group to share their facts.

- You can make it a relay race to see which group can finish the fastest. Have each student play both roles (listener and sharer), or have students play one role, then start a new game in which they play the other role. Once students have completed their role(s), they can sit down. Once everyone is sitting, the team is finished.

Guess Who

Social Skills: Eye contact, contributing relevant information, taking turns in a conversation, standing at an appropriate distance, tone, volume, asking questions, listening.

Motor Skills: Dribbling, running (or any other locomotor skill), warm-up.

Equipment: Index cards (one for each student), masking tape, one ball for each student if practicing dribbling.

Directions

1. Pick a general topic (e.g., animals, superheroes).

2. On an index card, write a word relevant to the topic. Make one card for each student in the class.

3. Inform students that you are handing them a card, but they may not look at it.

4. Put a piece of tape on each index card.

5. Hand out the cards and tell students to stick them on their foreheads.

6. Students dribble the ball around the designated space or use a locomotor skill to move around.

7. Every time a student comes up to a peer, he or she can ask the peer for a hint about what the card of his or her forehead says (e.g., "Am I an animal on the farm?"). The only rule is that the student answering the question may not use the word on the card as a clue.

8. Students continue dribbling around the space, trying to figure out what their cards say.

9. The activity can go until a percentage of the class (e.g., 50 percent) figures out the answer. Another option is to run the game for a specified time period (e.g., five minutes).

Modifications

- Take the activity a step further by breaking students into groups. When making the cards, repeat each word two or three times (e.g., 10 words, each repeated three times, can work for 30 students). Once each student figures out what his or her card says, he or she then finds classmates with the same card.

- You don't have to use cards. You can attach a piece of paper to funny sunglasses or make paper crowns to wear.

Helpful Tips

- Consider using material from students' other classes or materials related to health and nutrition. *Example:* Find out what they are discussing in science class and try to integrate it into the game. You can use nutrition, muscles or drug education as topics, as well.

- Students with ASD might need some help creating questions.

- If students with ASD have problems reading, you might want to use pictures instead of words.

Chapter 5 ────────────
Physical Education Curriculum Models: Implications for Students With ASD

Content

Introduction

"What will my classes be doing this week?" That's a question that K–12 physical education teachers typically ask themselves before each week begins, and the answer can usually be found in the school or district-level curriculum guide.

Using the formal curriculum of a school or district, physical education teachers typically plan and implement lessons within the framework of a particular curriculum or instructional model. This chapter provides descriptions of several popular curricula or instructional models and describes the features of each model that are consistent with the learning and social needs of students with ASD, along with the features of the model that might present challenges to those students.

Curriculum/Instructional Models

"Curriculum includes all knowledge, skills and learning experiences that are provided to students within the school program. A formal curriculum typically includes the planned and sequenced learning experiences that allow students to reach significant goals that teachers have determined worthwhile for students to achieve." (Lund & Tannehill, 2010, p. 6).

Typically, curriculum models represent a particular philosophy and favor particular learning outcomes. Teachers then choose instructional strategies that are compatible with the curriculum model they are using and the learning outcomes they look to foster. The curriculum models that are included in this chapter were chosen because they represent models typically found in K–12 physical education programs and/or the features of the models offer some unique opportunities for enhancing the learning experiences for students with ASD. The curriculum models described in this chapter are:

- Multi-Activity.

- Sport Education.

- Adventure Education.

- Fitness Education.

- Teaching Personal & Social Responsibility.

Multi-Activity Model

Model Description

This model might sound familiar: the Multi-Activity Model is the most common curriculum model found in physical education programs and has a long history, dating back to the "education through the physical" movement of the early 1900s (Hastie, 2003). The purpose of the model has been to provide students in the elementary grades with opportunities to develop basic motor skills that would enable them to participate in a variety of movement activities, including games that involve locomotor and manipulative skills, dance and rhythmic activities, and activities associated with developing and maintaining fitness. At the middle school and high school levels, the purpose of a multi-activity curriculum, typically, is to expose students to a variety of sports and movement activities so that each student can experience sports, games and activities that are personally enjoyable and relevant. The hope is that students then will make positive choices for continued participation throughout adulthood.

In this model, regardless of grade level, students participate in activities during relatively short (three or four weeks) units of instruction. Therefore, two or three different units might be included in the course of a marking period, with the potential to provide students with opportunities to experience eight to 12 different activities during the course of one school year. Teachers whose physical education programs reflect this model often identify the frequent shifts from one activity to another as necessary for preventing students from becoming bored. Teachers also identify the capacity to expose students to a wide variety of activities as an attractive feature of the model.

Figure 5.1 on p. 137 provides an overview of the main features of a Multi-Activity Model, as it is typically implemented, with implications for students with ASD.

The Multi-Activity Model is not without its critics, who maintain that, due to the brevity of the units and the repetition of sports and activities over the course of K-12 programs, students typically don't emerge from this model particularly well-skilled. This perceived lack of effectiveness of the model, however, seems to have more to do with the manner in which it is implemented than in the model itself (Hastie, 2003; Lund & Tannehill, 2010).

In units that focus on traditional sports and games beginning in grades 4 or 5 and particularly at the middle and high school levels, critics also identify the propensity of dominant, aggressive male students to control game play, which often results in lower-skilled students being marginalized or excluded and, as a result, disengaging from the activity (Ennis, 1999; Griffin, 1984).

Figure 5.1. Multi-Activity Model
Features & Implications for All Students

Feature	Implications
Predictable class routine: Warm-up, skill practice, game play or skill application.	Because of the predictability of the class routine, students — especially in the middle and high school levels — might not give their full effort.
The model accommodates a variety of activities that could involve individual as well as group participation. Units of instruction are relatively short, typically lasting 3–4 weeks (9–12 lessons).	Most students seem to react well to the variety offered by frequent changes in the activities.

Figure 5.2 Advantages & Challenges of a
Multi-Activity Model for Children With ASD

Advantages	Challenges
Individual lessons within a Multi-Activity Model typically follow a predictable routine: warm-up, skill practice, game play.	Length of a typical unit (3–4 weeks, 8–12 lessons) might be too short for students with ASD to learn the skills or activities.
The model accommodates a variety of activities that could involve individual as well as group participation, providing options for students with ASD.	Changing units so often fails to address the need that students with ASD have for consistency and predictability.
	Students with ASD might experience confusion amidst the sometimes-conflicting rules of different sports and games (e.g., soccer = no hands; basketball = no feet).
	Giving students with ASD different field or court positions during game play, with different performance expectations, can be confusing and unsettling.

Model Considerations

- Switching activities every three to four weeks does not provide students with ASD enough time to acclimate to an activity to the point that they begin developing the skills needed to engage in the activity successfully. Therefore, longer units might be better received by students with ASD. While increasing the length of the instruction units might be easy when teaching a self-contained class of students with ASD, it could prove challenging in an inclusive setting.

- Try to provide a diverse set of units to give students with ASD a better chance of being successful or enjoying a unit. In particular, individual sports/activities should be covered, along with team sports/activities.

- To help students with ASD transition between units, try to sequence activity units to maximize similarities from one unit to the next. *Example:* If the transition is from soccer to basketball, a student with ASD might have difficulty understanding why it's suddenly okay to dribble the ball with his or her hands, when doing so during the soccer unit was not allowed. Moving the class from outdoors (soccer) to indoors (basketball) also might be problematic, as it presents a change in routine, and the two environments provide different sensory experiences. These two games also require different sets of skills and have different rules (e.g., a goalie verses general defense). A better alternative would be to sequence lacrosse followed by floor hockey indoors. The class setting will change, from outdoors to indoors, but the sports are somewhat similar in strategy and skills required.

- Students with ASD will respond well to the predictable class routine associated with this model. Therefore, keep warm-up activities and skill-development activities as consistent as possible.

- In inclusive settings, adjust the model to encourage the active engagement of all students. Implementing rules that avoid dominance by the most-skilled players is recommended, so that all students will be able to participate and contribute.

Sport Education Model

Model Description

The Sport Education (SE) Model was introduced initially by Daryl Siedentop in 1995 as an alternative to the Multi-Activity Model and continues to grow in popularity (Siedentop, 1995). The SE Model offers all students the opportunity to participate in an "authentic sport experience," previously available to only the skilled athletes chosen to play organized extracurricular sports. Since the model was introduced in the mid-1990s, several authors have developed detailed descriptions and curricular materials to help physical educators who are attracted to the notion of providing meaningful sport experiences to all of their students (Siedentop, 1995; Siedentop, Hastie, van der Mars, 2011; Bulger, S.M., Mohr, D.I., Rairigh, R.M. & Townsend, J.S., 2007). The SE Model incorporates six features of organized sport (Siedentop, 1998), with modifications that emphasize educational outcomes for all students. These features are:

1. Seasons.

2. Affiliation.

3. Formal Competition.

4. Culminating Event.

5. Record-Keeping.

6. Festivity.

Teachers can use this model, with students beginning in grade 3 or 4, when children are ready developmentally to take on differentiated roles and assume leadership positions (albeit well-coached and supervised) within their teams *(see Figure 5.3 on p. 140)*. A good rule of thumb regarding readiness to participate in sport education for elementary students: If the students are at a grade level at which they're capable of serving in the school's student government or student leadership council, they're capable of participating in a Sport Education season (Bulger, et al., 2007).

When the SE Model is implemented at the middle or high school level, students can take more responsibility for leadership and autonomous functioning within their teams. *Example:* High school students should be capable of designing their own warm-up and team practices, while younger students will need teachers' help to script those activities. However, students with ASD might need extra assistance when given leadership roles, especially if an intellectual disability is present.

Figure 5.3 Sport Education Model
Features & Implications for All Students

Feature	Implications
Seasons. An SE season lasts two or three times longer than a typical Multi-Activity unit.	Students have time to improve skill and game-play ability.
Affiliation. Students join a team at the beginning of the season and stay on the same team throughout the season.	Students have time to build interpersonal relationships with teammates and to learn to work as a team.
Formal Competition. Game play and practice sessions are interspersed throughout the season to mimic a typical sport season.	When practice sessions and game play mimic a sport season, students have an opportunity to see the relevance and importance of practicing both individual skills and game tactics.
Culminating Event. A competitive event highlights the season and provides goals toward which students work.	With the provision of multiple ways to accumulate points for their teams, all students have the opportunity to contribute to team success.
Record-Keeping. Students are responsible for keeping individual and team statistics throughout the season.	Keeping individual and team statistics provides each student with data regarding what skills and tactics he or she can perform successfully and what skills/tactics each student needs to practice, as well as what the team needs to work on to be more successful.
Festivity. Teams come up with slogans or cheers, have team colors, hold celebratory interactions among and between teams, create team Web sites, etc.	The festive features of sport (e.g., assigning team colors, encouraging teams to adopt slogans or cheers, emphasizing the celebratory aspect of the season-culminating event) can enhance student engagement during the course of a Sport Education season and encourage team bonding.

Adapted from Siedentop, D. (1998). What is sport education and how does it work? Journal of Physical Education, Recreation and Dance, 69(4), 18-20.

Figure 5.4 Advantages & Challenges
of the Sport Education Model for Children With ASD

Advantages	Challenges
Longer seasons result in fewer transitions during the school year.	Students with ASD might lack the social skills needed to participate successfully in an SE season.
Team affiliation creates a stable and predictable group of teammates throughout the SE season. Given the social difficulties associated with ASD, it might be easier for students with ASD to interact socially with a small group of people with whom they are more familiar, rather than the entire class.	Students who lack an affinity for the sport being played don't have an alternative for the season.
Students have the opportunity to develop the ability to function within a team.	The complex concepts related to game strategy in particular and competition in general might interfere with students' ability to acquire the skills needed to play.
Teammates have the opportunity to get to know everyone on the team and find ways to capitalize on each student's strengths to benefit the team. Using differentiated roles will allow all students, including those with ASD, to choose a role that is best suited to their abilities to contribute to team success.	The celebratory significance of culminating events might not be apparent to students with ASD.
Students are involved in an authentic sport experience that can increase the likelihood of skill transfer to other recreation settings outside of school.	When score-keeping responsibilities are shared, students with ASD might struggle with the tasks of recording and evaluating individual and team data.

Continued on next page

Figure 5.4 *(Cont.)*

Advantages	Challenges
The many social interactions that occur throughout an SE season provides students with ASD with a safe and structured place to develop and practice appropriate social skills.	Students with ASD need to become familiar with the schedule of practice sessions and games so that the activities during each class session are predictable, and not surprising.
The record-keeping feature of the model provides visual representation of desired behaviors. Data also can be used as an assessment for IEP progress reports.	
Culminating events often involve tangible rewards (certificates), to help solidify the abstract nature of success.	
The culminating event is of particular importance for students with ASD because it provides closure at the end of the season, which helps signify that it's time to transition into a different unit or season.	

Model Considerations

- Because "team" is an abstract concept, concrete visual representations of the team can be helpful. Focusing on a team name, color and mascot will help define the concept.

- A clear definition of each student's role and expected contribution to the team activities can help students with ASD know what is expected of them.

- Provide students with ASD with a season schedule at the beginning of each season. A poster in the gymnasium outlining each day also will help students with ASD.

- Students with ASD will need specific instruction about what to expect during each part of the season (e.g., pre-season practice versus pre-season game play).

- You might need to tell students with ASD what is socially appropriate behavior when participating in different events (e.g., a team cheer) related to the festivity component of the SE Model. They also might need an explanation of the activity's social significance.

- Use a tangible reward system to encourage positive behaviors and decrease the abstract nature of the sport.

- Make a point to recognize the contribution of all students, acknowledging each student's strengths. This is important to emphasize that everyone is a valuable member of the class community.

- You might need to simplify the record-keeping process for students who have difficulty reading or writing.

- If you're measuring a social behavior (e.g., good sportsmanship), students with ASD will need to know how to perform the behavior and when it is appropriate (e.g., shaking hands with opponents at the end of each game).

- Warn students when the culminating event is approaching, to help them prepare for change.

Adventure Education Model

Model Description

Adventure education curricula have become increasingly popular over the past several years and provide an approach to physical education that favors learning outcomes in the affective domain. Typically, learning outcomes for adventure education programs include the development of students' abilities to:

- Work together toward a common goal.

- Engage in problem-solving and critical thinking.

- Develop feelings of trust in themselves and toward their classmates.

- Challenge themselves to try activities that might be outside their comfort zone.

Typically, the Adventure Education Model is included in middle and high school physical education programs, although elementary physical education teachers in grades 4 and 5 often use some of the ice-breaker activities and problem-solving initiatives with their students.

Figure 5.5 Adventure Education Model Features & Implications for All Students

Feature	Implications
The Full-Value Contract. The purpose is to create a sense of community and establish mutually agreed-upon behavioral expectations for class members.	Students identify expectations for behavior and participation that they agree to follow. Examples of expectations appropriate for middle school students: • Be here. • Be safe. • Be honest. • Set goals.
Challenge by Choice. The purpose is to help students understand that they have the right and the ability to choose what are appropriate challenges for them in adventure education activities, and, ultimately, in life.	Students choose which of the activities and initiatives they will attempt, and have the right to opt out of a particular activity if they decide that they aren't ready to attempt it. Students are not allowed to opt out of participation continually and are encouraged to attempt unfamiliar activities with help/encouragement from teachers and classmates.
Experiential Learning and the Experiential Learning Cycle. The purpose is to help students understand how concrete experiences in one situation (adventure education activities) can result in learning concepts that they can generalize and apply to new situations.	A period of reflection follows each activity, during which students are encouraged to reflect as a group (debrief) how an activity went, as well as reflect individually (journal) regarding the impact of an activity on how they view themselves and their classmates.

Adapted from Panicucci & Constable, 2003.

Figure 5.6 Advantages & Challenges of the Adventure Education Model for Children With ASD

Advantages	Challenges
The Adventure Education Model provides an opportunity for students to develop the social skills needed to interact with peers and, possibly, create a trusting relationship.	Students with ASD who experience a hypersensitivity to touch will have difficulty with the activities that involve physical contact with others and/or with equipment. Other sensory sensitivities, such as hypersensitivity to sounds or vestibular motions, can prove to be a problem for some students with certain activities.
The model provides an opportunity for students with ASD to engage in challenging activities outside their comfort zone. Students with ASD, as with all students, will have an opportunity to experience the feelings of success at having overcome one's fears and reaching a goal that, previously, they perceived as unreachable.	All adventure education activities require extensive interpersonal interactions, relying heavily on both expressive and receptive communication skills. Students with ASD most likely will have great difficulties contributing to the conversations held among students during the problem-solving activities and participating in the debriefing sessions that conclude activities.
When provided with guidance, children with ASD also do very well with motor patterns that are repetitive in nature. These types of skills are needed to complete many of the high elements.	The use of metaphoric language when describing the setting for problem-solving activities can make it difficult for students with ASD to understand, due to their difficulties with imaginative play.
For many of the activities in adventure education, students with ASD can watch their peers perform the activity and then be told of some efficient ways to perform it themselves.	
Many adventure education activities lend themselves to providing each person a specific responsibility. The specificity is ideal for students with ASD because they don't have to interpret the social aspect of the environment.	

Model Considerations

While this model can present a challenge for students with ASD, it carries enough benefits to make it worth trying. So, rather than avoiding adventure education activities because they might be problematic, physical education teachers who favor them for their potential for building trust, self-confidence and students' ability to solve problems together should find ways to modify typical adventure education activities to accommodate the needs of students with ASD. *(See Figure 5.7 for some suggestions on how to modify some adventure education activities to provide a comfortable learning environment for students with ASD.)*

Figure 5.7 Adventure Education Activity Modification Table

Activity	Purpose	Example	Suggested Modification
Ice-Breaker Activities	To provide opportunities for students to interact with and get to know one another in preparation for activities that will require a level of trust.	**Emotions Tag.*** Moving in an open space, each student who is tagged acts out the emotions chosen by the tagger. Play until everyone (or almost everyone) is displaying the same emotion.	If a student with ASD flees from the tagger and is tagged, tell him or her the emotion, and model an appropriate response. Provide a picture or video of someone demonstrating the same emotion and remind the student with ASD when he or she might experience the emotion.

Figure 5.7 *(Cont.)*

Activity	Purpose	Example	Suggested Modification
Problem-Solving Initiatives	To provide opportunities for students to practice working together as a group to devise a solution to a particular movement problem.	**Hot Chocolate River. ** Challenge a team of students to travel from one side of the Hot Chocolate River to the other stepping only on "marshmallows" (poly spots or wooden blocks) and pulling up the marshmallows after the last student crosses.	Forego the use of metaphoric language and state the problem in literal terms. Also, provide a visual map along with visual cues on the floor to help students understand the challenge. Depending on the activity, consider breaking the class into smaller groups so that students with ASD are not overwhelmed by the large social interactions.
Trust Activities*	To provide opportunities for students to practice working together and to learn to trust their classmates while engaged in low-risk activities.	**Trust Lean, Trust Fall**	Emphasize to students with ASD their roles in the activity. Have them watch two or three trials first, to get a visual.

Continued on next page

Figure 5.7 (Cont.)

Activity	Purpose	Example	Suggested Modification
Trust Activities* (Cont.)			Emphasize the importance of safety and the students' responsibilities. Place students with ASD in a location where other students can help compensate, just in case.
Low Initiatives	To provide students with opportunities to engage in challenging activities close to the ground that require problem-solving and teamwork, without the use of equipment (harnesses and belays).	**Mohawk Walk, Spider Web**	Have students with ASD watch others to gain a visual example of how to participate. Provide visual markers to help outline the task. Encourage students to create a few cues words or phrases to help guide one another.
Low & High Elements***	To provide students with opportunities to engage in challenging activities both low to and	**Zip Line**	Allow students to try wearing a harness before they perform activity to get used to the feel of the safety equipment.

Figure 5.7 (Cont.)

Activity	Purpose	Example	Suggested Modification
Low & High Elements*** (Cont.)	high above the ground that require problem-solving and teamwork, with the use of equipment (harnesses and belays).		Allow students to watch peers before trying the activity. Show students a video of the activity, if possible.

Panicucci (2003), p.5

**Panicucci & Constable (2001), pp.114-115*

****PE teachers without formal training in adventure education from one of the licensed providers (e.g., Project Adventure) would not have students engage in any adventure education activities involving low and high elements that require the use of safety equipment, but they would be able to have students participate in the Ice-Breaker Activities and the Teamwork and Communication Activities.*

Model Considerations

- Adventure education activities can be problematic for some students on the spectrum, especially those who experience hypersensitivity to touch and/or proprioceptive or vestibular hypersensitive. Pick only the activities that are appropriate for those students, given their sensitivity.

- While much of adventure education relies on students' coming to their own conclusions and "figuring it out themselves," students with ASD might require some guidance or assistance in making the task more concrete.

- Activities in which students are asked to engage in imaginative play most likely will need to be simplified and presented in a concrete fashion for students with ASD.

- The emphasis in adventure education activities on working together, building trusting relationships among students and group problem-solving provide an excellent opportunity for students in inclusive settings to learn about their classmates with disabilities and how to help these students participate in the activities successfully. In inclusive settings, students will need clear guidelines on how they should engage in each activity and how they can help students who are struggling with a particular activity.

- The debriefing discussions with students provide excellent opportunities in inclusive settings for classmates to acknowledge the accomplishments of all students. Also, the teacher can offer students feedback on how well they assisted classmates, including those with ASD.

- Students with ASD likely will have difficulty reflecting on their contributions and will need specific, concrete questions to help guide them. *Example:* "Did you help Jessica get through the spider web?" instead of "Did you contribute to your team's success?"

Fitness Education Model

Model Description

The purpose of a fitness education curriculum is to develop:

- Students' knowledge about the importance of fitness and physical activity.

- Students' knowledge about what kinds of activities promote different components of fitness.

- The skills needed to participate in a variety of activities that contribute to developing and maintaining appropriate levels of fitness.

- The attitudes and dispositions that contribute to the likelihood that an individual will engage in a variety of physical activities on a regular basis both as students, and later, as adults.

Fitness education curriculum materials, such as NASPE's *Physical Best* books, often include learning outcomes in the cognitive, psychomotor and affective domains. Typically, students assess their current fitness levels, set goals for improvement, design an individual fitness plan, implement the plan and assess their progress periodically.

Figure 5.8 Fitness Education Model
Features & Implications for All Students

Feature	Implications
Pre-Assessment of Fitness Levels	Provides students with a baseline measure of their fitness levels.
Setting of Individual Fitness Goals	Encourages students to reflect on their current fitness levels and make some decisions about what they would like to change.
Designing of a Personal Fitness Plan	Enables students to creat their own fitness plans, based on their levels, goals and interests.
Execution of the Plan	Students can engage in their personal fitness plans both in and outside of the physical education class.
Periodic Progress Assessment Progress & Plan Adjustment	Periodic assessment helps students see progress and can motivate them to continue participating in fitness activities.

Given the current emphasis on the importance of fitness for children and school-age students, fitness education units of instruction and activities are typically seen throughout the grade levels. Usually, elementary students are taught to monitor their pulse rates, use pedometers, and perhaps experience heart rate monitors, as well, during their physical education classes. As students progress through the grade levels, the emphasis shifts toward having students take more and more responsibility for their own fitness and for maintaining a healthy level of physical activity both in and outside of school.

Figure 5.9 Advantages & Challenges
of the Fitness Education Model for Children With ASD

Advantages	Challenges
Setting individual goals, which typically is part of a Fitness Education Model, is ideal for students with ASD. Students identify goals and select activities/exercises that are consistent with their capabilities.	Students with ASD will need assistance in setting appropriate fitness goals and identifying appropriate activities/exercises. Also, goals will need to be concrete rather than abstract.
Enacting their individual fitness plans in class will provide students with ASD the opportunity to operate independently and at their own pace. This is an ideal model for students with ASD for whom verbal interaction with others is problematic, because students can work independently on their own fitness programs.	Students with ASD will need assistance in pacing timed activities such as walking and/or running on a treadmill.
Activities tend to be repetitive in nature, which students with ASD often prefer because of the predictability.	Students who are hypersensitive to touch might struggle to work with certain equipment. Also, some assessments might be contraindicative of sensory sensitivities.
Activities tend to be concrete and easily tracked (e.g., 10 reps of biceps curl).	Students with ASD might need a concrete external motivator (e.g., a token system) to encourage them to persist with a desired behavior.
Fitness tests contain prescribed exercises that students with ASD can understand and perform.	Introducing new fitness options to the class (e.g., doing yoga for a day) might present a problem for students with ASD, because of the change in routine.

Model Considerations

- Modifications to activities or equipment might be necessary for students with ASD who struggle to complete some age-appropriate activities because of motor delays.

- Students with sensory sensitivity might struggle to use certain equipment (e.g., weight machines, Thera-Bands®), so make sure that alternatives (e.g., free weights) are available.

- Make considerations regarding sensory needs and general motor behaviors. *Example:* Students with very rigid movement might do better with a weight machine that guides their movements, rather than free weights.

- As with all students, students with ASD will need to be monitored for safety. You might need to review correct form and ways to use equipment properly more often than usual.

- In some instances, students with ASD might not be motivated to complete the assessment, might not understand the assessment's objective or might not understand how to complete the assessment. As a result, the student's assessment data may be inaccurate. Consider offering an external motivator (e.g., a token system), taking extra time to explain the importance of the test, providing visual demonstrations of the test, and having students with ASD observe their peers before performing the assessment themselves.

- Students with ASD will need help setting goals and will be better off identifying concrete goals rather than abstract ones. *Example:* "Increase number of sit-ups from 15 to 20," rather than "Increase abdominal strength." Also, providing students with ASD with two goals and asking them to choose between the two might work better than asking them to come up with their own goals from scratch.

- As with all students, encourage students with ASD to set SMART goals (specific, measureable, attainable, relevant and time-based) (Andersen, 2000).

- Represent goals visually in numerous locations to help students with ASD remember the point of the exercises.

- Using a visual outline (task card) of the lesson will help keep students engaged and on task.

- Assign students with ASD partners to help them start on the activities and keep them focused. To create an inclusive environment, have all students pair up, so that students with ASD are not highlighted as different.

- Let students with ASD know in advance when fitness assessment will replace their usual fitness routine.

Teaching Personal & Social Responsibility Model

Model Description

The Personal and Social Responsibility (TPSR) Model was developed by Don Hellison in the 1970s to encourage at-risk youths to take responsibility for the impact of their actions on their own lives and on the lives of others in the context of physical activity (Hellison, 1978). In the years since Hellison introduced the model, it has been modified and adapted for use in a variety of contexts, including school physical education programs, extra-curricular sports, before- and after-school programs, and community-based youth programs. The model, in its current form, challenges kids to identify levels or goals of responsibility at which they already are operating or seek to attain. *(See Figure 5.10 on p. 155 for a description of those levels/goals.)*

Figure 5.10 Teaching Personal & Social Responsibility Model Levels & Goals

Level/Goal	Description
0 = Irresponsible	The student interferes with the rights of other students to participate and learn.
1 = Self-Control	The student might not be actively engaged in class activities, but he or she is not interfering with other students' rights to participate and learn.
2 = Effort/Teamwork	The student is actively engaged in the class activities and is making an effort to meet the learning goals that the teacher has set.
3 = Goal-Setting/ Coaching Oneself	The student is actively engaged in class activities and is reaching beyond the expectations that the teacher has set for the class. The student has set personal goals and is actively attempting to reach those personal goals.
4 = Leadership/Coaching Others	The student has taken on a leadership role and is helping classmates reach the goals set for the class, as well as encouraging classmates to go beyond minimal expectations and set higher goals for themselves.
5 = Transfer/Being Responsible Outside the Gym	The student takes the notion of being personally and socially responsible outside of the physical education class and applies the responsibility levels in different contexts and to different aspects of his or her life (e.g., on the playground, at home, in the neighborhood).

Adapted from Hellison, D. (2011) Teaching personal and social responsibility through physical activity, 3rd ed. Human Kinetics, Champaign, IL.

Although the levels appear to be hierarchical, it's common for students to visit a few different levels during one class period. In fact, it's possible for the lesson activities and/or your instruction strategies to have an impact on the particular level or levels that are readily accessible to all students — including students with ASD — during the course of a single lesson.

At the outset of a lesson, the teacher describes the activities that will take place. Students are likely to be listening actively (Level 2), especially if the activities forthcoming are ones that they enjoy. During game play, students might be at Level 3 (highly skilled and motivated to be successful in the game), Level 2 (somewhat successful during game play), Level 1 (struggling to perform skills in the context of game play and appearing active on the court or field but actually are moving away from the ball and the action), or even Level 0 (disrupting game play out of boredom or frustration).

You can elicit particular levels of responsibility from students by using particular instruction strategies. *Example:* You can encourage students to set goals for themselves (Level 3) during a lesson in which skills are practiced at different stations in the gym and performance goals written on task cards encourage students to try to improve their scores as they practice. When you use peer checklists during skill practice in which students, in pairs, alternately observe their partners perform a skill and provide descriptive feedback based on skill components, students have the opportunity to help one another improve their skills (Level 4) just by following the directions on the peer checklist.

Given the possibility for students to visit different levels during a particular lesson, having students reflect on the extent to which they are being responsible is important. Implementing the model includes using particular strategies or lesson components intended to encourage each student to pay attention to his or her actions and how those actions affect the individual as well as the group. *(See Figure 5.11 on p. 157 for these strategies and their implications for students with ASD.)*

Figure 5.11 Teaching Personal & Social Responsibility Model Features & Implications for All Students

Feature	Implications
Relational Time	The teacher engages individual students in conversation at the beginning of class, with the purpose of determining how each student is feeling, and uncovering any issues that might be troubling students or that might be going particularly well in their lives.
Awareness Talk	The teacher and students discuss what will happen during class for the day and acknowledge the role that the levels will play during class activities. Students are encouraged to set goals for themselves related to the levels they hope to achieve and what they hope to accomplish during class that day.
Lesson Focus	Students engage in the class activities planned for the day while the teacher facilitates student engagement in the learning activities, as well as helping students focus on their levels of responsibility during class activities.
Group Meeting	Students and the teacher gather a few minutes before the end of class to engage in conversation regarding how the class went and how well students were able to interact and work together in productive ways. Other topics of discussion: difficulties that students encountered in reaching the lesson's activity goals and how class members might have interacted better with one another.
Self-Reflection Time	Each student reflects on his or her participation in the day's lesson and identifies the levels at which he or she operated. The teacher facilitates this reflection by asking questions such as, "How well did you work with your classmates today?"

The TPSR Model is well-suited to virtually all grade levels, with attention paid to students' developmental levels. At the younger elementary school grades, teachers can display posters depicting the goals or levels of responsibility with smiley, frowny and neutral faces indicating the relative desirability of the levels (Levels 0 and 1 = least desirable; Levels 2, 3 & 4 = most desirable). Conversations during awareness talks and group meetings should reflect students' developmental level, with the middle and high school levels involving more student-generated dialogue and discussion than at the elementary level.

It's important to note that the TPSR Model should not be implemented by itself. Rather, it needs a context in which it can be implemented. That context could be another curriculum model and/or particular physical education activities.

Figure 5.12 Advantages & Challenges of the TPSR Model for Children With ASD

Advantages	Challenges
The model encourages social interaction and awareness of others.	Students might have difficulties focusing on both movement skills and social skills simultaneously.
The model provides structured time for students to reflect on their behaviors and how their actions affect others.	Language difficulties can affect participation in certain components of the model (e.g., awareness talk, reflection).
The model provides a venue for incorporating social skills into instruction.	The abstract concepts (e.g., "participation," "giving maximum effort") can be difficult for students with ASD to comprehend.
The predictable structure of a TPSR lesson that includes relational time, awareness talk, lesson focus, group meeting and reflection will provide students with ASD a level of comfort in knowing that each lesson will follow the same structure.	Interpersonal skills that are difficult for children with ASD are necessary for participating in many components of the model, including awareness talk and reflection.
	Open-ended questions often used to structure components of the model such as awareness and reflection can be too vague for students with ASD to understand.
	Students with ASD might not know when it's appropriate to contribute to class conversations.
	As some students with ASD might have difficulty contributing to the conversations, others might dominate the conversation, pulling in irrelevant information.

Model Considerations

Although implementing the TPSR Model in either self-contained or inclusive classes that contain students with ASD can be very challenging, the model is particularly well-suited for students with ASD because it encourages students to be aware of the impact of their actions on others. In particular, the model's awareness talk and reflection time that are included in each lesson provide opportunities for all students — specifically, students with ASD — to consider their own behavior and actions and how those actions affect themselves and others.

A recurring theme of this book has been the importance of finding ways to adapt activities — in this case, the TPSR Model — to meet the needs of the students in your classes, and we encourage you to try the model, given the potential benefits.

- When using this model with students with ASD, the teacher directs or leads each of the lesson components of the model, including:

  - During relational time, the teacher engages in informal conversations with students as they enter the gym before the lesson begins, asking questions about, for example, how their day is going. For students with ASD, questions should be specific. *Example:* "What did you do over the weekend?" "Did you have fun in computer class today?"

  - During awareness talk, the teacher describes Levels 1 & 2 and gives examples of behaviors appropriate for each. For students with ASD, it's important to describe what they should do for the particular lesson, rather than providing general examples. An appropriate description for Level 2 in a basketball lesson: "Listen, dribble the ball, pass the ball to your partner and stop at the red cone." In the beginning, the teacher might need to provide students with ASD with an appropriate goal. As time progresses, they might be able to pick a goal from two or three options and might eventually be able to come up with their own goals.

  - During the lesson, the teacher integrates a focus on Levels 1 and 2 with attention to the lesson's skill or game-play focus. *Example:* In addition to providing specific skill feedback, the teacher might say, 'Nice job stopping!"

  - During group meeting, the teacher asks what the students liked and disliked about the lesson. In addition to asking that general question, the teacher could ask questions that would be easier for students with ASD to respond to. *Example:* "What did you enjoy more, being the goalie or playing forward?" This is also an appropriate time to apply Pick-a-Hand *(see p. 35)* to assist with communication.

- During reflection time, the teacher asks students to respond to how well they performed at the different levels. The reflection can be informal (thumbs up, thumbs down) or formal (writing in a journal). For students with ASD, an informal "thumb vote" is reasonable, with the teacher asking a specific question, such as "Did you give Jean a high five when she made a goal?"

- Students with ASD most likely will have a difficult time contributing to conversations that lean toward the abstract, as in the group meeting. To assist with that:

  - Let students with ASD know how group meetings work and the social etiquette involved.

  - State a question to which students with ASD can respond. The question should be direct and focused on one behavior. *Example:* A student with a limited vocabulary might be able to respond to a question such as "Did you pass the ball?" A student with an adequate vocabulary might be able to reflect on his or her own performance or emotions and could respond to a question such as "Was the game fun?" or "What part of the game was fun?"

  - Establish a subtle cue for the student to let you know when he or she is ready to talk, so that you can create a gap in the conversation.

  - Conversely, if a student with ASD is dominating the conversation, help control the conversation by using a "talking stick" or ball that is to be held by the person currently talking.

  - Having students sit in a circle, rather than in random spots, will help provide order for students with ASD.

- If you are trying to apply all levels of the TPSR Model with the class, you should note that Level 5 of the model — Transfer/Being Responsible Outside the Gym — might present problems for children with ASD. The level refers to the goal of having students incorporate the notion of personal and social responsibility into all aspects of their lives, not just in the physical education class. It will be difficult for children with ASD to reach that goal because it requires them not only to apply information in an abstract manner but also to generalize information from one setting to another. Nevertheless, having students with ASD reflect on the levels experienced in their physical education class can result in worthwhile experiences with personally and socially responsible behaviors.

Conclusion

Teachers choose curriculum models for a variety of reasons. Sometimes (with the Multi-Activity Model, in particular), the curriculum has been in place for so many years that it has become part of the culture of the physical education program. Another model might be adopted because it captured the interest of the program coordinator or the teacher(s) during a workshop or convention presentation. And sometimes, a curriculum model is chosen because it's consistent with the philosophy and value orientations of a program director or physical education teacher who might be especially committed to the importance of fitness and encouraging students to be physically active.

We encourage physical education teachers to choose curriculum models that reflect what they believe are important for students to learn in physical education and then look for ways to modify the model so that it can be implemented successfully in any school setting. Students with ASD have the potential to achieve the learning outcomes of any of the curriculum models described in this chapter, once the teacher has examined each model in relation to the abilities of his or her students and has made any modifications that might be necessary to accommodate the needs of those students.

Resources

Bulger, S.M., Mohr, D.I., Rairigh, R.M., Townsend, J.S. (2007). *Sport education seasons*. Champaign, IL: Human Kinetics.

Siedentop, D. (1998). What is sport education and how does it work? *Journal of Physical Education, Recreation and Dance,* 69(4), 18-20. Reston, VA: American Alliance for Health, Physical Education, Recreation and Dance.

Chapter 6 —————
Behavior Management:
Proactive Strategies

Content

Introduction

It's difficult to facilitate student learning in a class environment that is disorganized and with students who are inattentive or distracted. This chapter describes preventive strategies you can use to encourage all students — especially students with ASD — to behave appropriately in your physical education class. The chapter begins with some general considerations regarding behavior management and student misbehavior, and follows with several strategies that will provide a context in which appropriate behavior is likely to occur.

General Considerations

When thinking about misbehavior and behavior management, it's best to apply some general considerations before you start to think about the strategies you will put in place. While these considerations are important for all students, they are particularly relevant when addressing students with ASD.

Determining the Cause

Before you can even begin to address misbehavior in the classroom, you must determine why the student is demonstrating a problem behavior. In fact, what appears to be misbehavior on the part of any child might be the child's way of communicating that something is wrong. It will be difficult to rectify the situation until you understand the reason for the behavior.

Some strategies might be counterproductive, depending on the cause of the misbehavior. *Example:* David is normally a well-behaved student, but he has been disruptive since the class has started working on jump rope skills. He wanders around the gym, bothers other students, uses his jump rope as a lasso and talks with peers while you are delivering instructions. After giving David three warnings, you finally put him in a time-out. As soon as David returns to the activity, though, the misbehaviors start again.

Usually, taking away a child's privileges (e.g., giving the child a time-out) extinguishes misbehavior, but what if the student doesn't consider what's being taken away a fun activity? In this example, David cannot jump rope and doesn't want his peers to know. By putting him in a time-out, you give David exactly what he wants: an excuse not to jump rope. So, David's punishment has become a reward. Without assessing the situation fully, you end up doing the exact opposite of what you intended. To prevent this frustrating experience from occurring, you must identify why the student with ASD is acting out.

Our emphasis throughout this book has been that children with ASD are similar to other children in many ways. As a result, they misbehave for many of the same reasons that other children misbehave. Don't assume that a student's misbehavior is a direct result of his or her having ASD! It might be that the child is being a typical kid. Misbehavior is simply a way to communicate problems.

Children with ASD also have some unique circumstances that can lead to misbehavior, and those circumstances relate to their disability characteristics. *(See Figure 6.1.)* *Example:* While you are delivering instructions, Andrew talks continuously to himself, distracting the students around him. You ask Andrew to stop talking and listen to the instructions. He stops for a few seconds, and then starts humming very loudly. Chances are, Andrew is hyposensitive and needs to create an auditory stimulus for himself. He's not trying to defy you; he's just trying to make himself comfortable.

Figure 6.1 Some Common Causes of Student Misbehavior

Universal	Disability-Specific
Boredom	Over-stimulated
Frustration	Under-stimulated
Hunger/ thirst	Communication problems
Exhaustion	Pain
Fear	Medication imbalance/recent change
Problems at home	Not knowing appropriate behavior
Desire for attention	Poor social skills
Embarrassment	Lack of predictability/routine
Physical discomfort	

Accounting for Time of Day

The time of day can have a big effect on what you should expect from students with ASD. In an ideal world, students with ASD would have the coping skills to deal with the craziness of a typical school day. That isn't always the case, though. By the end of the day, some students are fatigued from coping with the extensive amount of stimulus they have encountered throughout the day. Other students might be overloaded from an overwhelming situation that they just left and need a few minutes to regain composure. *Example:* A student who takes the bus to school might still be a little frazzled in first period PE class. The noise and chaos of a school bus can overwhelm someone with poor social skills and heightened senses. As a result, the student might distance himself from the group or misbehave. But if given a few minutes at the beginning of class to sit quietly and bring his body to a comfortable level of stimulus, he might have no problems in class.

Try to stay aware of periods of time that students with ASD might be struggling, and accommodate as needed. It might mean that you allow a student some time to recuperate by himself or herself (under the supervision of a paraprofessional), or you might recognize that you don't have a student's full attention, so he or she won't benefit much from an instructional task.

Figure 6.2 Times That Might Be Difficult for Students With ASD

1. After getting off the school bus, because of the excessive amount of stimulus and social contact.
2. The very beginning of the school day (particularly on Mondays), because of the transition into a structured school day.
3. Right after lunch, because of the excessive amount of stimulus and social contact.
4. After a change in routine (e.g., school assembly, fire drill), because of reliance on schedule and possible sensory overload.
5. Right after taking an exam, because of mental fatigue.
6. After recess, because of the excessive amount of stimulus and social contact.
7. The end of the school day, because of general fatigue.

Setting Realistic Expectations

For some children with ASD, a 50-minute period feels like eternity. Keep in mind that children are asked to behave for an entire school day, which typically is six-and-a-half hours long. For children with ASD who are trying to balance sensory perception problems, communication barriers and difficulties with social skills, six-and-a-half hours is a long time! It might not be practical to expect students with ASD to behave for your entire class period. That doesn't give them a pass to run around and cause mass chaos, but it might mean that half-way through the class period, you give a student with ASD a five-minute break to go to a quiet location and regroup.

Each student is different, and you will need to assess each one's abilities to determine when or if he or she needs a break. Keep all students' attention limits in mind when planning the lesson. If you know that students will be attentive and productive for only 30 minutes, make sure that you put the important parts of the class (e.g., instructional components) in the first 30 minutes.

Avoiding Assumptions Regarding Communication

If a student is bouncing a ball during instructions and you ask him to stop, you probably assume that the rest of the class will be forewarned that bouncing the ball is an unacceptable behavior. Children with ASD, however, don't always think that way. Children with ASD often don't interpret information given to someone else as applying to them. So, instead of addressing one student when correcting a behavior, remind the entire class of the rule that you want to see all students follow. If you still want to address the child who is demonstrating the misbehavior, follow up using the child's name. *Example:* "When I am giving instructions, we all need to hold the ball in our hands. That includes you, Jacob."

Use a similar tactic for delivering positive reinforcement to students for a behavior that you want the entire class to emulate. *Example:* Jackson is standing at the door waiting quietly, as you want all students to do. So, you announce to the class: "Everyone should stand by the door quietly when he or she is ready to leave. Jackson is waiting very nicely!"

Teachers often use body language or facial cues to communicate to students that they would like a change in behavior. The hope is that students will interpret the cue, and the correct behavior will spread throughout the group. A common example of this is when the teacher stops talking and waits for students to become quiet: students usually catch on to the fact that the teacher is not pleased, and silence spreads quickly throughout the group. Students with ASD, however, might not catch on. They might continue to talk until someone says: "You need to stop talking. The teacher is waiting." One way to help students with ASD in this situation is to announce, "I am going to wait for the class to stop talking before I continue." If you think the student with ASD didn't hear you, repeat the announcement as more of the class quiets down.

Sharing Strategies

Parents, classroom teachers, paraprofessionals and other service providers (e.g., speech therapists) can be your allies when it comes to behavior management. They can tell you what tends to trigger misbehavior, what different misbehaviors usually mean, what signals students might give you right before they misbehave and what strategies can help redirect or control the misbehavior. That can save you a lot of time and energy!

Example: Trisha has ASD and was attending a local sporting event. In the distance, she saw a team mascot. With an odd smile on her face, Trisha ran toward the mascot. Assuming that Trisha was excited to see the mascot, the paraprofessional let her go. But as soon as Trisha neared the mascot, she tried to tackle it to the ground while kicking wildly. As people ran over to intervene, Trisha ran and hid behind the bleachers. She sat rocking and humming for a half hour before she would come out. When Trisha's mother came later in the day, she apologized and explained that Trisha is terrified of mascots and responds violently. She also reported that the odd smile was the telltale sign that Trisha was about to be aggressive, but that, if you have Trisha face away from the mascot and say "Friend," she is fine. If someone had asked about Trisha's trigger before the sporting event, a difficult situation could have been avoided.

If you can't meet with the parents face to face, send home a letter asking about what triggers misbehaviors, what cues the student might show before he or she misbehaves, ways to prevent the misbehavior and strategies for responding if the misbehavior occurs. *(Find a sample letter on the CD-ROM that accompanies this book.)*

When sending the letter home to a child's parents, emphasize that you're asking for this information to help the child have a positive experience in PE. Some parents won't want to give too much information because they're afraid that you will exclude their child or develop a negative perspective of their child. So, emphasize that you are asking so that you can help the child cope with adverse circumstances and make PE enjoyable, as well as productive. Parents and classroom teachers will appreciate that you are trying to keep behavior-management strategies consistent!

Talking to the Student

Teachers can't read students' minds (although that would be nice!). Don't be afraid to ask students why they are misbehaving. As stated earlier, misbehavior usually occurs as a way to communicate a problem, whether it is physical discomfort, anxiety, a need for attention or general frustration. If you can't figure out why a student is misbehaving, ask him or her to identify the problem. Often, the student will be able to tell you exactly what is bothering him or her. If the child is nonverbal or has limited verbal abilities, consider asking him or her to show you. Many times, the student will be able to take you to something that is bothering him or her, or give you some sort of signal to show you the problem.

You just have to remember to be patient enough to watch and/or listen. You also could try the Pick-a-Hand approach discussed in Chapter 2.

Sometimes, students won't know why they are demonstrating a problem behavior, or they might not be able to identify their own emotions. In those cases, try giving them a few suggestions of what could be causing the problem, to help them identify the irritant. *Example:* "Are you frustrated because you missed the goal?" Keep in mind that being able to identify one's emotions is an important life skill that should not be overlooked. If people cannot identify what is bothering them, they can't help themselves remedy the situation. So, it's important to help students with ASD learn to recognize their own emotions and frustrations.

Mixing & Matching Your Strategies

Most teachers have two or three behavior-management techniques that generally work for them and their students. Don't be afraid to apply those techniques to students with ASD. Many of your general behavior-management strategies will work wonderfully for children with ASD. Also, don't be afraid to mix and match strategies, depending on students' needs. What works with one student might be completely ineffective with another.

Unless the student's IEP states otherwise, you should always be using at least two or three strategies. Using only one strategy tends to make it become ineffective. Instead, try to use a progression of strategies: one for minor misbehavior, one for moderate misbehavior and one for serious misbehavior. If you always jump to the strategy for serious misbehavior, when a serious misbehavior actually does occur, you will lack the tools to address it.

You also don't want to use too many strategies. Students should know what to expect if they are misbehaving; it shouldn't be a surprise. So, pick a few strategies that you feel fit your teaching style, meet the needs of the students and address the cause of the misbehavior appropriately.

Established Behavior Plans

Many children with ASD already have pre-established behavior plans in their IEPs. Particularly if a child's behavior tends to be problematic, the child study team will agree upon a strategy for managing the child's behavior. The strategy will outline when and how to apply it, along with appropriate consequences and rewards. If a child already has an established behavior plan, you must abide by it. So, you must use the IEP's behavior-management strategy in your class. To avoid confusing the child, mix in other strategies only if they don't interfere with the behavior plan. Most of the preventive strategies provided in this book are designed to create an environment in which students can be successful and will not interfere with a child's behavior plan. Instead, they will help you create a positive environment for *all* students.

If you have trouble incorporating a child's behavior plan into your class format, talk to the child study team to determine whether a modification for your class is possible and practical. Unless told otherwise, though, you must continue to use the established plan.

Proactive Strategies

Establishing Rules & Routines

What It Is: **Rules** are statements of behavior expectations that define acceptable ways of behaving and interacting in physical education class. Rules should be stated in positive terms that reflect what students *should* do, rather than what they *shouldn't* do. *Example:* "Put the ball at your feet when I am giving instructions," instead of "Don't bounce the ball while I am talking." Be sure to reinforce rules consistently.

Routines are pre-established patterns of behavior that apply to frequently occurring events during a lesson. Typically, they're used to define acceptable behavior when engaging in common events such as entering the gym at the beginning of class, taking attendance, performing warm-up exercises, distributing and collecting equipment, managing lesson closure and dismissal at the end of class. When students know what they are expected to do when they enter the gymnasium, and how they are expected to retrieve and return equipment, you can spend more time on instruction and less time repeating directions that might be the same for each class. The predictability of routines also creates a sense of comfort for children with ASD.

How to Apply It: Always! It's important to establish rules and routines that describe acceptable student behavior, and it's essential that you always spell out exactly what is expected of students and that you keep these expectations consistent throughout the semester. Students will know how they are expected to behave in your physical education classes only if you tell them, and students with ASD are no different.

Example: Paul was having difficulty entering the gymnasium in an acceptable manner. He often would run in, rummage through the equipment, then run around the gym's perimeter. The teacher established a routine to help modify the behavior. Paul was instructed to walk into the gymnasium, walk over to his poly spot within his group and sit on the poly spot with his hands folded in his lap. He had to be reminded of the routine for the first few weeks, but once he got it, the teacher could jump right into instruction time instead of wasting time trying to get Paul to join the group.

Example: Quinn didn't like to participate in the practice activities that were designed to lead up to game play, but he loved participating in the actual games. The class decided to make a rule that students were not allowed to participate in the game if they didn't complete at least 75 percent of the practice activities. When Quinn refused to practice, he was reminded of the consequence of his choice. For the first two classes, he still refused to participate and grew very angry when he was told he couldn't participate in game play. By the third class, however, he started to participate in the practice activities.

Considerations/Helpful Tips

Rules

- Describe acceptable behaviors and responses in detail, while avoiding general or abstract terms. Rather than simply stating the "Always listen" rule, you might want to state it this way: "When the teacher is talking, stop talking, stand still and listen to the teacher." If a student has difficulty with receptive communication, you can shorten the statement to "Quiet, freeze, listen."

- When working with children with ASD, you might have to limit the number of rules you put in place to between three and five. So, choose which rules you feel are most important for a child with ASD to be able to participate safely and effectively.

- State all rules in simple words. Especially if some students have difficulty with verbal communication, you might need to explain your expectations in a limited number of words. *Example:* Instead of saying "Keep your hands to yourself," you might say "Hands on legs" (while putting your hands at your side) or "Hands in lap."

- Many students with ASD are "rule police": once they learn the rules, they perceive them as black and white and follow them to the letter. If they or someone else breaks a rule, children with ASD might feel compelled to report and address the infraction. So, when setting rules, make sure that they apply to all situations throughout the entire school year. *Example:* You set a rule that all students must keep their hands to themselves. During a unit in dance, though, you want students to hold hands and elbow-swing. A student with ASD might be quick to point out that this is not allowed because students are not keeping their hands to themselves, as the rule states. To avoid that problem, add a clause to the rule, such as "... unless given permission."

- While some students are sticklers for rules, others have difficulty applying rules to different situations. So, it's important to review established rules and appropriate behaviors with students at the beginning of class, particularly when you plan to change something about the class that might lead students with ASD to believe that the routine or rules don't apply. *Example:* Derek, a student with ASD, knows that he should not hit classmates in the gymnasium. But he doesn't transfer that rule when you move the class outside. So, when the class starts playing soccer outside and someone steals the ball from him, he retaliates by hitting the student.

- Provide visual demonstrations of your expectations. This includes demonstrating what the correct behavior looks like, highlighting a student who is demonstrating the behavior correctly and showing a short video of people demonstrating the correct behavior. When a student struggles with the correct behavior, refer him or her to the visual.

- Use visual aids to help students remember the rules. Hang a poster with both pictures and written words illustrating the rules. But avoid using a picture of the unacceptable behavior with a line through it. Instead, show the behavior that you want to see.

Routines

- For routines, rely on task cards *(see p. 94)* or other visual cues that help to provide reminders. *Example:* If students are expected to enter the classroom and gather in their groups, put poly spots on the floor to remind students with ASD of where they're supposed to stand. Provide visual pictures on the equipment carts to help remind students where to place equipment during clean-up.

- Students with ASD thrive on routine and schedule, but you sometimes might need to change the routine. Create a back-up plan for what will happen if you need to make changes. In some instances, it might help to share your plan with students with ASD, so that they're not caught off-guard. It's almost like teaching students the emergency evacuation route in case of a fire. You hope you don't have to use it, but it's better that they know it than trying to learn it during an emergency. When telling students about the back-up plan, give them enough information so that they'll have a general idea of what to expect. *Example:* You've been holding class outside for the past three weeks, but rain and thunderstorms are forecast for today. Given the chance that the class will need to be indoors, you modify your lesson plan. Warn students with ASD in advance that class might be moved inside to the main gym, and inform them how the lesson is to be modified.

- Decide whether to share the back-up plan with students with ASD, based on their levels of functioning and their rigidity with schedule. Some students will gain comfort knowing that a back-up plan is in place. Others, though, will become preoccupied with the thought that you might make a change and will focus exclusively on that possibility.

Assessing Skill Levels

What It Is: The practice of pre-assessing students' skill levels at the beginning of a unit of instruction is an essential pedagogical strategy that you should use for *all* students. The source of disruptive behavior in all students (including those with ASD) can stem from a situation in which students are being asked to perform a skill or participate in an activity for which they don't have the requisite skills to succeed, resulting in frustration. On the flip side, you might ask students to complete an activity that is far below their performance abilities, which results in boredom. In either situation, students are not being challenged appropriately, and they sometimes demonstrate inappropriate behaviors. Pre-assessing students' skill levels before engaging on class instruction and activities can prevent them from becoming frustrated.

How to Apply It: Assess students' skill levels at the beginning of a new unit. Never assume that you know what a child is capable of simply because of his or her disability. Just as with the other students in the class, some children with ASD are very good in athletics and some are not so skilled.

Example: The class is starting a unit on jumping rope. Miguel often self-stimulates by jumping up and down, so the teacher figures that he is going to do well in this unit. Students complete a quick evaluation, in which they try single-hop and double-hop, counting how many times in a row that they can jump for each. The teacher looks over and Miguel is having a horrible time. He can't even figure out how to swing the rope to complete the assessment.

Example: Amber tends to be delayed in her motor skills, particularly in skills that require hand/eye coordination. So, the teacher assumes that Amber will struggle with foul shots in basketball. The teacher asks students to practice foul shots until they make at least five baskets out of 10 shots. Amber is able to make seven of 10 shots on the first try. Then she grows bored and starts to throw the ball at the wall. After talking with the paraprofessional, the teacher finds out that Amber shoots hoops regularly with her older brother at home.

Considerations/Helpful Tips

- Don't be afraid to reassess a student's skill level if you feel that the initial assessment was not accurate. If students with ASD are over-stimulated or are trying to cope with the change of a new unit, they might not perform to the best of their ability during the initial assessment. They also might perform poorly if they are not motivated to complete the task. *Example:* Jennifer had participated in swim meets for years and always swam pretty slowly. At this swim meet, instead of being awarded medals for placing, the winner is to be awarded a baseball hat. Jenifer loves hats. She jumps in the water and takes almost four seconds off her 25-meter swim time, setting a new personal best. Apparently, she never was really interested in medals, but she really wanted the baseball hat.

- Be sure that you're assessing skill level and not a disability factor. Consider how your instructions, students' sensory perception and their communication skills affect their performance. *Example:* Your class is participating in the PACER test. A student with ASD is moving slower than usual and seems very rigid. You realize that the noise of the PACER test is too much for him to handle and is distracting him. Once you turn off the beeper and give basic verbal cues, the student is fine. *Example:* You notice that, while jumping rope, Miguel lands continuously on the rope. You assume that it's because he doesn't have the necessary hand/eye coordination and try to decrease the level of difficulty. Something doesn't feel right, though, because you have seen Miguel perform other tasks that require the same level of skill. You realize that Miguel has misunderstood the purpose of the activity and thinks that he is supposed to jump and land on the rope.

- Allow students with ASD to watch other students perform the assessment before asking them to try it. That way, they can see what is expected of them and understand what they're supposed to do. Be sure to focus students' attention on the essential components of the assessment and what aspects you want to see them perform.

Using Help Cards

What It Is: Help cards give students a way to let you know that they need help, before their frustration leads to misbehavior or a meltdown. Give students an index card at the beginning of class, and instruct them to hold up the card or hand it to you when they're unclear about instructions or are frustrated. By providing them with the card, you eliminate the need for students with ASD to formulate the words to ask for help.

How to Apply It: When a student has difficulty asking for help or expressing his or her confusion or frustration. This approach usually is successful with students who tend to struggle with social skills but don't have other difficulties such as an intellectual disability.

Example: Lawrence has difficulty remembering instructions. He usually is able to get half-way through an activity but then forgets what he is supposed to be doing. Lawrence has a task card, but sometimes, he still is unsure of what is expected of him based on the limited information presented on the card. In the past, he would wander over to the equipment and help himself to something to keep himself entertained. The teacher gives Lawrence a help card at the beginning of class. The teacher instructs Lawrence to hand him the card if Lawrence forgets what to do or is thinking about retrieving a piece of equipment.

Example: Jamil has a very difficult time figuring out how to respond to his peers when they are in game play. Sometimes, he grows so frustrated that he ends up screaming at teammates; while other times, he behaves inappropriately, including laughing at peers when he thinks their mistakes are funny. After watching Jamil, the teacher can see that he is processing the situation and thinking about how to respond, but is choosing the wrong approach. So, the teacher provides Jamil with a help card. When Jamil hands the teacher the help card, she quickly suggests an appropriate social response to the situation.

Considerations/Helpful Tips

- Asking for help is an important skill for students to develop. So, the help card shouldn't be used as a substitute for communication, but rather as a crutch to help bridge the gap. When a student presents the card, help him or her work to formulate the words needed to express the confusion. Keep in mind that you need to consider the student's level of frustration before going into a teachable moment.

If the student is already overwhelmed and frustrated, that's not the time to work on verbal communication skills. But if the child is mildly flustered, you can walk him or her through how to ask for help in the future.

- To help save paper and time, decorate a few index cards as help cards and then have them laminated. If you don't have access to a laminator, you can use clear shelving paper/contact paper on both sides of the index card.

- You can use help cards for all students, not just those with disabilities. It's a discreet way for students to tell you that they're stuck. Students who are shy or embarrassed by their skill level often respond well to this technique because the cards are so discreet. Keep the cards in a manila envelope that is attached to the equipment cart, the equipment closet door, the locker room door or any other central location.

- Help cards present good opportunities to use peer teaching. Encourage students to help one another if they see a peer holding up a card. For this to work, you need to teach students how to provide one another with help.

Following Your Rules

What It Is: Enforcing the rules consistently is a cornerstone of effective class management and behavior management. Unfortunately, some teachers become lax with the rules if they have a student with ASD in the class. While extenuating circumstances sometimes dictate bending your rules, in general, it's best to enforce — and reinforce — the rules you have set for the class. Not only does that ensure safety and classroom order, but the consistency provided when you enforce rules equally also helps keep students with ASD at ease and helps them understand what is expected of them.

Particularly at the start of a new school year or new unit, remind students of the rules at the outset of class. If there is one rule that you know a student with ASD struggles with, remind him or her of the rule — and the consequences for breaking it — one on one. If the student can communicate verbally, ask him or her to state the rule and the consequences for not following it. Remember to focus on the behavior you want and not to place emphasis on the behavior you don't want.

How to Apply It: When a student's behavior is not in compliance with the established class rules, you should enforce the consequences for noncompliance. Having said that, the notion of picking one's battles is important. *Example:* If a student's misbehavior is minimal and non-disruptive, then you might choose to ignore a minor rule infraction and focus on a larger issue. If you have addressed the student with ASD specifically, though, and reminded him or her of the rule, follow through with the appropriate consequence.

Example: You have established a rule that students must stop moving and listen on your signal. A student with ASD doesn't stop on your signal, even after you remind him about the rule, so you follow up with the pre-established consequence (give a strike).

Considerations/Helpful Tips

- Ensure that the consequence is appropriate for students with ASD. *Example:* Asking a child with ASD to explain why his or her actions are not safe might be beyond his or her verbal and intellectual abilities.

- Keep the consequences of rule-breaking consistent from one class to the next. If you use the "three strikes and you're out" rule on Tuesday, use it on Thursday, as well.

- Provide students with a warning before moving right to the consequence. The only time this doesn't apply is when students display a behavior that puts themselves or other students in danger (e.g., hitting a peer). In that case, jump right to the consequence.

Using Prompts & Cues

What It Is: Prompts and cues are auditory or visual messages given to students to remind them what is expected of them or to help them recognize when and how to act appropriately. You might use a verbal cue as simple as the word "Go" or a visual cue such as a picture of a green light to show a student that it's his or her turn. The cues can be visuals that are posted permanently and that you refer to throughout the class (e.g., a list of responsibilities), or they can be something you show the student when you want to deliver a specific message (e.g., a picture of an ear to remind the student to listen). Other common cues are playing music to communicate when the student should be active, holding up cards to show the intended behavior (e.g., a stop sign to show that you want him or her to stop) and saying agreed-upon words such as "Freeze."

How to Apply It: When a student is having difficulty understanding or remembering what is appropriate behavior (e.g., when it's his or her turn), providing a prompt or cue can help clarify and remind him or her what is expected.

Example: Brad loves to lead the class in stretches, and he would like to do it every class period. When you tell Brad that it's someone else's turn to lead stretching, he has a meltdown and refuses to participate. The same thing happens when you tell him that he may not help with clean-up. To help with the behavior, you post a chart that has each student's name on it. You then explain that each class period, a different student will lead stretching; when the picture of a person stretching appears next to your name, it's your turn to lead the class. You can do the same with other tasks, such as clean-up and set-up. When Brad insists that he lead, you refer to the chart and count how many students have to go before it's his turn again.

Example: Kevin doesn't stop an activity when you're trying to deliver instructions. You set up the rule that when the music is playing, students may perform whatever activity is planned. As soon as the music stops, students should stop what they are doing and sit on the floor.

Considerations/Helpful Tips

- For the system to work, it must be clear and concise. You want the cue to be very obvious (e.g., when the music is on, you move your body).

- Keep the system consistent. If you hold up a red poly spot to show students that you want them to freeze, don't use a red poly spot for any other purpose.

- Expect a transition time as students learn the system. In the beginning, you will need to review the cue at the beginning of each class and also provide some instruction when you implement it.

Confirming Your Words

What It Is: Because students with ASD take words literally, they sometimes struggle with sarcasm, slang or expressions that can be interpreted in different ways. This misunderstanding can lead to inappropriate behavior because students might not fully understand what is being stated. So, it's important to explain the meaning of a phrase, saying or word as it pertains to the situation. You confirm your words to clarify what they mean in the current context to prevent students from doing something inappropriate or growing frustrated because they don't understand. It also can mean that you clarify a rule or statement with an exception clause (e.g., "You don't interrupt me UNLESS it's an emergency").

How to Apply It: When misbehavior follows because a student doesn't understand what you want him or her to do.

Figure 6.3 Restating Common Rules to Improve Understanding

General Rule	Example of Rule Reworded for Students With ASD*
Enter the gym in an orderly fashion and go to your floor spots.	Walk into the gym without talking. Sit on your poly spot, hands in your lap.
Stop activity and listen on my signal.	When you hear the whistle, stop moving, face me and listen to instructions.
Retrieve equipment in an orderly fashion.	When I call your squad, walk to the cart, pick up one ball and take it back your spot.
Return equipment in an orderly fashion.	When I say "Clean up," carry your ball to the bin and place it inside the bin.
Be a good sport during game play.	When you are playing, keep your hands on your body only, say "Good job" to friends and think about your body only.
Share equipment with classmates.	(Use a timer to show the number of minutes each student will be in possession of equipment.) You play with the ball until the timer rings, then you are all done and it's Sharon's turn.
Raise your hand when you have a question.	When you have a question, raise your hand and wait for me to call your name.

* If a student has difficulty with long phrases, these directions need to be shortened.

Example: While the teacher is explaining the rules of a game, one student says he wants to "beat the other team." The student with ASD gets a concerned look on his face and suddenly moves away from the group. He then starts saying "No hitting! No hitting!" The teacher realizes that the student took the term "beat" as literally hitting someone physically. To clarify, the teacher states, "What Jason means is he wants to try to score more points than the other team."

Example: At the beginning of class, the teacher tells students that they are going to work on their badminton serves. He then asks that they try a drill but states that he doesn't want them to ask any questions until they complete the drill, because he wants to get a basic sense of where their skill levels are. About two-thirds of the way through the activity, the teacher notices that Kaitlin has wet her pants. When he asks what happened, Kaitlin says, "You said not to ask any questions." In retrospect, the teacher realizes that he should have said, "Don't ask any questions about serving in badminton."

Example: You explain to the class that in soccer you shoot the ball at the other team's goal. In the middle of the game, Kevin runs up to the opposing team's goalie and uses his hand to make a pretend gun that he fires at the goalie.

Considerations/Helpful Tips

- You might need to clarify common expressions that are incorporated into rules. *(Find examples of common phrases used in PE that can be misinterpreted on the CD-ROM that accompanies this book.)*

- When rewording the rules or instruction to make them clearer, be careful not to make them too wordy so that the child cannot remember all the information. Consider breaking the rules or instructions into multiple parts.

Giving Reinforcement

What It Is: Be prepared to provide students with reinforcement for their compliance with class rules and routines. Often, you can do that by providing the child with something he or she likes after demonstrating the desired behavior. *Example:* If a student really likes to be captain, you could give him or her that responsibility for the last 10 minutes of class as a positive reinforcement for listening to instructions.

Examples of reinforcement include: providing verbal acknowledgement, awarding stickers, providing student choice of activity, allowing students to take a desired role in the class, participating in preferred duties (e.g., team captain), giving positive cues (e.g., thumbs up), and giving checks on a chart as a means for acquiring a larger reward (e.g., "Once you get 10 checks, you can choose an item from the treasure chest").

When providing students with reinforcement for their behavior, it's important to tell them exactly why they're being rewarded. Particularly with students who have ASD, don't assume that they know what behavior has led to the reward. So, state the behavior the student is displaying and why you like it, followed by the reward the student will receive. Also, be sure to acknowledge the positive behavior immediately; don't wait until the end of class. *Example:* "Abdul, I really like how you are waiting your turn quietly. You may pick out a sticker to put on your chart." If you wait until the end of class, Abdul won't know which behavior he's being rewarded for. The immediate feedback allows him to reflect on his current behavior.

How to Apply It: Teachers typically establish reinforcement at the beginning of the school year to delineate compliance with class rules and routines. Also, a child study team might have established particular reinforcements for the child, and you will be asked to implement them in the gymnasium to maintain the reward system throughout the child's day.

Example: At the beginning of the unit, you introduce to the class a poster that has each student's name and 10 boxes after each name. You inform students that they have multiple ways (e.g., showing good sportsmanship, sharing equipment, helping a classmate) in which to earn stars to fill in each box. When a student earns 10 stars, he or she is allowed either to lead the class warm-up for a day or to lead the line back to the classroom.

Considerations/Helpful Tips

- Make sure that students perceive the reward favorably. If the reward results in a change of schedule, it might be distressing to a child with ASD. *Example:* Setting up stations of different activities and allowing students to pick what they would like to do as a way of rewarding good behavior over the past month is not always a good option for students with ASD. The chaos of the situation, combined with the change in routine, can be distressing and perceived as a negative.

- Elementary school children usually like to receive stickers, and a high school student might like stickers, too, depending on his or her level of functioning. Consider the child's intellectual abilities, as well as his or her biological age when choosing rewards.

- While students with ASD might be excited about receiving a sticker, they might not like to have it placed on their clothing. They might find the sticker distracting and a change in their normalcy. Instead, consider putting stickers on children's task cards or on index cards that they can carry around.

- This is a great place to incorporate a child's object of obsession! When you incorporate the object of obsession into the reward, it makes the reward all the more appealing. You can use stickers or music related to the object of obsession, let the student talk about the object of obsession, and play a game that mimics or incorporates the object of obsession.

Applying Regulated Permission

What It Is: Everyone has a really bad day once in a while, when no matter what you try to do, things just don't seem to go right. For children with ASD, having a really off day can prevent them from being able to cope with their environment. With regulated permission, you recognize that the child has an extenuating circumstance and that he or she is going to act up. As a result, you give the child another activity or are more lenient in applying your rule. Don't use this strategy too often, though: no more than once per child per marking period. Use it only when you realize that, no matter what strategies you put in place, the student doesn't have the capacity to comply with your behavior expectation.

How to Apply It: Apply regulated permission when an extenuating circumstance (e.g., fire alarm the period before, doctor appointment that morning, relocating PE to the cafeteria because of an assembly, death in the family), has thrown the child off for the day.

Example: Andrew, a student with ASD, had a dentist appointment early in the day to have a tooth filled. As a result, his entire schedule has been thrown off and his mouth is tender. When Andrew walks into the gymnasium, you can see that he is having a tough day: He is self-stimming more than usual, has an agitated look on his face and is yelling. As you start the class, you see that Andrew is melting down and realize that he can't function in the class. You ask the paraprofessional to work with Andrew on the side, performing an activity that he has enjoyed in the past.

Example: Earlier this morning, the fire alarm sounded because of a small fire in the cafeteria. Zachary, a boy with ASD, was in a part of the building where it took him a little bit of time to get out. Being very sensitive to noise and visual stimuli, he really struggled. The noise from the alarm, combined with the busy hallways and the flashing lights, were too much. Zachary's paraprofessional comes to the gym and says she can't even get Zach to come in today. He has had his hands over his ears for the past hour and has been rocking nonstop. You recognize that being in the loud gym will not help Zachary's senses and that he doesn't have the ability to focus on class material today, so you suggest that the paraprofessional take Zachary to the library, where you have reserved three books on soccer, the sport being covered in your class.

Considerations/Helpful Tips

- Allowing a student who is extremely schedule/routine-oriented to do something different from his or her normal day will just make the student more flustered.

- Students have to recognize that you will not grant regulated permission often. Tell them why it's occurring, so that they understand it's not a punishment or a reward for an undefined behavior.

- Regulated permission is another strategy that relies on having a paraprofessional available, because it often requires someone to supervise the student. If you don't have that option, you can assign the student a different role within the class activity.

- If a student with ASD is incredibly overwhelmed from past stimuli (e.g., a fire drill), it might be best for him or her to go to a quiet, calm location (e.g., library, special education room, nurse's office, guidance counselor's office). Consider arranging for that quiet spot at the beginning of the school year.

Providing Socially Acceptable Behaviors

What It Is: Because social skills are such a struggle for children with ASD, it's not uncommon for them to demonstrate a socially unacceptable behavior in an attempt to interact socially with a peer. Sometimes, students just don't know how to initiate a social interaction, so they go with whatever they can figure out — hitting, laughing at or poking a child — to elicit a response. And when students with ASD don't realize that tears mean that a person is upset, they continue the negative behavior because they have received a social response.

So, you need to help teach students with ASD how to start conversations, join groups or express their thoughts in a socially acceptable manner. It's particularly important to give them some skills that pertain directly to the activity your class is undertaking at the time. *Example:* When someone misses a shot, urge students with ASD to say "Next time" or "Good try," instead of yelling or laughing at the classmate.

How to Apply It: Provide socially acceptable behaviors when a student is misbehaving (e.g., hitting a peer) in an attempt to create social interaction or to be accepted by his or her peers.

Example: Xavier is notorious for running up and poking Robert. Every time he gets poked, Robert starts to cry, and then Xavier starts laughing. At first, it appears that Xavier is a big bully. But, once Xavier is taught how to say "Want to play?" the poking stops.

Example: David runs out of the locker room and tries to join a group of peers who are talking. He wants to be part of the conversation, so he goes up to the group and just starts laughing. David then starts saying "Hi! Hi! Hi!" without really addressing anyone in particular and while talking over everyone. The group stops talking and breaks apart, so David starts following one student, still saying "Hi! Hi! Hi!" You teach David that, when he comes out of the locker room and walks up to the group, he should listen to what the kids are saying.

He then may say "Hi" once to each student in the group while looking the student in the eyes.

Considerations/Helpful Tips

- Try to foresee where a social skills difficulty might arise. When giving instructions about the game or activity, have students provide you with some ideas about appropriate things that they could say or do when seeing their peers do well, as well as when they struggle. This often will benefit all students, not just those with ASD.

- Ask a paraprofessional to help with positive feedback when a student performs a social skill correctly.

- When possible, encourage students not to respond to an inappropriate social response or action from a child with ASD.

Contracting

What It Is: Sometimes, it's helpful to have a visual outline of the rules that states what is unacceptable, what is acceptable and what happens when a student doesn't behave. One way to do that is to create a formal contract on which you and a student with ASD can agree. The contract should stipulate the behaviors that you expect to see, the behaviors that are inappropriate, the consequence that occurs when the student performs an inappropriate action and the reward that he or she will receive when completing the appropriate actions. Once you have created the document, you both sign it and both get a copy of it. In class, you use it as your reference for how to discipline/reward based on what you agreed upon. *(Find a sample contract on the CD-ROM that accompanies this book.)*

How to Apply It: Use contracting only when the student does not have an intellectual disability and can understand the concept of cause and effect. Use a contract when a student continually acts inappropriately because he or she doesn't know the correct behaviors or is not motivated to behave.

Example: Darren has been having difficulty participating in class. When you give the class instructions, he talks over you without raising his hand, and he doesn't wait his turn in line. You sit down with Darren during homeroom period and draft a contract that lists the behaviors that are not appropriate and behaviors he should display instead (e.g., raise his hand before talking). The contract then states that you will give Darren two warnings when he performs an inappropriate action. If he continues to perform the action, he will be given a time-out. If Darren displays appropriate action, he will be allowed to sort the equipment during clean-up and can stand at the front of the line at the end of class, both things he really likes.

Example: During a basketball game, Fernando becomes very aggressive when the opposing team scores a basket. He yells at his teammates and throws the ball out of bounds. You devise a contract with Fernando in which you identify the inappropriate responses to an opponent's score, and instruct Fernando to do the following: "When the other team scores a basket, walk to the end line on your team's side of the court, touch the end line with your foot and return to your position on the court." Failing to adhere to the contract leads to a three-minute time-out. Adhering to the contract earns points toward a reward that is appropriate for Fernando (e.g., permission to shoot baskets at the beginning of class).

Considerations/Helpful Tips

- Students with intellectual disabilities or who have difficulty with communication won't understand this approach conceptually. So, contracting is only for students who can help contribute to creating the contract and who understand what a contract between two people means.

- Don't simply hand a contract to a student and tell him or her to follow it. Instead, discuss it with the student and come to some agreement. Usually, contracts are created outside of class, during a lunch period, detention, before school or after school. You can create a general outline of what you want to see and what behaviors you will not accept, but you need to allow the student to add to the document. Also, let the student help come up with the consequences and the rewards. That way, it's more meaningful to the student, and he or she has a sense of ownership.

- If the student can't read but can understand the concept, use pictures to outline the information.

- You must follow through with the contract. Don't include consequences that you can't deliver. Allow no flexibility in applying the contract. Once it's created, apply it consistently in your class.

- The reward can be something small, so long as it's meaningful to the student. *Example:* If the student really likes to help organize and put away equipment, his or her reward can be helping to clean up at end of class. Or, if the student enjoys announcing the end of the game, his or her reward can be yelling, "Time to get changed" when the class is complete.

- Students often find it helpful to track performance toward their goals. Consider giving a student with ASD and/or the paraprofessional a sheet that they can use to record how many times the student is performing the appropriate and inappropriate behaviors. Review the sheet with the student briefly at the end of class and before giving out a reward. *(Find a sample "Tracking My Goals" sheet on the CD-ROM that accompanies this book.)*

Scheduling Time to Regroup

What It Is: Because of their hypersensitivity, students with ASD often become overwhelmed by the end of the class period. To help prevent that problem, provide students with an opportunity to decrease their level of stimulus so that they can contribute to the class. How? Schedule a chunk of time for students with ASD to remove themselves from the situation to calm their senses and regroup. This is different from sending students to the Cool-Down Zone when they've already become over-stimulated. Instead, have students take this break at a scheduled time in an attempt to prevent them from becoming overwhelmed. Usually, this means that a student with ASD will leave the gymnasium for a short period of time to get away from the chaos of the class. Or, the student might simply sit in a corner of the gym for a few minutes. A paraprofessional or aide is needed to complete this strategy.

How to Apply It: Schedule time for regrouping before the student becomes over-stimulated by the end of the class period, which could lead to misbehavior, or when the student starts to lose focus or become easily agitated due to mental fatigue or over-stimulation.

Example: Half-way through the class period, Kayla walks with her aide to the water fountain that is down the hall. Whether she is thirsty or not, Kayla always takes that five-minute water break. The purpose is to provide Kayla with some quiet down time to regain her composure.

Example: During the first three minutes of class, while the teacher takes attendance, Matthew stays in the locker room with his paraprofessional. He sits on a bench and looks at his task card to organize his thoughts on what he will be doing in that class.

Considerations/Helpful Tips

- Remember that the point of scheduling time to regroup is to give students the opportunity to remove themselves from classroom stimulus before being overwhelmed or over-stimulated. They don't have to go far; just away from the stimulus.

- Tap into the paraprofessional. You can't keep an eye on the class and a student in the hallway at the same time. Come up with a system that incorporates the student and the paraprofessional.

- Don't be afraid to ask students with ASD when they think it would be helpful to take a break and what they could do to help themselves calm down.

- Don't make a big deal about it. Either tell the student quietly that it is time to take his or her walk or just allow the paraprofessional to go.

- Give students who are higher-functioning the option each class to go or stay. *Example:* Tell Kayla that it's half-way through the class, and she might like to take her walk now, or she can finish the class if she feels comfortable.

- Consider creating a cue system so that students can tell you whether they need to move their scheduled time-out. Sometimes, they might start to feel that they are becoming over-stimulated before their scheduled time. If they have a cue (e.g., a help card, a hand signal, a phrase they say, such as "water walk"), they can remove themselves quietly from the situation before they lose control.

Conclusion

This chapter has reinforced the importance of effective preventive behavior-management strategies as necessary prerequisites for establishing a class environment in which learning can occur. In fact, as emphasized throughout the chapter, the preventive behavior-management strategies that will help students with ASD function well in a physical education class setting are the same strategies that will work for *all* students. In that regard, this chapter contains some of the most commonly used preventive behavior-management strategies in physical education programs, while emphasizing those aspects of the general strategies that are especially important to students with ASD. In addition, the chapter provides suggestions that should help you tailor the implementation of these strategies to help students with ASD participate effectively in physical education class.

Chapter 7

Behavior Management: Reactive Strategies

Content

Meeting the Physical Education Needs of Children With Autism Spectrum Disorder

Introduction

Despite their best efforts to establish a class environment in which students know how to behave and interact appropriately, teachers occasionally are faced with students who misbehave and disrupt the learning environment to the extent that some action is warranted to help restore order and productivity. The strategies described in this chapter are meant to be used as responses to student misbehavior that is sufficient to warrant teacher intervention.

Establish as Preventive, Apply as Reactive

The first few strategies described in this chapter require some preparation before they can be used effectively and, therefore, might appear to be preventive strategies. But, even though they are established in advance, these strategies are not to be used until or unless a student with ASD encounters a situation in which compliance with class rules and routines becomes problematic.

Boosting Interest

What It Is: As with all children, sometimes, an activity doesn't appeal or interest a child with ASD. It could be that the child doesn't see the purpose of the activity or doesn't perceive the activity as enjoyable. To combat that problem, incorporate something into the lesson to make the student more interested in the activity. It could be giving students facts about the sport being played or activity being performed, incorporating their favorite theme or explaining to students when they would use the skill outside of the class so that they understand its relevance.

How to Apply It: Boost a student's interest when he or she is bored or uninterested in the activity.

Example: Jimmy, a boy with ASD, loves to learn everything he can about reptiles but has difficulty staying engage during PE class. You plan a class in which you want students to be physically active and work on basic motor skills. So, you set up an obstacle course in which students need to hop like a frog from one line to the other, slither like a snake under a pole, jump from poly spot to poly spot (with pictures of different reptiles on them) and collect all of the bugs that frogs eat (with some pictures of bugs spread on the floor, along with pictures of other objects such as fruits, dairy products and sports equipment).

Example: Caleb, who is really into math and numbers, often refuses to participate in PE drills. You number index cards 1 through 20, and then attach them to the gym wall. When the class works on soccer shooting drills, you tell Caleb to shoot the soccer ball at the even numbers only. If he hits one with his ball, he is allowed to take the number off the wall. His goal is to collect all the even numbers.

Considerations/Helpful Tips

- Because children with ASD tend to have an object or theme of obsession, incorporating it into your lesson is an excellent way to pique their enthusiasm. And because students with ASD tend to be very visual learners, it often helps to include pictures that are related to their interests. *Examples:* Use pictures of their objects of obsession to aim at in a throwing or shooting task, to collect by walking or running between designated spots, to land on in a gross motor task such as jumping or hopping, or to "squish" on a ball in a kicking or striking task.

- Remember that if a student with ASD has difficulty with imaginative play (as many do), having the student imitate or pretend to act like his or her object of obsession might be difficult. That doesn't mean you shouldn't encourage students with ASD to use their imagination; just recognize that it's a struggle for them. To help them with it, you can demonstrate and include pictures. You might want to consider a theme month, incorporating the theme into each class period. That kind of repetition might make it easier for children with ASD to participate in imaginative play.

Cool-Down Zone

What It Is: As discussed in Chapter 3, the Cool-Down Zone is a place where students go to recompose themselves. Students can use it to put their emotions back in check or simply to remove themselves from too much stimulation. The Cool-Down Zone is different from the scheduled regrouping time because it's used only on demand, when students feel overwhelmed or over-stimulated. The Cool Down Zone is not a time-out and should not be seen as a punishment. Instead, it's a tool that you provide for students to help them manage their own behaviors. Here's how it works:

You designate a spot in the gym or on the field that is to be used only for the Cool-Down Zone. It should be a location that is still within your line of sight but removed enough from the class that it is away from most of the stimulus. Usually, it's in a corner of the space. When a student feels that he or she is losing control of his or her emotions or is over-stimulated, he or she goes to the Cool-Down Zone for a few minutes until he or she feels ready to participate in the activity.

How to Apply It: Establish the Cool-Down Zone on the first day of class and then employ it when a student becomes frustrated, angry or overwhelmed by stimulus.

Example: Adam loves parachute activities. When the teacher announces that the class will be using the parachute, Adam grows so excited that he screams and jumps up and down. After about 30 seconds, the teacher realizes that Adam is all worked up and can't calm himself enough to participate in the activity. She guides Adam to the Cool-Down Zone and says: "Adam, I see that you are very excited to play parachute. Before you can play, you need to stop yelling and calm down. Take three deep breaths (demonstrating breathing with him). When you are able to sit without yelling for one minute, you can play." The teacher then leaves Adam in the Cool-Down Zone with a paraprofessional. When Adam is calmer, the teacher welcomes him back by saying: "You look much calmer now. Are you ready to join the class?" She then includes Adam in the activity immediately.

Example: During a ball-handling and shooting activity, Laura becomes overwhelmed from all the noise in the gym. She puts her fingers in her ears and starts to rock back and forth. Laura walks over to the Cool-Down Zone but is not able to calm herself. Because the entire gym is loud, the teacher suggests that Laura and the paraprofessional walk around the hallway for a few minutes so that Laura can get away from the noise. Because Laura is already over-stimulated, the teacher doesn't try to talk to her; that will simply add to the extra stimulus. Instead, she tells the paraprofessional to bring Laura back to class when she is comfortable taking her fingers out of her ears and stops rocking. When Laura returns, she is placed on the edge of the group to help lessen the amount of noise she hears.

Considerations/Helpful Tips

- When a student is already over-stimulated (particularly from an auditory stimulus), the last thing you want to do is add to the amount of stimulus by talking to him or her. Instead, try to use visuals and demonstrations. Allow the student to calm down and regain some composure in the Cool-Down Zone before trying to give him or her spoken information or instructions.

- Don't assume that students will automatically go to the Cool-Down Zone when they're overwhelmed. They most likely will need to be directed there, especially when they are still learning to use it or are overwhelmed. Encourage the paraprofessional to step in and direct students to the Cool-Down Zone when needed.

- When directing students to the Cool-Down Zone, provide them with some tools to help them regain composure. Students with ASD often don't know how to help themselves relax. You can suggest deep breathing, give them a motor task such as bouncing up and down on a playground ball or playing with a squishy ball, or have them perform a rote task, such as counting to 100. This also is an appropriate time to reference an emotions chart.

- Ask the paraprofessional, classroom teacher and/or parents for ways to help the student relax. Often, you'll discover an agreed-upon strategy (e.g., taking three deep breaths) that they are trying to have the student implement.

- Many times, children with ASD cannot define the emotions they are feeling. To help them, tell them what emotion it appears that they are experiencing. *Examples:* "Thomas, you look frustrated." "Kathy, it looks as though you are angry." It's important to help them label their emotions so that they can express them in the future.

- See Chapter 2 for more helpful tips and considerations.

Reactive Strategies

Removing the Distracter

What It Is: Because of their general sensitivity to different stimuli, children with ASD could be distracted by any of a number of things. In some cases, the stimulus might simply deflect their attention, while in other situations, it might make them uncomfortable. In either case, it's often helpful to remove the variable that is distracting the student or making him or her uncomfortable so that he or she can focus. This strategy includes moving the student to a different part of the gym to avoid excess noise, turning off a light because it's buzzing or is too bright for the student, turning down the volume on music, modifying the rules of a game to prevent physical contact or allowing students with ASD to wear hats so that the sun isn't in their eyes.

How to Apply It: Remove the distracter when a student is being disruptive because of discomfort brought on by over-stimulus or when a student can't focus on the task at hand because of a distraction.

Example: Larry, a student with ASD, doesn't like any form of physical contact because he is hypersensitive to touch. The teacher designs a relay race in which students tag the next student in line to signify when that student may start. Larry becomes very agitated at the thought of someone touching him. The teacher quickly alters the activity so that the student who is running must touch the *poly spot* beside the next student in line.

Example: Marshal loves to play with the water fountain and would be happy to spend the entire class period turning it on and off. Before class starts, the teacher hangs a poster over the fountain so that Marshal can't see it and makes sure that Marshal is in a small group that is assigned to the other side of the gym.

Considerations/Helpful Tips

- Sometimes, a distracter also can serve as a necessary stimulus. Therefore, you can't simply remove the distracter, because the child with ASD will become flustered from the lack of stimulus. Instead, you need to provide the student with another stimulus or use the distracter as a reward. *Example:* Silvia loves the feeling of her pinnie and pulls on it continuously. She becomes so enthralled with it that she doesn't participate in the drill. If you were to take the pinnie away from her, Silvia would become agitated. Instead, you tell Silvia that she has to shoot the ball five times before she can play with her pinnie for 30 seconds.

- Apply good teaching strategies when considering distracters. Never have students with ASD face the sun when you address them, for example. Or, try to address the class with your back to a blank wall and not a wall covered with posters.

Warning System

What It Is: With small misbehaviors, we sometimes need to remind students that their misbehavior is unacceptable before we move right into a consequence. Many times, teachers refer to this approach as "Three strikes and you're out." You give the student two warnings. The third time results in a consequence (e.g., time-out or loss of privilege). Because many children with ASD need specific and concrete information, it's important that you provide them with the correct instructions when providing a warning. Complete the steps in Figure 7.1 to do that successfully.

Figure 7.1 Implementing the Warning System

1. Tell the student what behavior he or she is demonstrating that is not appropriate. Remember to be specific!

2. Provide the student with a behavior that you want to see, instead.

3. Remind the student of the consequence if he or she receives three warnings about the misbehavior.

4. Remind the student which warning (e.g., first, second, third) he or she is on.

5. Repeat steps 1 – 4 until the behavior stops or the student receives the consequence.

Before implementing this strategy, you must determine why the misbehavior is occurring! Remember that students with ASD might not realize that they are misbehaving and, if that's the case, giving them a consequence for "misbehavior" is ineffective. *Example:* During a catching drill, Kevin consistently catches the ball but intentionally throws it back over his partner's head. The teacher warns Kevin three times and eventually takes away a privilege. But Kevin might not be misbehaving intentionally; he might have misunderstood the purpose of the activity. Because the class worked on throwing for distance last week, Kevin is still under the impression that he is supposed to throw the ball as far as he can.

How to Apply It: Use the warning system when behavior is disruptive but doesn't endanger another person. Often, the teacher establishes the warning system at the beginning of the school year. As new behaviors arise during the year, you might need to amend the rules to address the new behaviors and expectations.

Example: Caitlin is having difficulty remembering to stay in line and wait her turn. At the beginning of class, the teacher gives her three clothespins with pictures of "Dora the Explorer," her favorite cartoon, on them and explains to Caitlin that each time she gets a warning, she loses a clothespin. The teacher then reminds her that the appropriate behavior is to wait behind Suzy until it is her turn. As class progresses, the teacher notices that Caitlin jumps to the front of the line. So, the teacher takes away a clothespin, tells Caitlin that it's not okay to cut in line, and reminds her to stand behind Suzy.

Example: During a throwing-and-catching drill for softball, Kevin yells at a peer who drops the ball. At the beginning of class, the teacher had reminded Kevin that when a peer drops the ball, he should say something nice, such as "That's okay" or "Good try" or stay quiet. When Kevin laughs at his peer, the teacher gives him one of three index cards labeled "Strike 1," "Strike 2" and "Strike 3."

The teacher then reminds Kevin that laughing at a peer's mistake is not acceptable behavior and provides him with the socially acceptable options. He also reminds Kevin that if he gets all three "Strike" cards, he loses the privilege of helping to choose the team name for game play, which is something he looks forward to doing.

Considerations/Helpful Tips

- It's helpful to give students with ASD a visual representation of the strikes to help them remember and understand. You can start them out with three items and take away one each time they receive a warning, or you can give them an item each time they receive a warning. Just make sure to keep the system consistent. If you alternate between taking away and giving an item, the student might become confused. Some suggested visual representations:

  - Popsicle sticks or clothespins. Decorating them makes them more fun.

  - Paper clips.

  - Small cards that students keep in their pockets.

  - Sad-face stickers that you can attach to a task card or to a card designated specifically for managing a student's behavior.

  - Marks on a dry-erase board.

- To help students, remind them of the appropriate behavior at the beginning of class, as well as the warning system and consequence if they don't follow the rules.

- Keep your description of the desired behavior specific and concrete. "Sitting nicely," for example, doesn't convey what you want. Instead, say "Sitting with your hands in your lap."

- When expressing that a behavior is unacceptable, emphasize that you are not pleased with the student's actions but that you still value him or her as a person. Many times, children — particularly those lacking in social skills — misread a reprimand as "The teacher hates me."

- Once you have given a student a warning and pointed out the inappropriate behavior, have the student repeat the desired behavior or show it to you to ensure comprehension. *Remember:* If the student has echolalia, simply repeating what you said doesn't ensure understanding!

- One way to encourage good behavior is to provide children with rewards if they don't receive any warnings. As with contracting, the reward doesn't have to be a big deal, so long as it's important to the student. Perhaps the student receives a sticker (age-dependent) or is allowed to do something that he or she he really enjoys. At the very least, provide verbal praise (or a signal, if that's more appropriate for the student).

- If you must deliver the consequence to a child, ensure that it occurs immediately after the unacceptable behavior. Otherwise, the child often won't associate the negative behavior with the negative consequence.

- Never use physical activity as a consequence! The old "Go run three laps for being late" approach is the last thing you want to implement. It teaches students to dislike physical activity and suggests that physical activity is a punishment.

- If a student has acted out in another class, don't dole out the punishment during PE. While it might seem logical to take away an activity the student enjoys, such as physical education, it sends a mixed message to the student.

- Determine whether the consequence is appropriate for the student. While detention might be an appropriate consequence for high school students without a disability, it might not be an appropriate punishment for a student with ASD. Remember that the purpose of the consequence is to deter the child from repeating the behavior. Make sure that the consequence really meets that goal.

Figure 7.2 Tips for Making the Warning System More Effective

1. Give a visual representation of the warning.
2. Remind students of the appropriate behavior and the warning system at the beginning of class.
3. Describe the desired behavior.
4. Emphasize that you like the student; it's the behavior that you don't like.
5. Have the student repeat the correct behavior to you verbally.
6. Provide an award in the absence of warnings.
7. If a consequence is needed, deliver it immediately after three warnings.
8. Make sure that the consequence is appropriate for the student.

Time-Out

What It Is: A time-out removes a student from the class activity for a brief time. During the time-out, students should think about the behavior that was inappropriate, as well as what behavior is considered acceptable. For a time-out to communicate the problem successfully to the student, you must identify the unacceptable behavior, state what behavior the student should be demonstrating, inform the student of the consequence of the misbehavior, including how much time to be spent in time-out, and tell the student what he or she needs to do to return to the activity.

Once the student's time-out is finished, follow up with a short question-and-answer session. Ask the student to tell you what he or she did wrong and then tell you what appropriate behavior he or she will display in the future. Then, welcome the student back into the activity with a positive attitude.

Figure 7.3 Administering a Time-Out

1. Identify the unacceptable behavior.
2. Identify the behavior that you expect.
3. Identify the duration of the time-out.
4. Require a behavior before returning.
5. Follow up at the end of the time-out with a quick Q&A.
6. Welcome the student back to activity with a positive attitude.

How to Apply It: Give a student a time-out when you know that he or she enjoys the current activity but is not demonstrating appropriate behavior or following class rules. For many students with ASD, it is appropriate to use this from K-12, although young children will struggle with it.

Example: Adrienne continuously bites the Nerf® balls during an activity. The teacher informs her that it is not acceptable to bite the ball; balls are for throwing and catching. The teacher then tells Adrienne that she is receiving warning No. 1 by handing her an index card with a big sad face on it. The teacher then tells Adrienne that if she receives two more warnings, she will be given a time-out. When Adrienne continues the misbehavior, the teacher gives her a time-out, first reminding her that balls are for throwing and catching, not for biting. The teacher instructs Adrienne that she must sit on the sidelines for three minutes before she may return to the class. After three minutes, the teacher chats quickly with Adrienne and then welcomes her back in to the activity.

Considerations/Helpful Tips

- A time-out is different from a Cool-Down Zone in that a time-out is a forced removal from the activity, and the student is being reprimanded for his or her behavior. When a student *chooses* to use the Cool-Down Zone, he or she does so as a means of helping himself or herself regain control.

- Provide students with a visual so that they see how much longer they have to stay in time-out. An egg timer is perfect for this!

- The length of a time-out for a student without a disability often is not appropriate for a student with ASD. Five minutes could seem like an eternity to for a 12-year-old with ASD. Keep time-outs short for students with ASD.

- Never give a time-out during instruction time. Removing a student from instruction time denies him or her important information, and the student can fall behind in class material. The only exception to this rule is when a student is hurting himself or herself, or another student.

- You might need to tell students with ASD what they are supposed to do during a time-out. Instead of giving a general statement (e.g., "Sit nicely and think about what you just did"), provide them with the behavior that you want them to demonstrate during the time-out. *Example:* "You must show me that you can keep your hands to yourself before you can return to the group. So, sit with your hands in your lap without touching anyone else for two minutes."

- Some children with ASD will have difficulty telling you what they did wrong and what the appropriate behavior is. You might need to provide them with prompts and cues, or allow them to give you a one- or two-word answer. *Example:* You remind a student that he was yelling at his peer and then ask, "What will you do when you get angry at your teammate?" Make sure that you have provided the student with a strategy that can be communicated in a few words. For example, the student might say "Good try." You know that by saying "Good try," the student with ASD intends to replace yelling with the phrase "Good try." You also can use the Pick-a-Hand approach (see p. 35), in which you provide two different behaviors from which the student can choose. *Another option:* Allow the student to use a sign to communicate with you or the other students. *Example:* The student can sign "Sorry" to the team instead of offering a spoken apology. The student also can use communication devices or pictures.

- Follow up on time-outs with positive reinforcement once the student is demonstrating the appropriate behavior. That further reinforces the appropriate behavior, while squelching the negative behavior. One of the easiest ways to do that is to use verbal praise. *Example:* "Great job saying 'Good try'!"

Signal Interference

What It Is: Signal interference is a visual cue or signal that one gives to students to tell them that you don't approve of their behavior. It could be shaking your head "No," signing "Stop" or something else that you have agreed upon in advance with the student. After you give a signal, indicate the behavior the student should be demonstrating. Either model the behavior or provide another agreed-upon signal that denotes the desired behavior.

How to Apply It: Use signal interference when a student's misbehavior is just beginning and is not yet too disruptive to the class. The student has to be able to see you, know which behavior you want to stop, and know what your signals mean.

Example: After completing a bean-bag toss activity, Jason tends to hit himself in the head on the way back to his spot. You place your hand on Jason's shoulder and gently press down to help give him the necessary stimulus, as well as remind him that hitting himself is inappropriate. You then hand him a yarn pompon to play with as he sits and waits his next turn.

Example: As you give the class instructions, Kenneth asks the student next to him several questions. You look at Kenneth, shake your head "No" and then point to your ear. This is a signal that you introduced on the first day of class to mean "Stop talking and listen."

Considerations/Helpful Tips

- Remember that a student with ASD often won't recognize subtle cues. Standing with your hands on your hips and discreetly shaking your head "No" will not communicate effectively with a student who has ASD, especially if you haven't discussed this cue with the student previously. So, make sure that your cue is obvious and straightforward. (The "evil eye" is not a good choice.)

- Tell the student what to look for and what it means. *Example:* "When I sign 'Stop,' that means I want you to stop what you are doing. If you are unsure of what you should do, ask me." For students who are not verbal or not high-functioning, you might need to follow the signal immediately by a verbal cue and a demonstration of the behavior you want.

- Students with ASD must see you make the signal, so be sure that they are looking at you when you make it.

- Try to use a signal that is used in other settings, including at home or in other classes.

- Designate only one signal to represent a command, and use it consistently. *Example:* Use shaking your head "No" only to communicate that you want the student to stop that behavior. Don't use shaking your head, signing "Stop" *and* snapping your fingers interchangeably.

Modifying the Activity

What It Is: When a student is frustrated because the skill is too difficult, it might be helpful to modify the task so that the child is successful. Completing the task decreases the student's frustration and allows him or her to participate productively. Modify the task to overcome the hurdle that is preventing the child from completing it. You can modify the performance expectations (e.g., moving the target closer, giving the student more time to complete the task), modify the equipment (e.g., use a larger ball to make it easier for the student to catch) or modify the motor pattern (e.g., allow the student to catch the ball with both hands, not just one). As the student develops his or her skill level, you can decrease the amount of modification until no modification is needed.

How to Apply It: Modify the activity when a student exhibits signs of frustration that might lead to misbehavior because he or she is not able to complete the task.

Example: Gretchen is having difficulty completing a throwing-and-catching activity. She continually misses the ball when it's thrown to her. The teacher can see that Gretchen is becoming frustrated: she throws the ball at the ground and wanders away from her partner. The teacher stops the activity and moves on to a different drill. This time, the teacher gives students a variety of balls from which to choose, and encourages Gretchen to pick a larger Nerf® ball instead of the tennis ball. The Nerf® ball will move a little slower through the air, giving Gretchen more time to respond. The ball's larger size also gives her more surface area to grasp, increasing her chances of catching it. The teacher then encourages Gretchen's partner to focus on his form, so that he continues to develop his skill, as well.

Example: Ricardo is growing frustrated because he can't hit the volleyball over the net when he serves; his serves fall short or go into the net. After failing at the task in the previous class, Ricardo now refuses to serve. The teacher announces to the class that, when serving the ball, all students (not just Ricardo) may take up to four steps toward the net. As Ricardo improves a little at serving the ball, the teacher encourages him to take fewer steps forward until he is standing in the designated spot.

Considerations/Helpful Tips

- As with all modifications, don't overdo modifying the activity. Start with small modifications before making dramatic changes. Also, consider your objective for the unit. If you want the student to be able to participate in a recreation-league version of the activity, make modifications that are realistic for the student's parents to request in the community program.

- Try to anticipate the modification before starting the activity. Changing an activity in the middle of class — after students have been given directions and have seen the equipment being used — can confuse students with ASD. So, if you think before starting the activity that students are going to struggle, introduce the activity with the modification already in place. If that's not possible, make the modification as fluidly as possible.

- When you modify an activity, make the modification available to the entire class, or make it seem to be part of the curriculum. That helps to ensure a positive experience for students with ASD and doesn't portray them as "helpless" or "lacking in skill."

Figure 7.4 Make Modifications for All!

When modifying an activity, try to make it class-wide or make it seem to be part of the curriculum. By doing that, you:

1. Help all students succeed, including those who are not skilled in sports.

2. Avoid making the student with a disability feel bad about himself or herself.

3. Encourage students without disabilities to recognize the potential of students with ASD, instead of focusing on how students with ASD are different and need accommodation.

Strategies That Usually Don't Work

Some strategies that are used commonly in the physical education setting generally are not successful when used with students with ASD. Proximity control, "The look" and planned ignoring often don't work because children with ASD don't perceive the nonverbal messages those strategies are intended to communicate. In general, avoid any strategy that relies on children with ASD perceiving or interpreting subtle cues or messages. Instead, apply other strategies suggested in this chapter that are direct and specific.

Conclusion

Occasional student misbehavior is inevitable, even when you have put effective preventative behavior-management strategies in place. Having an arsenal of strategies to use in response to student misbehavior can help restore the effective learning environment in a lesson if it's disrupted, making life much easier and more pleasant for both you and your students. Before applying any strategies, it's essential to first determine the cause of the misbehavior. Then, match the cause of the misbehavior with a strategy that will address the problem and not simply discourage the student from participating in the activity.

Chapter 8 ————————————
Working With Others

Content

Introduction

Helping students with ASD achieve the learning goals set for them in physical education is much easier if approached as a team effort. This chapter explores how physical education teachers can partner with classroom teachers, paraprofessionals, staff members who provide special services (e.g., physical therapists, behavior specialists), other students and parents to help students with ASD attain their learning goals and objectives.

Communication is central to the success of any partnership, and this is no exception. It's important to communicate the ways in which each of you — as partners — can contribute to the benefit of a student with ASD. Each partner in this endeavor has a different and unique relationship with the student, and the strategy that you use when working with each partner should reflect that relationship.

The purpose of this chapter is to describe the perspective that each potential partner brings to the table in providing an effective learning environment for students with ASD and to suggest ways in which each partner can contribute to students' development. The chapter begins by describing the roles that the child study team and a student's individualized education program (IEP) play in the education experience of a child with ASD. It then describes the role and contributions of each potential partner to the success of students with ASD in a physical education setting, and suggests strategies for working with those students.

The Roles of the Child Study Team & the IEP

Any student classified as eligible for services under the Individuals with Disabilities Education Act (IDEA) will have an IEP, which identifies education goals for the student and describes plans for attaining those goals. The IEP is developed and implemented by a child study team, which typically includes a representative of the school's administration, a guidance counselor or advocate for the child, a regular classroom teacher (if the child is in an inclusive classroom during any portion of the day), a special education teacher and a legal guardian. Other people who might participate include the school nurse, the school psychologist, those offering other services (e.g., physical therapist), the student (depending on age and the disability's nature) and anyone else recommended by the school staff or identified by the parents and/or student. These team members meet once a year and come to agreement on what is in the child's best interest.

Physical education is a required service under IDEA, meaning that all students with disabilities — including students with ASD — must be provided with appropriate physical education. To ensure that those services are available, physical education teachers should contribute to the IEP process. By doing so, they can provide input on including learning goals specific to physical education, request equipment or materials needed to assist the student, and establish a working relationship with the parents and the classroom teacher toward attaining the goals within the IEP. While it might not be practical for physical education teachers to attend IEP meetings for each student, they at least can suggest to the team some physical education goals and appropriate assessments for each student. By talking to the classroom teacher or parent before the IEP meeting, you can contribute your expertise to the process and help avoid the possibility of including unrealistic PE-related goals for the student or even failing to include any PE-related goals for the student at all.

Figure 8.1 Sample Physical Education-Related Goals for a Student's IEP

Sample Goal	Assessment*
Elementary School: Throw and catch a ball with a classmate.	Skill checklist completed by teacher.
Middle School: Participate with classmates in a team sport.	Game-play assessment completed by teacher. Record number of touches/passes/goals attempted with the ball.
High School: Develop an individualized fitness plan that the student can complete at home.	Individualized fitness plan evaluated by teacher.

* Often, assessments included in IEPs are defined broadly (e.g., assignment). These, however, are suggestions of ways to assess goals in physical education.

Communicating With the Team

Of course, the demands on a teacher's time and energy — especially when teaching large classes — make it difficult, if not impossible, to interact with all of the people who might have knowledge about every student with a disability. Yet, the wealth of information that can be exchanged between you and the many people who have contact with a student with ASD has the potential to affect that student's learning and growth in a positive manner. Because people who see the child in different environments (e.g., at home, in class, in physical therapy) have very different perspectives, it's important to ask a variety of people (e.g., parents, classroom teachers, the physical therapist, the speech therapist) about each child.

You can obtain information from these team members in a variety of ways. At the very least, try to have a brief conversation focusing on some specific areas of interest. Although each child is unique, some general pieces of information tend to be helpful for all students *(see Figure 8.2)*.

It also might be helpful to arrange an easy means of communication in case something happens during the school year that affects the child. For example, if the classroom teacher is informed that the student's parents divorced recently (creating change in the home), the child's behavior might be affected dramatically. As the PE teacher, you might not be privy to that information, unless you had prearranged with the classroom teacher to alert you to such changes in the student's life. The classroom teacher might even be able to share a strategy with you that is working to help the child in the classroom.

Figure 8.2 Topics to Discuss With Others in the Child's Life

1. Sensory sensitivity (i.e., what the child needs to avoid).

2. Instructional strategies that seem to work well with the child.

3. Behavior-management strategies that have succeeded. (Especially helpful if a behavior plan is not in place.)

4. Communication strategies that encourage reciprocal interaction.

5. Areas of interest or ways to motivate the child.

6. Behavior patterns that might signify that the child is in distress.

Working With Classroom Teachers

All teachers, regardless of the grade level or subject matter they teach, encounter some of the same difficulties as physical education teachers when they work with students with ASD in their classes. For example, the difficulties that students with ASD experience with social skills will affect them throughout the school day and, most likely, will interfere with their ability to attain learning goals.

Developing students' social skills provides common ground for you and classroom teachers to identify consistent messages that you can convey in your respective settings. Helping all students learn to work together in inclusive settings also is a goal that you share with classroom teachers. Typically, the strategies that work to encourage positive social interaction are unique to each child. The extent to which you and classroom teachers share strategies for positive social interaction that work for each student will affect the success that students with ASD have with these strategies. So, it's important to talk with classroom teachers to ensure that everyone is using the same strategies.

Working with classroom teachers for the purposes of sharing strategies that help students with ASD engage and learn will be somewhat different at the elementary level than doing so at the middle/high school levels. At all grade levels, teaming up with a classroom teacher or teachers responsible for teaching your students with ASD when they are not in physical education will help you provide consistent messages regarding what is expected of the students in each of the learning environments. Efforts to coordinate with classroom teachers might become more complex at the middle/high school levels, because the students have several classroom teachers during the course of the school day. In that case, the paraprofessional who travels with the student can help provide consistency and can facilitate the communication among teachers in the different subject matter classrooms.

Figure 8.3 Strategies for Working With Classroom Teachers

1. Have a notebook that travels with the child and that teachers can use to note difficulties and/or successes of the day.

2. Use the paraprofessional for verbal updates about other class performances and information from other teachers.

3. Take advantage of formal faculty meetings and professional-development days to touch base with classroom teachers and/or other subject matter teachers.

4. Exchange information with other teachers regarding how best to contact them during the year. Use all tools, including e-mail, phone, Skype, common prep periods, before/after school meetings, etc.

5. Request that some time set aside for faculty professional development be devoted to meeting with other teachers to discuss different students and their needs and progress.

Working With The Paraprofessional

The Teacher's Aide & the Paraprofessional

Depending on the level of ability, students with ASD have paraprofessionals assigned to them as part of their IEPs. Unlike a teacher's aide, the paraprofessional is given information on how to assist the student with a disability appropriately and is responsible only for the child to whom he or she has been assigned, not the entire class. Each state has its own requirements and definitions of what a paraprofessional does, but, typically, the paraprofessional's job is to ensure that a student with a disability is kept safe, remains focused on the material, is enabled to complete the learning objectives and is assisted with any basic personal needs (e.g., bathroom). The paraprofessional accompanies the student throughout the day. Because the paraprofessional's role applies more to students with ASD than the teacher's aide's role *(see Figure 8.4)*, this chapter focuses on the paraprofessional.

Figure 8.4 Classroom Aides Versus Paraprofessionals*

Classroom aide/teacher assistant:

- Often is a part-time employee or volunteer.
- Provides instructional and clerical support in the classroom.
- Might supervise students in the cafeteria, on the schoolyard, in the hallways or on field trips.
- Is most common in elementary schools.

Paraprofessional:

- Is assigned to work directly with a student with a disability.
- Usually remains with the student throughout the school day.
- Assists the student with academics, and — when appropriate — personal hygiene/medical needs.

* Definitions and job descriptions might vary by state.

The level of a paraprofessional's involvement in a student's engagement in learning activities can vary greatly. In the least ideal situation, the paraprofessional might be involved only minimally in the physical education lesson and might confine his or her activities to monitoring the student's behavior and intervening only when the student is behaving inappropriately. In that instance, physical education teachers have described the paraprofessional as "just another body in the room." Instances of minimal involvement on the part of a paraprofessional might result from both the paraprofessional and the physical education teacher being unclear on exactly what the paraprofessional's role is in the class. Ideally, the paraprofessional and the physical education teacher act as a team to which each contributes to enhancing the quality of the learning experiences for the child (Davis, Kotecki, Harvey, Oliver, 2007). An ideal partnership between the paraprofessional and the physical education teacher is possible when the PE teacher takes an active role in redefining the working relationship between the two professionals.

Paraprofessionals observe and monitor student behavior but they have the potential to contribute to students' progress toward learning goals in physical education at all grade levels. Typically, paraprofessionals have earned high school diplomas and have completed some postsecondary coursework. As such, they are capable of assisting students in learning physical education-related skills and concepts ... but only with direction from the physical education teacher about what they should do to assist a student with ASD. If students are practicing a specific motor or sport-related skill, for example, the paraprofessional can assist the student by repeating the performance cues that the physical education teacher has given the students. If students are participating in a game, the paraprofessional can record how many times the student with ASD is involved directly in game play. For fitness-related activities, the paraprofessional can assist the student with ASD in performing exercises, record fitness scores, provide encouragement, etc. *(see Figure 8.5)*.

Note that the paraprofessional's role is *not* to serve as a partner for a student with ASD. If students are practicing skills in pairs, a student with ASD should partner with a classmate. It's important that students with ASD practice with classmates so that they perceive themselves — and fellow students perceive them — as members of the class learning community. It's also important that students with ASD be given ample opportunities to intermingle with their peers without the paraprofessional, to provide opportunities for natural social interaction. Lastly, don't ask the paraprofessional to take his or her focus off of a student with ASD to help another student.

Figure 8.5 The Role of the Paraprofessional in a PE Setting

Learning Goal	Activity	Paraprofessional's Role	Tips
Develop motor skill or sport-related skill.	Skill practice alone or with partner.	Reinforce performance cues provided by the teacher.	Pair students with ASD with other students, not the paraprofessional, when practicing in pairs. Provide the paraprofessional with a list of performance cues.
Develop game-play skills & tactics.	Small-sided game play.	Record involvement in game play; provide verbal encouragement. Buddy with the student with ASD so that the student stays engaged in the game.	Let the paraprofessional know that he or she will need appropriate shoes during physical education, to allow the paraprofessional to move easily.
Develop & maintain appropriate levels of fitness.	Exercises performed in stations.	Assist with exercises; provide verbal encouragement. Help record performance on task card.	Give the paraprofessional some tips about how to perform each station effectively.
Develop the ability to move rhythmically to music.	Students participate in a dance or rhythmic activity performed to music.	Reinforce performance cues; model steps or movements.	Provide the paraprofessional with the dance before class so that he or she can become familiar with it.

Increasing the involvement of a paraprofessional in a physical education lesson will take some time and effort. But the benefits realized from taking this initiative will make your time worthwhile! Suggested steps for engaging the paraprofessional in your physical education lessons include:

Establish the context. Talk with the paraprofessional at the beginning of the school year regarding his or her role in the class. Emphasize the contributions that he or she could make in helping attain the learning goals for the student with ASD. It might be helpful to provide the paraprofessional with a checklist *(see Figure 8.6)* that describes how he or she can help the student during each segment of a typical physical education lesson. Find a sample checklist, along with a blank checklist form, on the CD-ROM that accompanies this book.

Provide guidance. Give the paraprofessional a copy of your lesson plan, with his or her role highlighted, or provide a checklist of skills or performance cues that you want him or her to reinforce with the student. Figure 8.7 provides a sample lesson plan for a fitness stations lesson that includes a description of the paraprofessional's role during each segment of the lesson. You might find that it's more helpful and less confusing to the paraprofessional to provide an abbreviated form of the lesson plan that includes the paraprofessional's role. *(See Figure 8.8 and find downloadable versions of Figures 8.6, 8.7, and 8.8 on the CD-ROM that accompanies this book.)*

Give feedback. Provide the paraprofessional with verbal guidance, encouragement and reinforcement during the physical education lessons, and praise and gratitude at the end of lessons, when appropriate.

Get feedback. To establish a working relationship with the paraprofessional, it's important to get feedback from him or her throughout the year. Taking a few minutes to ask the paraprofessional's opinion about how things are going and whether you can do anything to help, for example, will go a long way toward establishing a strong working relationship.

Figure 8.6 PE Class Routine/Paraprofessional's Role

Teacher's name: Sally Smith

Class location: 2nd-floor gymnasium

Lesson Segment	General Routine	Paraprofessional's Role
Locker Room	Students enter the locker room and have five minutes once the period begins to change clothes and move to the gymnasium.	• Help student change clothes. • Help student place belongings into locker and lock it. • If student needs extended time to change, supervise and encourage student to move in timely fashion. • Accompany student to gymnasium.
Beginning of Class	Students report to designated floor spots for attendance and warm-up. Students are expected to sit quietly.	• Help student find designated floor spot. • Assist student as needed to remain seated. • Retrieve task card from teacher.
Warm-Up/ Attendance	Class completes a series of warm-up exercises/activities in group places, followed by jog around the gym. Teacher takes attendance while students are completing warm-up.	• Refer to task card as needed to help student focus. • Redirect student to complete warm-up activities and stay on designated spot. • Encourage student to remain with class during jog.

Continued on next page

Figure 8.6 (Cont.)

Lesson Segment	General Routine	Paraprofessional's Role
Learning Tasks	Students complete a series of activities related to the lesson goal.	• Ensure that student is using equipment in a safe & appropriate manner. • Provide cue words or direction to student, as needed. • Remind student to remain in designated spot. • Redirect and remind student of activity goal, as needed.
Game Play	(Not included in every lesson.) Students engage in game play. Teacher provides rules and teams assignments.	• Stand on the sideline as much as possible, but remain within close proximity of student in case intervention is needed. • Redirect inappropriate social interaction that disrupts the game or becomes a risk to others. • Remind student of the rules or game objective (e.g. which goal to shoot at), as needed.
Lesson Closure	Teacher initiates a question-and-answer discussion, followed by a summary of the lesson's goals and activities.	• Remind student to stand with the rest of the class. • Help student to contribute to the conversation in whichever way is appropriate (e.g., ask student a "Yes/No" version of the teacher's question).
End-of-Class Routine	Students return to locker room and have until the bell rings (about five minutes) to change into school clothes.	• Assist student in changing clothes. • Ensure that student has all his or her belongings. • Encourage student to leave locker room in timely fashion.

Figure 8.7 Sample Lesson Plan With Paraprofessional's Role Included

Fitness Stations

Objectives: Develop muscle flexibility, strength and endurance.

Develop ability to work independently and in small groups.

Equipment Needed: Fitness equipment to complete stations.

Time	Lesson Plan Segments	Assessment	Accommodations	Paraprofessional
	Instant Activity/Attendance **Dance Party:** While students stand in designated groups for attendance, they dance to music playing in the background. Music includes a variety of tempos & styles, and students match the beat.	None	• Student with ASD placed in back corner of group, so that he or she is away from the music.	• Ensure that student is in own spot. • Encourage free dance.

Continued on next page

Figure 8.7 *(Cont.)*

Time	Lesson Plan Segments	Assessment	Accommodations	Paraprofessional
	Warm-Ups **Color-Coded Warm-Up Sequence:** Pre-established warm-up routines, usually activity-specific (e.g., soccer) that are color-coded and, typically, are posted on gymnasium wall. Teacher announces which color warm-up is being used for the day.	None	• Provide student with 8x10 version of color-coded exercise chart. • For a non-reader, include a picture next to each written activity. • Use cue cards with images that match color-coded exercise chart.	• Remind student of day's designated color. • Hold copy of chart so that student can see it. • Remind student where class is on the chart if student loses focus.
	Introduction/Motivation/ Anticipatory Set Provide students with their task cards Describe each station. Divide students equally among stations.	None	• Simplified task card for a non-reader. • Instructions kept short, with visual demonstration. • All terms concrete.	• Remind student to focus on teacher if attention wanders.

Figure 8.7 *(Cont.)*

Time	Lesson Plan Segments	Assessment	Accommodations	Paraprofessional
	Learning tasks/experiences	Students record individual performance at each station on their individual task cards. At start of lesson, students set personal goals for performance and effort.	• Music played at reasonable volume.	• Help record progress on task card.
	10 stations for 3 minutes each. Signify start and stop of station with music starting and stopping		• Quiet zone available if needed.	• Ensure that student moves to correct stations.
	• Crunches		• Option not to have partner hold one's feet in crunches.	• Help foster social interaction with peers.
	• Medicine ball toss (variety of weights and sizes, including basketball for weaker students)		• Visual reminders at each station.	• Ensure safety with jump rope.
	• Lunges		• Stations numbered clearly.	• Provide student with assistive prop (e.g., ball on stomach for crunches) as needed.
	• Wall sit		• Feet positions marked on floor for lunges & hopping activity.	
	• Hop through hoops and ladders			
	• Crab walk and wheelbarrow			
	• Superman			
	• Hamstring and quad stretch			
	• Triceps, deltoids and pectorals stretch			
	• Jump rope			

Continued on next page

Figure 8.7 *(Cont.)*

Time	Lesson Plan Segments	Assessment	Accommodations	Paraprofessional
	Learning tasks/experiences (cont.)		• For visual learner: squishy ball to put on stomach and squish with crunches; tape wall marker for students to feel with their fingers when they are in the right squat position. • If jump rope with the rope becomes problematic, allow jumping motion without rope.	

Figure 8.7 *(Cont.)*

Time	Lesson Plan Segments	Assessment	Accommodations	Paraprofessional
	Lesson Closure Reinforce importance of using a variety of activities to affect flexibility, cardiac health & muscle strength. Reflect on attainment of goals & effort expended.	Informal assessment of students' responses to teacher's questions and personal reflection on progress toward goals.	• Use some "Yes/No" or Pick-a-Hand questions. • After class, give concise summary.	• Reword question, if needed, for child with ASD. • Encourage participation in discussion in whatever form appropriate for student.

General Teaching Suggestions for Substitute:

Kayla (Period 4): Use small phrases; allow to go into hallway, as needed; place in group on the edge of gymnasium.

Tommy (Period 7): Allow extra time in locker room; make sure he gets a simplified task card; allow to leave class five minutes early.

Figure 8.8 Sample Lesson Plan, Abbreviated Version, for the Paraprofessional

Fitness Stations

Objectives: Develop muscle flexibility, strength and endurance.
Develop ability to work independently and in small groups.

Time	Lesson Plan Segments	Paraprofessionals
	Instant Activity/ Attendance **Dance Party:** Students dance to music while teacher takes attendance.	• Ensure that student is in own spot. • Remind student of day's designated color. • Encourage free dance.
	Warm-Ups Color-Coded Warm-up Sequence	• Hold copy of exercise chart so that student can see it. • Remind student where class is on the chart, if student looses focus.
	Introduction/Motivation/ Anticipatory Set Teacher describes stations.	• Remind student to focus on teacher if attention wanders. • Help simplify instructions, as needed.
	Learning Tasks/ Experiences 10 stations for 3 minutes each. Signify start and stop at each station with music.	• Help record progress on task card. • Ensure that student moves to correct stations. • Help foster social interaction with peers. • Ensure safety with equipment. • Repeat performance cues already provided from teacher.
	Lesson Closure Questions & answers.	• Reword questions, if needed, so they're understandable to student. • Encourage participation in discussion in whatever form appropriate for school.

Notes:

Working With Other Support Staff

The assignment of support staff is determined by the student's needs. Therefore, a student with ASD might work with a host of different professionals, based on the fact that he or she has difficulties that could be addressed in different manners. *(See Figure 8.9 for possible support staff and their roles.)*

Figure 8.9 Support Staff & Their Roles With Children With ASD

Title*	Role
Speech Therapist/ Pathologist	Assists with verbal communication or use of an augmentative communication device.
Physical Therapist	Focuses on developing basic motor skills, a typical walking gait and balance needed for basic activities of daily living.
Occupational Therapist	Often works on sensory perception. Also might focus on developing skills in everyday life (e.g., tying shoes, using a spoon).
Behavior Specialist	Works with a child with ASD and people in the child's life to help decrease problem behaviors. Observes the child's environment and behaviors, then recommends and sometimes helps implement different behavior plans/ interventions.
School Psychologist/ Psychiatrist	Primary role is to identify the child's disability.
School Nurse	Administers medication and help with medical complications often associated with ASD (e.g., seizures). His or her office might be used as a resource for the student to use as a safe zone.

* Includes professionals who often work with students with ASD, but the list is not all-inclusive.

The most useful conversations with any of the individuals identified in Figure 8.9 would focus on the goals that each one might have for a particular student, along with techniques that have been successful. In addition, talking about ways to integrate goals and strategies from each specialist into physical education — and vice versa — has the potential to enhance the student's learning and growth. *Example:* If the child is working with a physical therapist to decrease toe walking, can the PE teacher incorporate something into class activities to help enforce walking with a heel-to-toe gait?   The physical therapist might be able to share strategies and games that he or she uses to encourage the correct gait.   In turn, you could discuss some games in PE that the physical therapist might use.

Working With Classmates

Classmates of a student with ASD have a different perspective from any of the adults involved and have a unique opportunity to participate in that student's education and social development. Emphasizing that treating every student with dignity and respect is the best way to encourage positive student/student interactions without drawing undue attention to a student with ASD. Here are some strategies for encouraging positive interactions:

- During game play, require that all students on a team must be involved in a play before anyone may attempt a goal.

- Award points to a team during game play for genuine (not gratuitous) expressions of encouragement given to teammates and/or opponents.

- Make a point to organize activities to focus on different skill sets throughout the semester, allowing all students — including those with ASD — to demonstrate their strengths. *Example:* Be sure to include a balance of individual and team sports, as well as activities that require rhythmic movement, problem-solving and fitness activities.

- Use a variety of strategies when forming groups or partners for skill practice, so that students have the opportunity to practice with a variety of other students.

- Emphasize the importance of treating one's classmates the way one would want to be treated.

- Employ Thumper's Rule from the movie "Bambi": If you can't say something nice about somebody, don't say anything at all.

- Take privileges away from those students who taunt or mistreat other students for any reason.

Not surprisingly, those strategies are no different from the techniques that teachers typically use with their classes to encourage positive behavior and social interaction, regardless of the presence or absence of students with ASD.

In addition, if a student with ASD exhibits particular behaviors in social situations that other students might find unsettling, scripting a response for classmates helps them react appropriately. It's then up to you to explain to the child with ASD what the appropriate response should be if someone makes the scripted statement. A scripted response also helps the child with ASD respond to the request in the future, given that the request has already been stated and the appropriate response modeled.

Example: A student with ASD might stand too close to a classmate, violating the classmate's "personal space" and causing him or her to feel uncomfortable and avoid the student, or even push the student away. If you witness this behavior, offer all students in the class an appropriate response, such as: "If a classmate is standing too close to you, say 'Please take one step back' to that classmate." It's important to offer that scripted response to the entire class without drawing attention to any one student; in this case, the student with ASD.

You also should model using the scripted phrase, and intervene when necessary. *Example:* If you notice that a student with ASD is drawing too close to a peer, say: "Jake, you are standing too close to Kate. Please take one step back." Then, help Jake follow through with the request. Students need to see that, when you make that request, the behavior of the student with ASD changes. In this case, the student with ASD gives his peer more personal space.

If a student with ASD doesn't respond to your request, students won't try to apply that approach. So, either you or the paraprofessional must intervene to ensure that the student with ASD complies with your request. *(Figure 8.10 offers some general scripted responses to particular situations that might arise with students with ASD.)*

Figure 8.10 Sample Scripted Responses to Behaviors That Might Bother Classmates

Behavior	Scripted Response
Standing too close to a classmate.	"If a classmate is standing too close to you, say 'Please take one step back' to that classmate." Use an agreed-upon term — such as "Bubble" — that students can use if they feel that their space is being invaded.
Touching or stroking a classmate's clothes or hair.	"If a classmate is touching you in a way that makes you uncomfortable, say 'Please stop touching me' or 'Hands to yourself' to that classmate."
Making inappropriate comments during conversation.	"What you're saying makes me feel (sad, upset, etc.). Remind the student to focus on topic at hand (e.g., "We are talking about baseball.").
Failing to make eye contact.	"Please look at me while you're talking." Use an agreed-upon phrase, such as "Eyes up."
Speaking with inappropriate volume (yelling).	"Please talk more quietly." Use an agreed-upon phrase, such as "Soft voice" or "Inside voice."
Using equipment inappropriately.	"Please stop. You might hit me."

Sometimes, a student with ASD might exhibit a behavior that frightens or confuses other students in the classroom. *Example:* The student might become overwhelmed and start rocking, biting himself or yelling. Trying to ignore that behavior doesn't help other students understand it and, in turn, leads students to perceive the student with ASD as "odd." Instead of focusing only on the student with ASD, you instead could hold a class discussion about what it's like to be stressed, what can stress us out, and ways in which we cope with our stress. Place emphasis on how everyone handles things differently. Then, discuss what to do when you see that a classmate is stressed. In this part of the conversation, discuss how different people like different kinds of help. Some people like to be left alone, while others like to talk to a friend. Lastly, discuss how the Cool-Down Zone *(see Chapters 3 and 7)* could be applied. The most important part of the conversation is helping students recognize that each person copes with stress differently and that all students have unique behaviors!

Peer Teaching

Using a peer-teaching strategy can help students with ASD in a variety of ways. It can provide social interaction, decrease feelings of being overwhelmed associated with large groups, provide helpful feedback needed for skill development and help keep the child engaged in the lesson. The peer teacher can be a classmate or a cross-age peer.

When the peer teacher is a classmate, students are expected to take turns being observers and performers, reflecting reciprocal roles. Based on the recommendations of Mosston and Ashworth (2002), peer teaching is successful when students are provided with an observation checklist. Typically, the checklist describes three to five essential skill components that students can observe easily. Students are paired up, with each pair given a checklist. One student of each pair then observes the other performing the motor skill, with the observer determining whether or not the components of the skill included in the checklist are being performed. The observer then provides feedback to the performer before switching roles.

The intent of this strategy is not to place the student with ASD with a more skilled partner, but to create an environment in which students with ASD can participate and benefit equally in the peer-teaching partnership. It's essential that students with ASD are paired with a variety of students and not a selected handful repeatedly. For peer teaching to be successful for children with ASD, you might need to modify the checklist. Also, students with ASD might need to be provided with prompts to help them offer and receive appropriate feedback. *(See Figure 8.11 for suggested accommodations.)*

Figure 8.11 Accommodations in Peer Teaching

Modifying the Peer Checklist

1. Replace or augment skill component descriptions with pictures.

2. Modify the vocabulary used to describe the skill component to make it appropriate for reading levels.

3. Provide alternative ways (e.g., Bingo markers instead of a pencil) to mark off whether the skill component is observed.

Modifying the Post-Observation Conversation

1. Provide some questions or statements that the observer can use to inform the performer about the skill component observed (e.g., "I saw you ...").

2. If a child is nonverbal, give the observer the option of pointing to picture that represent the skill component not observed.

3. If a child is nonverbal, provide basic communication cards (as done with Picture Exchange Communication System) or augmentative communication devices to provide a means of communication.

4. Encourage the paraprofessional to assist with both receptive and expressive communication during the conversation.

5. Teach the student serving as a partner to use limited verbal communication. *Example:* Use short phrases or rely primarily on pictures or demonstrations of the skill.

Cross-age peer teachers from higher grade levels also can help all students. You might be able to arrange that within the same school (e.g., a 5th-grader peer-teaching 1st- or 2nd-grader), or from another school in the district (e.g., a middle school student peer-teaching an elementary school student during lunch or study hall period as part of a service learning project).

Cross-age peers are brought in to help *all* students in the classroom, not just those with disabilities. They can demonstrate skills, assist with class management and help set up equipment. It might be beneficial to provide the peer teacher with some suggestions on how to communicate effectively with all of the students, especially those students with ASD.

Another advantage of cross-age peers is that they can serve as social-skills role models and can help foster social interaction. Just remember that they might need some guidance about how to help a child with ASD become engaged in a conversation and interact socially in an appropriate manner.

Working With Parents

Because you don't have many opportunities for parental interaction, it might be difficult to ask parents about how best to teach their children. But parents offer a wealth of information! If you can't arrange to speak with a child's parents in person (e.g., at parent/teacher conferences), send a letter home that asks for information about the child. *(Find a sample letter on the CD-ROM that accompanies this book.)* If designing your own letter, consider what information would help you teach the student effectively. Ask questions about any stimulus that the student might find offensive, what topics might motivate him or her, strategies that tend to work well with the child, etc. You can give a similar form to the paraprofessional who works with the child.

In addition to seeking general information from parents, it's also important to keep parents informed about learning objectives for their children throughout the school year. Sharing insights about what activities their child is undertaking in physical education can encourage parents to engage the child in the activities at home, helping to increase the student's skill level.

Providing students with physical education "homework" is an under-used strategy that could benefit all students, not just those with ASD, although students with ASD will be more likely to need assistance from parents to benefit from engaging in out-of-class activities. Providing parents with some guidance and direction regarding what the child can do at home to help attain physical education goals can help enhance the student's sport- and fitness-related movement skills (Fiorini, Stanton & Reid, 1996; Folsom-Meek, 1984).

If possible, meet with parents (during parent/teacher conferences is ideal) to discuss the child's physical education goals for the school year and to provide them with a checklist of skills/tasks/activities that the child can do at home. The activities that you provide to parents might be related to the learning goals established in the child's IEP for the school year, or they might be specific to a particular unit of instruction. If you create a generic list of skills, along with appropriate activities, you then can choose the skills that are appropriate for each child. Often, you will use the same list for numerous children, as their skill levels and developmental needs are similar.

Once you have provided parents with that information, establish a means for reporting the child's progress. Some parents will be eager to incorporate physical activity into their homes, but others might not be willing — or able — to complete the activities with their children. Regardless, never penalize a student whose parents don't participate and who cannot complete the activity by himself or herself.

Some examples of "homework" assignments for students at three different grade levels follow. Although the activities are different, the common factors include:

- Description of the assignment and the intended outcome.

- Checklist of activities, with performance cues.

- Method for assessing and recording student progress.

Homework Examples

Elementary School

Locomotor Movement Skills: Elementary school, suggested grades 1-3

Purpose: Provide an opportunity for students with ASD to practice the locomotor movements that they are learning in physical education at home, with some help from parents.

Process: Parents play "Follow the leader" with the child, either indoors or outdoors, using different locomotor skills, such as walking, hopping or galloping. Encourage parents to take turns being the leader with the child. Figure 8.12 presents a sample task card that you might send home with parents. The card provides performance cues for the locomotor skills, as well as some helpful hints to help parents perform the skills with their child.

Figure 8.12 Sample Task Card for Parents

Learning Activity	Performance Cues	Outcome	Tips
Sliding: **Step** with the lead foot. **Touch trail foot to** the leading foot. Move to the right, right foot leading. Move to the left, left foot leading.	**Apart** (step with lead foot). **Together** (touch trailing foot to lead foot).	___ (number) successful slides to the right. ____ (number) successful slides to the left. Goal: 10 slides in succession.	• After showing your child the skill, physically move the child's feet. • Provide objects for your child to step on to help with the motion. For example, place pictures of bugs on the floor and have the child squash the bugs. • If your child has difficulty bringing feet together, put a sticker on the inside sole of each shoe and encourage the child to make the stickers touch.

Middle School

Manipulative Skills: Typically, middle school physical education programs include a variety of sports and games that involve throwing and catching. The sample homework activity for middle school students with ASD, therefore, focuses on the overhand throw, both to a stationary and a moving partner.

Purpose: To provide middle school students with opportunities to practice throwing and catching at home, because those skills are used in many sports and games typically played in physical education classes.

Process: Parents play catch with their child at home, using a ball (or object such as a beanbag) that is comfortable for the child to throw and catch. Suggest that parents stand relatively close to the child at first and then increase the distance gradually as the child shows success at throwing and catching.

Also, suggest that parents vary the object thrown, so that when the child has mastered throwing and catching a beanbag or yarn ball, he or she progresses to a Nerf® ball, then a plastic or rubber ball.

High School

Fitness Activities: Typically, goals for high school physical education programs include preparing all students for a physically active lifestyle as adults. That emphasis should not differ for students with ASD. So, a homework assignment for high school students with ASD might include coming up with activities that they could undertake at home to address the different components of physical fitness (e.g., muscle strength, flexibility, cardiovascular endurance). While it's possible for students to engage in muscle-endurance and flexibility exercises at home, the cardiovascular component might require specialized equipment (e.g., stationary bike) or an outside facility (e.g., swimming pool).

Sometimes, parents just need to be provided with a list of different activities that would be beneficial to the development and maintenance of different fitness components. A homework assignment helps them see what is available in their homes and community.

Performance Outcome: The student will be able to complete three sets of eight to 10 repetitions of selected exercises.

Process: Choose exercises that emphasize development of muscle groups and components of fitness that will contribute to the student's overall fitness levels. Figure 8.13 provides an example of a homework assignment that targets muscle endurance, flexibility and cardiovascular endurance. But if students are engaged in a fitness unit in school as part of their physical education curriculum, it might make sense to include the exercises that students are experiencing in school in the fitness homework assignment.

Figure 8.13 Sample Home Exercises That Target Muscle Endurance, Flexibility & Cardiovascular Endurance

Muscle Endurance

Sample Exercise	Exercise Description	No. of Reps or Duration	Hint
Biceps curl	Start with your arm extended at your side, hand facing forward. Keeping your elbow pressed against your side, bring your hand toward your shoulder and then return to original position in a slow, smooth movement.	Begin with two sets of 3-5 reps and gradually increase # to three sets of 10 reps. Then, increase weight by 2 or 3 lbs.	Use soup cans, or plastic soda bottles filled with sand or water as weights.
Wall squats (for quads)	Stand with your feet shoulder-width apart and your back against a wall. Place your feet far enough away from the wall that your knees stay over your ankles at all times. Slide your body down the wall until your thighs are parallel to the ground (like sitting in a chair). Return to original position.	Hold sitting position for 30 seconds (if possible) and gradually increase number of reps and duration of squat.	Ensure that there's enough traction under feet so that child doesn't slip. Instead of counting out a time, sing a song (e.g., "Row, Row, Row Your Boat"). Put marker on wall of how far child should go down.

Continued on next page

Figure 8.13 (*Cont.*)

Flexibility

Sample Stretch	Stretch Description	No. of reps or duration	Hint
Toe Touch	Keeping legs straight, reach toward your toes as far as is comfortable, and hold the position.	Hold stretch for 15 seconds and repeat 3-4 times.	Can be performed either standing or sitting. Modify to child's comfort. Encourage child to stretch farther by showing how far he or she was able to reach last time. If sitting, place an object on student's legs/feet and have him or her reach for it. Help students remember to keep legs straight by *gently* placing hands on knees.
Huggers	Reach with your arm across your chest, keeping the arm extended. The opposite hand then lightly pushes the extended arm against your chest until you feel a stretch in the back of the extended arm.	Hold stretch for 15 seconds and repeat 3-4 times.	Ensure that child extends arm and is not simply hugging him- or herself. Keep shoulders square while stretching.

Figure 8.13 *(Cont.)*

Cardiovascular Activities

Activity	Duration	Hints
Walk around the neighborhood.	About 30 minutes at a brisk pace, or break it up throughout the day.	Make it a scavenger hunt, in which students look for a few things (e.g., a blue car, a stop sign, a squirrel). Consider using a pedometer so that the child can see how many steps he or she takes. Go as a family and engage in conversation.
Play tag in the backyard, or at the park.	About 15 minutes, paired with another activity.	If the child doesn't like being touched, tuck a bandana in a back pocket and have the "tagger" pull it out. If the child is obsessed with a topic, play a modified version of "TV tag."
Play a physically interactive computer game (e.g., Wii or Kinect).	About 30 minutes of active engagement.	Choose games that accommodate numerous players. Consider using games with a fitness component. Switch games if the child becomes frustrated or bored.

The at-home activities suggested in this chapter are just samples of the kinds of activities that students would do in class and that students with ASD could be expected to do at home with help from their parents. Some parents might welcome guidance on physical education activities that they can help their children perform outside of school, while other parents might be focusing on their child's social-skills development and might not be interested in additional responsibilities outside of school. As has been suggested throughout this book, it's important to assess each child's situation and provide the kinds of learning experiences that can best assist that child.

Be realistic about your own workload and resources available to you. If providing descriptions of at-home activities places an unreasonable demand on your time and energy given the number of classes you teach, the number of students in your classes and the number of students with ASD, then providing your students with ASD with accommodations in class to the activities all students are performing is a reasonable and respectable goal. You are the best judge of what is possible in your physical education program. With that said, creating generic descriptions of at-home activities that can be used for a large number of students is another option for teachers who are strapped for time but believe that home activities could be beneficial.

Conclusion

This chapter emphasizes the importance of working with others to best accommodate the needs of students with ASD in physical education class, as well as in the academic classroom, on the playground and at home. Knowing that you are not alone in your quest to provide an effective learning environment for your students can be a comforting notion, and exchanging ideas and information with parents, classroom teachers and paraprofessionals can benefit the students, as well as the stakeholders. Finding ways to help classmates engage effectively with one another also will enhance the learning environment for all students.

The examples offered in this chapter are just that: examples. The needs and strengths of students with ASD are unique to each student. One must learn what works best for each student and then share that information with all involved in the student's education.

Glossary

Adventure Education Model: A curriculum model that emphasizes the development of interpersonal and intrapersonal skills through the use of challenging physical activities. (p. 143). In adventure education activities, students are challenged to solve movement problems in groups within a context of mutual respect and trust. Activities typically include ice-breakers, trust activities and problem-solving initiatives.

Asperger's disorder: One of the five pervasive developmental disorders. (p. 4). Often called Asperger's syndrome, it is characterized by impairment of social skills, and restrictive, repetitive behaviors or interests. Asperger's differs from autism in that no impairment in language and no intellectual disability are present. Asperger's is a spectrum disorder, with a wide variation of abilities: some people with Asperger's are high-functioning and can live independently; some are lower-functioning and need much more assistance; others span the different levels of functioning in between.

Augmentative communication systems: Sometimes referred to as "alternative communication systems," this term refers to communication methods used to supplement or replace spoken and/or written communication. (p. 34). Augmentative equipment can range from low-tech (a series of pictures) to high-tech (an expensive computer system controlled by breathing into a straw). The term also can refer to communication techniques that don't rely on equipment, such as sign language or body language.

Autism: One of the five pervasive developmental disorders. (p. 4). Autism is characterized by impairment in social skills, expressive and receptive communication skills, and restrictive, repetitive behaviors or interests. All characteristics must be present before age 3. Autism also is often associated with an intellectual disability, and is much more common in males than females. It is a spectrum disorder, with a wide variation of abilities: Some people with autism are high-functioning and can live independently; some are low-functioning and need constant assistance; others span the different levels of functioning in between.

Childhood disintegrative disorder: One of the five pervasive developmental disorders. (p. 3). A rare disorder, it is characterized by typical development for at least two years of life, followed by a significant decrease or loss of language skills, social skills and motor skills before age 10.

Closed skill: A motor skill that is performed in a relatively stable and predictable environment. (p. 100). A foul shot in basketball would be considered a closed skill, because the only player moving at the time the shot is taken is the player taking the shot. Success in performing closed skills depends on the performer's ability to repeat particular movements or movement patterns consistently.

Communication board: A piece of equipment used by people who have difficulty communicating through speech. (p. 36). Communication boards come in the forms of computer systems, a series of flip cards, a poster with a series of images or a poster with a keyboard imprinted on it. The person with communication difficulties selects images or keys on the device to relate his or her message to another person.

Cool-Down Zone: A behavior-management strategy that helps students control their emotions. (pp. 89, 191). Teachers designate a location where students can go to regain their composure and/or become less stimulated, so that they can return to the activity and be comfortable. Any student in the classroom (not just those with disabilities) may use a Cool-Down Zone. To use it effectively, students need assistance and instructions on how to regain composure and how to express their emotions appropriately.

Cue card: A large piece of paper or poster that contains an image/word that is shown to the class (usually by the teacher) to communicate the current activity or expectation. (p. 52). It can be used to show the general category of the activity (e.g., warm-up) or to communicate a specific activity within the category (e.g., jumping jacks). It also can be used to communicate class expectations (e.g., a picture of an ear for "listening").

Diagnostic and Statistical Manual of Mental Disorders (DSM): A book published by the American Psychological Association that provides medical professionals with agreed-upon definitions of all mental disorders recognized in the United States. (p. 3). Medical professionals use the criteria specified in the DSM to diagnose patients with specific disorders. The DSM-IV-TR was produced in 2000. The DSM-V is expected to be published in May 2013.

Echolalia: A type of communication approach seen in children with ASD as well as other disorders, in which the person repeats or echoes what he or she hears. (p. 14). The repeated phrase or word could be from something the person heard immediately prior, or it could be something he or she heard hours, days, weeks or even months ago. Usually, the repeated words are out of context, or they disrupt the conversation. *Example:* The teacher asks "How are you today?" and the student responds "How are you today?" Children with ASD also use echolalia to express an emotion or feeling when they are unable to express themselves. *Example:* A student who loves to watch "Shrek" yells, "Donkey, no!" over and over again when you have the students start running the mile. He is trying to express "I do not want to run today" but cannot generate the phrase, so he reverts to something he has heard that expresses the same emotion.

Expressive communication: The ability to convey one's thoughts or feelings to another person through spoken word, body language, written communication, a communication aide, sign language or other communication tool. (p. 14).

Fitness Education Model: A curriculum model that prioritizes the development of students' knowledge about fitness, an increase in student fitness levels, and the development of students' favorable dispositions toward engaging in physical activity. (p. 150).

Generalizability: The ability of the individual to apply a learned skill in another situation or environment. Often, it refers to applying life skills or social skills learned in school to similar situations at home or in the community. Example: If a student learns in school to make eye contact when he or she is talking with peers, he or she makes eye contact when talking with parents and siblings at home.

Hypersensitivity: A heightened level of perception to a stimulus. (p. 56). A stimulus such as sound is perceived as much louder than how people in the general population would hear it. A person can have one sense that is heightened (e.g., hearing), some senses heightened (e.g., sight and hearing) or all senses heightened. The amount of sensitivity also varies from person to person, running on a spectrum from mild to extreme sensitivity. As a result of the sensitivity, the person might perceive everyday stimulus (e.g., classroom lights) as painful or distracting.

Hyposensitivity: A significant decrease in one's level of perception to a stimulus. (p. 58). A stimulus such as a noise is perceived as much softer than how people in the general population would hear it. A person can have one sense that has decreased sensitivity (e.g., hearing), some senses with decreased sensitivity (e.g., sight and hearing) or all senses with decreased sensitivity. The amount of sensitivity also varies from person to person, running on a spectrum from a mild decrease in sensitivity to an extreme loss of the perception. As a result of the decreased senses, the person might seek extra stimulus (e.g., be drawn to loud music), use equipment to provide extra stimulus (e.g., a weighted vest) or perform actions that provide extra sensations (e.g., spinning around in circles).

Inclusive classroom: A classroom in which students with disabilities not only are included in class activities, but also are seen as equally contributing, valuable members of the classroom community. While that label often is used by school systems to describe classrooms in which children with disabilities are present, it is very difficult to truly accomplish.

Intellectual disability (ID): A term used to describe a person who has difficulty learning at the expected level and functioning in daily activities. (p 24). ID often is measured through the person's IQ and his or her ability to function independently in society. The level of intellectual disability can vary dramatically, with four general categories: mild, moderate, severe and profound. Other terms used to describe the disability include mental retardation and cognitive impairment, although both terms can be considered offensive. Intellectual disability is considered the preferred and politically correct term.

Multi-Activity Model: A curriculum model characterized by relatively brief units of instruction (typically, no more than 12 lessons long), in which a particular sport or movement activity is the focus of each unit. (p. 136).

Open skill: A motor skill that is performed in a relatively unpredictable environment. (p. 100). A set shot in basketball would be considered an open skill, because — in addition to the player taking the shot — teammates and opponents also potentially are in motion. Success in performing open skills depends on the performer's ability to adjust his or her movements in response to relevant environmental factors.

Paraprofessional: The definition can vary depending on state and school district, but typically, a person hired to assist students with disabilities. (pp. 116, 211). A paraprofessional is responsible only for the child to whom he or she has been assigned and accompanies the student throughout the day. Usually, the paraprofessional's job is to ensure that the student is kept safe, remains focused on the material, is enabled to complete the learning objectives and is helped with any basic personal needs (e.g., bathroom). Qualifications for paraprofessionals vary among states, although they usually are similar to those required of a substitute teacher. Paraprofessionals sometimes are referred to as "paras," aides or assistants.

Pervasive developmental disorder (PDD): A disability category that includes autism, Asperger's syndrome, Rett's disorder, childhood disintegrative disorder and pervasive developmental disorder – not otherwise specified (PDD-NOS). (p. 3). This category also is called autism spectrum disorder (ASD). Students within this category all have significant delays and difficulty with social skills and social interactions.

Pervasive developmental disorder – not otherwise specified (PDD-NOS): One of the five pervasive developmental disorders, PDD-NOS is characterized by impairment in social skills, and expressive and receptive communication skills; and restrictive, repetitive behaviors or interests. (p. 3). But, while a student with PDD-NOS has the characteristics of the other pervasive developmental disorders, he or she does not meet all of the criteria outlined in the definitions to result in a specific classification. People with PDD-NOS are sometimes said to have "atypical autism."

Picture Exchange Communication System (PECS): A communication system in which one creates sentences using images. (p. 37). Images of items used commonly in the child's life are placed into a binder. The cards are attached to the pages with Velcro®. To use PECS, the child removes the cards that specify his or her thoughts (e.g., "I want," "cookie"), place the cards on another strip of Velcro® designated for communicating with others, and then hands that strip to the intended recipient (e.g., teacher). PECS is different from other communication systems in that students are required to initiate the conversation, not just respond to other people.

Poly spot: A flat vinyl disc used to mark a spot on the floor for a variety of games and activities. Poly spots come in different colors, and some have letters or numbers on them for use in interdisciplinary activities typically included in elementary physical education programs.

Positive reinforcement: A reward provided to a student to increase the likelihood that he or she will repeat a desired behavior or response. (p. 181). Alternately, a response to a desired student action or behavior intended to increase the likelihood that the student will repeat the desired behavior. In physical education classes, positive reinforcement can take the form of verbal or nonverbal feedback.

Proprioceptive sense: Often referred to as the "sixth sense," it is the brain's ability to know where one's body parts (e.g., hands) are in relation to the rest of the body, as well as the environment. (p. 26). It also allows one to touch parts of the body that one can't see (e.g., nose) without using a mirror. Without this sense, most basic motor tasks would be virtually impossible because one would not be able to coordinate the different parts of the body to complete the movement.

Receptive communication: A person's ability to receive and understand another person's spoken or body language. (p. 15). It refers to being able to interpret the message that is being presented by another individual.

Rett's disorder: One of the five pervasive developmental disorders, Rett's disorder — also known as Rett syndrome — is characterized by normal development until age 5 months. (p. 3). Between ages 5 and 48 months, a significant deceleration of the head circumference is observed, combined with the loss of previously acquired skills (both social and motor). The child will develop a severe or profound intellectual disability and also will demonstrate self-stimming behaviors. This disorder is seen primarily in females.

Self-contained classroom: A classroom in which children with similar disabilities are completely segregated from students without disabilities. Also known as homogeneous grouping. Students often are grouped together by disability label (e.g., a self-contained autism classroom), although classrooms in some schools might contain students with a variety of disabilities, depending on the number of students within the district. Also, self-contained classrooms often mix grade levels, again depending on the number of students in the school or district.

Sport Education Model: A curriculum model intended to provide students with an authentic sport experience in the context of instructional physical education. (p. 139). The model is characterized by six features: 1) seasons (rather than units of instruction); 2) team affiliation; 3) formal competition, 4) a culminating event for each season, 5) record-keeping and 6) festivity. The goal is for all students, regardless of physical ability, to become competent, literate and enthusiastic sportspersons.

Self-stimming: Also referred to as repetitive movements, stereotypical behaviors or self-soothing. (p. 22). A repetitive movement/stereotypical behavior that is believed to fulfill a sensory need within a person with ASD. Self-stimming usually helps a child with ASD calm down or feel more in control and comfortable. It can be any stereotypical behavior, although the motion usually correlates with the sense that needs additional stimulus. If touch is the sense that is craved, for example, the child might bite his hand or hit his leg. If visual stimulus is craved, the child might flap his fingers in front of his face. *Other examples:* Spinning around in circles, rocking back and forth, humming and jumping up and down. More aggressive and concerning behaviors include hitting oneself, pulling one's hair, picking at one's skin and banging one's head against a hard surface.

Task card: An outline of the lesson plan or schedule that has been created for the student. (p. 94). The card lists what will occur during the day or class period and how long each activity will last. The card contains a column where the student can document the completion of each activity. The purpose of the card is to decrease anxiety that is associated with the uncertainty of upcoming events and to provide a visual representation of the class schedule.

Teaching Personal and Social Responsibility Model: A curriculum model intended to encourage students to take both personal and social responsibility for their actions and behaviors in physical education class. (p. 118). Originally developed for working with at-risk youths, the model has been used widely in both school and non-school programs that involve sport and physical activity.

Vestibular system: The inner-ear structure that is directly responsible for one's sense of balance. (pp. 19, 20, 64). It also helps one determine where he or she is in space.

About the Authors

 **Melissa Alexander** is an assistant professor at Montclair State University in the Department of Exercise Science and Physical Education. She completed her Ph.D. in Kinesiology at Michigan State University, with an expertise in Adapted Physical Activity. Her primary teaching responsibilities at Montclair State University include adapted physical education for undergraduate and graduate students, as well as assessment strategies for physical education teachers. She also is the program coordinator for students pursuing a Master of Arts degree in teaching (MAT in physical education).

Dr. Alexander's research interests include exploring appropriate pedagogical strategies to implement for children with ASD in the PE setting, as well as integrating social-skills development into physical education and sport. Her research has been presented and published within regional, national and international venues.

Over the past nine years, Dr. Alexander has applied her expertise in the field through the following roles: coordinator of an adapted aquatics program for a diverse group of individuals with disabilities; coach for Special Olympics soccer and aquatics; instructor trainer for Special Olympics aquatics certification; event volunteer at Special Olympics, Dwarf Games and other local disability sport festivals; and consultant with local school districts regarding their efforts to address the needs of students with disabilities.

When she is not working, Melissa enjoys spending time with her son Zachary, her husband Marv and their two dogs.

 **Susan Schwager** retired recently from her position as professor at Montclair State University in the Department of Exercise Science and Physical Education. She earned both her Master's degree and Ed.D. from Teachers College, Columbia University.

During her 28 years at Montclair State University, Dr. Schwager's scholarly work focused primarily on teacher socialization, as well as teacher and program development in physical education. Her primary instructional responsibilities included teaching both undergraduate and graduate courses in curriculum, teaching and supervision.

Dr. Schwager has published articles in numerous academic journals, including the *Journal of Teaching in Physical Education, Teaching and Change,* and *The Physical Educator*. She has been an invited and peer-reviewed speaker at numerous local, state, national and international conferences.

Within the American Alliance for Health, Physical Education, Recreation and Dance, Dr. Schwager has served as chair of the Curriculum and Instruction Academy, publications coordinator for the National Association for Sport and Physical Education (NASPE), and the Alliance Board of Governors' representative from NASPE. She currently is a PIPELine clinician and plans to continue in that capacity, as well as teach on an adjunct basis.

Dr. Schwager enjoys spending time with her husband Rich, as well as her son Rob and daughter-in-law Tatiana.

Acknowledgements

We wish to acknowledge the following people, who generously contributed their knowledge and expertise to the information and strategies in this book.

Marvin Alexander

Sarah Doolittle

Francine Reinitz

Marty Siegel

Noelle Sullivan

Joann Telesh

Brienne Von Rosendah

References

American Medical Association. (2004). *Immunization safety review: Vaccines and autism*. Washington, DC: National Academic Press.

American Psychological Association. (2000). *Diagnostic and statistical manual of mental disorders* (4th ed.). Washington, DC: Author.

American Psychological Association. (in press). *Diagnostic and statistical manual of mental disorders* (5th ed.). Washington, DC: Author.

Andersen, M.B. (Ed.). (2000). *Doing sport psychology*. Human Kinetics, Champaign, IL.

Autism Speaks Inc. (2011). *Be informed*. Retrieved March 9, 2011, from autismspeaks.org.

Auxter, D., Pyfer, J., Zittel, L. & Roth, K. (2010). *Adapted physical education and recreation* (11th ed.) Boston, MA: McGraw-Hill.

Bulger, S.M., Mohr, D.I., Rairigh, R.M., Townsend, J.S. (2007). *Sport education seasons*. Champaign, IL: Human Kinetics.

Chadsey-Rusch, J., Rusch, F. R. & O'Reilly, M. F. (1991). Transition from school to integrated communities. *Remedial and Special Education, 12*, 23-33.

Coyne, P. & Fullerton, A. (2004). *Supporting individuals with autism spectrum disorder in recreation*. Urbana, IL: Sagamore Publishing.

Davis, R.W. Kotecki, J.E., Harvey M.W. & Oliver, A. (2007). Responsibilities and training needs of paraeducators in physical education. *Adapted Physical Activity Quarterly, 24*(1), 70-83.

Edgar, E. (1987). Secondary programs in special education: Are many of them justifiable? *Exceptional Children, 53*(6), 555-561.

Edgar, E. (1988). Transition from school to community: Promising programs. *Teaching Exceptional Children, 20*(2), 73-75.

Elksnin, N. & Elksnin, L. K. (1998). *Teaching occupational social skills*. Austin, TX: Pro-Ed Inc.

Elksnin, N. & Elksnin, L. K. (2001). Adolescents with disabilities: The need for occupational skills training. *Exceptionality, 9*, 91-100.

Elksnin, L. K. & Elksnin, N. (1995). *Assessment and instruction of social skills*. San Diego: Singular Publishing Group.

Ennis, C. (2000). Canaries in the coal mine: Responding to disengaged students using theme-based curricula. *Quest, 52*(2), 119-130.

Fiorini, J., Stanton, K. & Reid, G. (1996) Understanding parents and families of children with disabilities: Considerations for adapted physical education. *Palaestra, 12,* 16-23.

Folsom-Meek, S.L. (1984). Parents: Forgotten teacher aids in adapted physical education, *Adapted Physical Activity Quarterly, 1*, 275-281.

Friend, M. (2007). *Special education: Contemporary perspectives for school*. Upper Saddle River, NJ: Pearson.

Graham, Holt-Hale & Parker (2007). *Children moving: A reflective approach to teaching physical education* (7th ed.). New York, NY: McGraw-Hill.

Griffin, P.S. (1984). Girls' participation patterns in a middle school team sports unit. *Journal of Teaching in Physical Education*, 4(1), 30-38.

Hastie, P. A. (2003). Teaching sport within physical education. In Silverman, S. & Ennis, C. (Eds.) *Student learning in physical education: Applying research to enhance instruction*, 2nd edition. Champaign, IL: Human Kinetics.

Hellison, D. (1978). *Beyond balls and bat: Alienated (and other) youth in the gym*. Washington, DC: AAHPER.

Hellison, D. (2011). Teaching personal and social responsibility through physical activity (3rd. Ed.). Champaign, IL: Human Kinetics.

Houston-Wilson, C. (2011). Autism spectrum disorders. In Winnick, J.P. (Ed.), *Adapted physical education and sports*. Champaign, IL: Human Kinetics.

Kasari, C., Chamberlain, B. & Bauminger, N. (2001). Social emotions and social relationships: Can children with autism compensate? In J. Burack, & Charman, T. (Eds.), *The development of autism: Perspectives from theory and research*. (pp. 309-323). Mahwah, NJ: Lawrence Erlbaum Associates.

Kohler, F. W., Anthony, L. J., Steighner, S. A. & Hoyson, M. (2001). Teaching social interaction skills in the integrated preschool: An examination of naturalistic tactics. *Topics in Early Childhood Special Education*, 21(2), 93-103.

Konig, C. & Magil-Evans, J. (2001). Social and language skills in adolescent boys with Asperger's syndrome. *Autism, 5*, 23-36.

Laushey, K.M. & Heflin, L.J. (2000). Enhancing social skills of kindergarten children with autism through the training of multiple peers as tutors. *Journal of Autism and Developmental Disorders, 30*(3), 183-193.

Levinson, L.J. & Reid, G. (1993). The effects of exercise intensity on the stereotypical behaviors of individuals with autism. *Adapted Physical Activity Quarterly, 10*, 255-268.

Libby, S. (1998). Spontaneous play in children with autism: A reappraisal. *Journal of Autism and Developmental Disorders, 28*, 487-497.

Lund, J. & Tannehill, D. (2010). *Standards-based physical education curriculum development*. Sudbury, MA: Jones & Bartlett Learning.

Manjiviona, P. & Prior, M. (1995). Comparison of Asperger's syndrome and high-functioning autistic children on a test of motor impairment. *Journal of Autism and Developmental Disorders, 25*, 23-39.

Mari, M., Castiello, U., Marks, D., Marraffa, C. & Prior, M. (2003). The reach-to-grasp movement in children with autism spectrum disorder. *Philosophical Transactions of the Royal Society of London. Series B, Biological Sciences, 358*, 393–403.

McGee, G. G., Krantz P. J. & McClannahan, L. E. (1984). Conversational skills for autistic adolescents: teaching assertiveness in naturalistic game settings. *Journal of Autism and Developmental Disorders, 14*(3), 319-330.

Morin, B. & Reid, G. (1985). A quantitative and qualitative assessment of autistic individuals on selected motor tasks. *Adapted Physical Activity Quarterly*, 2(1), 43-55.

Mosston, M. & Ashworth, S. (2002). *Teaching physical education* (5th ed.). San Francisco: Benjamin Cummings.

Nadel, J. (2005). *Emotional development: Recent research advances.* Oxford University Press, USA, p. 365-372.

National Center for Learning Disabilities Inc. (2011). *LD Basics.* http://www.ncld.org/ld-basics. Retrieved November 4, 2011.

Ozonoff, S., Dawson, G. & McPartland, J. (2002). *A parent's guide to Asperger's syndrome and high-functioning autism.* New York: Guilford Press.

Panicucci, J. (2003). *Adventure curriculum for physical education: High school.* Project Adventure Inc.

Panicucci, J. & Constable, N.S. (2003). *Adventure curriculum for physical education: Elementary school.* Project Adventure Inc.

Park, A. (2011, January 6). Study linking vaccines to autism is 'fraudulent'. *Time.* Retrieved June 22, 2012, from http://healthland.time.com/2011/01/06/study-linking-vaccines-to-autism-is-fraudulent/

Provost, B., Lopez, B.R. & Heimeri, S. (2007). A comparison of motor delays in young children: Autism spectrum disorder, developmental delay and developmental concerns. *Journal of Autism and Developmental Disorders,* 37(2), 321-328.

Reid, G. & Collier, D. (2002). Motor behavior and the autism spectrum disorders — Introduction. *Palaestra,* 18(4), 20–27.

Rink, J.E. (2010). *Teaching physical education for learning,* (6th ed.). New York, NY: McGraw-Hill.

Siedentop, D. (1995). *Sport education.* Champaign IL: Human Kinetics.

Siedentop, D. (1998). What is sport education and how does it work? *Journal of Physical Education, Recreation and Dance,* 69(4), 18-20.

Siedentop, D., Hastie, P. & van der Mars, H. (2011). *Complete guide to sport education with online resources.* Champaign, IL: Human Kinetics.

Staples, K.L. & Reid, G. (2010). Fundamental movement skills and autism spectrum disorders. *Journal of Autism and Developmental Disorders,* 40(2), 209-217.

U.S. Bureau of Labor Statistics. (2009). *Occupational outlook handbook, 2010-11.* http://www.bls.gov/oco/ocos153.htm. Retrieved November 4, 2011.

Walsh, D. (2008). Strangers in a strange land: using an activity course to teach an alternative curriculum model. *Journal of Physical Education, Recreation and Dance,* 79(2), 40-44.

Wicks-Nelson, R. W. & Israel, A. C. (2000). *Behavior disorders of children.* Upper Saddle River, NJ: Prentice Hall.